Model Business Letters

L Gartside

Former Chief Examiner in Commercial Subjects,
College of Preceptors

FOURTH EDITION

Revised by
Shirley Taylor Cert Ed DLCC MIQPS

PITMAN PUBLISHING
128 Long Acre, London WC2E 9AN

A Division of Longman Group UK Limited

© Longman Group UK Limited 1992
First published in Great Britain 1992

British Library Cataloguing in Publication Data
A catalogue record for this book is available
from the British Library.

ISBN 0-273-03799-4

Typeset by Medcalf Type Ltd, Bicester, Oxon.
Printed in Singapore

Model Business Letters

Contents

Preface to the first edition

Few business transactions are carried through successfully without correspondence at some point. Enquiries must be answered, quotations given, orders placed, complaints dealt with, transport and insurance arranged and accounts settled. Letters must be written to customers, salesmen, agents, suppliers, bankers, shipowners and many others; they cover every conceivable phase of business activity. They are the firm's silent salesmen and, often enough, represent its only contact with the outside world. Hence the need to create a good impression, not only of the writer's firm, but also of the writer himself as an efficient person eager to be of service.

In the pages that follow are to be found over five hundred specimen letters dealing with a comprehensive range of transactions of the kind handled in business every day. They are represented, not as models to be copied, for no two business situations are ever quite alike, but rather as examples written in the modern English style to illustrate the accepted principles of good business writing.

Every business letter is written to a purpose; each has its own special aim, and one of the features of this book is its use of explanation to show how the various letters set out to achieve their aims. Basic legal principles relevant to different types of transaction are also touched upon, but only where there is a need to clarify legal relationships. Where the book is used in class, the letters provide material for teachers who may wish to enlarge on these matters and the exercises the means for students to apply in practice what they have been taught.

The many letters included are written in the straightforward and meaningful style of the modern age and should be of special help to the overseas user, and especially to students in schools and colleges where commercial correspondence is taught either as a general business accomplishment or as a preparation for the various examinations.

November 1971
L.G.

Preface to the fourth edition

When it was decided to revise this book three main areas were given attention – the overall structure, the content and the general appearance. From studying the original structure of chapters, it was decided to split them into units, with each unit comprising letters which could be specifically grouped.

The result was four main units. **Unit 1 Techniques of Business Letter Writing** deals with the general theory of writing letters, their composition and display. **Unit 2 Routine Business Letters** deals with business letters and documents involved in everyday business transactions, with the final chapter in this unit showing a typical business transaction from beginning to end. **Unit 3 Special Business Letters** contains letters on various topics which most businesses will have to send at some time or other: goodwill, circular, sales, personnel and travel. Finally, **Unit 4 Classified Business Letters** is devoted to more specific business dealings: agencies, international trade, banking, transport and insurance.

In revising the structure, it was also decided to place all assignments in a separate Appendix rather than including them at the end of relevant chapters as previously. At the same time assignments have been included from major examining bodies, thus taking away the previous emphasis on free-writing tasks and placing it on realistic assignments involving students in studying a given situation and planning and composing suitable letters.

After the initial restructuring came the difficult decision of which letters to retain and which could be omitted. While trying to retain the comprehensive range of model letters which made previous editions so useful, I had to be fairly selective in cutting out letters which I felt were repetitive or unnecessary.

As far as content is concerned, the language and terminology had to be amended throughout in order to bring the model letters up to date. The emphasis today is firmly on brevity and conciseness while retaining courtesy and professionalism without overformality.

With speed being essential in business transactions today, many communications take place by telephone, telex or, more so, by fax. Many of the model letters shown, therefore, could easily be used as fax messages.

(It has to be stressed that all the models are presented as examples of well-structured letters written in modern English. No two business situations are ever identical, so they are not models to be copied wholesale.)

The publishers have, in turn, made this edition more attractive by improving its overall appearance. The text and the models are now presented in a format which should result in easier reference and increased usability.

In updating this book, I received considerable assistance, often at short notice, from the following people who provided their advice and expertise in helping to revise areas of specialism: Mr Terry Richards, Head of International Trade at Leeds Chamber of Commerce (International Trade and Transport), Mr Dennis Metcalfe, Parson Cross College, Sheffield (Insurance) and Mr Don Parrish (Banking). I am very grateful for all their help.

Thanks also to Pitman Examinations Institute and the London Chamber of Commerce and Industry for their kind permission to reproduce some of their previous examination questions.

Finally, I must thank the publishers for giving me the opportunity to revise a book by an author for whom I have always held a great deal of respect, and which must have initially involved him in a mammoth research task. I hope I have succeeded in bringing this edition into the Nineties, and, most importantly, that Mr Gartside would have approved of the changes.

1991   Shirley Taylor

Unit 1
Techniques of business letter writing

Technological developments in every area of business and commerce have imposed new demands for ever higher standards of clear, concise and understandable business communication. Despite the range of modern communication methods available today, the business letter remains an extremely important method of communication. Business letters convey the impression of a company in the way they are displayed, the language and tone used, and in the quality and printing of the letterheaded paper. High standards in a company's correspondence in the form of business letters suggest similarly high standards in business generally.

The grammatical structure of sentences, punctuation and spelling are all essential ingredients in good writing. However, they do no more than provide the tools for the job. Good writing demands more than an ability to handle the technicalities of language: it also includes the ability to transfer thoughts, ideas and feelings from one mind to another. Any business letter has three points of focus – the writer, the recipient and the message. As the writer, you must keep in mind that you are dealing with a person as well as with a situation. Hence you must have a clear idea of what you are going to include in your message before you express yourself. Your message should not only have unmistakable clarity, but also be received and understood in the spirit in which it was sent. So it is important to develop the ability to collect and classify facts and to present them in a form suited to the occasion.

The presentation of the business letter should also be considered. A consistently displayed, well-presented business letter will do much to enhance the image of the organisation which you represent.

Effective writing, therefore, combined with attractive and consistent display, has to be of paramount importance when writing business letters. This unit aims to illustrate the importance of these vital aspects in letter writing today.

Chapter 1

Introducing the business letter

In recent years the fully blocked layout has become the most popular method for displaying business letters (see Fig. 1.1). Some companies, however, still prefer to use the indented layout (see Fig. 1.2).

The letterhead

The paper a company uses for business letters expresses the personality of that company. Experts are often engaged to design such letterheads, especially an eye-catching logo with which the company can be associated. A letterhead will comprise:

1 **The company's name.** Companies formed with limited liability in the United Kingdom use the word 'limited' (or 'Ltd') in their name. In the United States the abbreviation 'Inc' (Incorporated) is used, while, in Australia, 'Pty Ltd' (Proprietary Limited), and in the Far East 'Pte Ltd' (Private Limited) are the terms used.

  In the UK the abbreviation 'plc' (or 'PLC') is used to show that the company is a public limited company.
2 **The full postal address.** The company's full address should be shown so that replies may be correctly addressed.
3 **Contact numbers.** For ease of future contact, telephone, telex and fax numbers should also be shown.
4 **Registered office and registered number.** When the registered office of a company is different from that shown at the address section of the letterhead, it is customary to print the registered address normally at the foot of the notepaper, along with the registered number.

Mechanical details

Apart from the main body (message), business letters should contain the following mechanical parts:

BOON & LEE LTD Building Contractors

PJD/ST	78–80 Still Road Singapore 1527 Tel: 3684721	Branch Manager R A Lim Telex: Habo 5821 Fax: 3683216

13 November 19--

Mrs Ethel Wright
25 Imperial Road
LEEDS
LS4 8JT

Dear Mrs Wright

FULLY BLOCKED LETTER LAYOUT

This letter layout has become firmly established as the recommended way of setting out letters. Its main feature is that all typing lines begin at the left-hand margin.

Open punctuation is usually adopted with this letter layout; that is to say no punctuation marks are necessary except in the body of the letter. You will notice, for example, an absence of punctuation marks from the date, the inside address, the salutation and the complimentary close.

With equal spacing between all sections of the letter (one clear line space), most people agree that this layout is very attractive and easy to type as well as business-like.

Yours sincerely

P J DREW
General Manager

Fig. 1.1 Fully blocked letter. This style has become increasingly popular in recent years and is now firmly established. It is the style adopted for all specimen letters in this book. It is thought to have a business-like appearance and also that absence of indentations reduces typing time. Open punctuation is now often used with the fully blocked layout.

FOOTSTEP PRODUCTIONS LTD.

8, Driscoll House, 19 Southampton Street, London WC2E 7QG
Telephone: 071-836 9990

Our ref: RBN/ST   20th September, 19--

Mrs. E. Hughes,
100 South Street,
PURLEY,
Surrey.
CR2 4TJ

Dear Mrs. Hughes,

<u>Indented Letter Layout</u>

This letter is typed in the traditional indented style, often called 'semi-blocked layout'.

The date appears on the right-hand side, and the inside name and address has commas at the end of each line with a full stop after the last item (no punctuation must be inserted in the post code).

Each paragraph of the letter is indented 5 spaces, although some typists prefer to indent 6 or up to 10 spaces.

Traditional spacing for this layout is to leave 2 clear line spaces after the date and inside address, with just one clear line space before and after the subject heading and also between paragraphs.

The complimentary close may be centred over the typing line, with the name and designation of the sender similarly centred; alternatively these items may be blocked commencing at the centre point, as in this example.

This layout is rarely used in business today.

Yours sincerely,

R. B. North
Managing Director

Fig. 1.2 Indented letter. The indented (or semi-blocked) layout is no longer used widely. Some people do prefer it, however, because of its balanced appearance and the indented paragraphing which reading of printed matter has made so familiar. Others dislike the indentations because they waste the typist's time.

1 Reference

Many letterheads have 'Our ref' and 'Your ref' printed on them. A reference will normally include the initials of the writer (usually in upper case) and the typist (which may be in upper case or lower case). A file or department reference may also be included.

Examples

GBD/JB   GBD/jb/Per1   GBD/JB/526

2 Date

It is usual to show the date in the order day/month/year, and this is always typed in full.

Example

26 June 19--

3 Inside address

The inside name and address of the recipient should be typed on separate lines as it would appear on an envelope. Care should be taken to address the recipient exactly as they sign their letters. For example, a person signing as 'James Leighton' would not be pleased to be addressed as 'J Leighton'. If a person's title is known, it should be used in this section immediately after the name.

Example

Mr James Leighton
General Manager
Leighton Engineering Co Ltd
12 Bracken Hill
MANCHESTER
M60 8AS

When writing letters overseas, you should always include the name of the country on the final line of the inside address. As the letter will be sent by airmail, this should be indicated one clear line space above the inside address.

Example

AIRMAIL

Mr Glen Courtland
Eagle Press Inc
24 South Bank
BOSTON
Mass 02110
USA

---

4 Special markings

If a letter is confidential it is usual to incorporate this as part of the inside address, one clear line space above it, either in upper case or in initial capitals/underscore.

Example

CONFIDENTIAL

Mrs Vera Jackson
Personnel Director
Soft Toys plc
21 Windsor Road
BIRMINGHAM
B2 5JT

An 'attention line' may be used if you wish to address the letter to a particular member of the company. This should be placed one clear line space above or below the inside address, as preferred. It should be typed in initial capitals/underscore or in upper case, as shown in the example.

Example

FOR THE ATTENTION OF MR JOHN TYLER, SALES MANAGER

Garden Supplies Ltd
24 Audrecia Street
ROTHERHAM
R45 9JT

---

5 Salutation

If your recipient's name has been used in the inside address, it is usual to use a personal salutation.

Example

Dear Mr Leighton

Dear Mr Courtland

Dear Mrs Jackson

This is better than being too formal by using 'Dear Sir' or 'Dear Madam'.

If your letter is addressed to a partnership (e.g. 'Holmes and Hatton Co' or 'Utility Furniture Co') or if an attention line has been used, the more formal salutation 'Dear Sirs' is used.

If your letter is addressed to a head of a department or the head of an organisation whose name is not known, then the salutation 'Dear Sir or Madam' or 'Dear Sir/Madam' would be used.

6 Heading

A heading gives a brief indication of the content of the letter. It is usually placed one clear line space after the salutation in upper case, or initial capitals/underscore.

Example

Dear Mr Leighton

ORDER NUMBER 4546

Dear Mrs Jackson

INTERNATIONAL CONFERENCE – 24 AUGUST 19--

7 Complimentary close

Like the salutation, the complimentary close is simply a matter of custom and a polite way of closing a letter. The expression used for the complimentary close must match the salutation, as shown here.

Example

Dear Sir
Dear Sirs
Dear Madam   Yours faithfully (formal)
Dear Sir or Madam

Dear Mr Leighton
Dear Mrs Holmes
Dear Jacqueline
Dear Steven
} Yours sincerely (informal)

8 Name of signatory/designation

After leaving 4/5 blank lines for a signature, the name of the sender should be shown, either with initial capitals or in upper case as preferred. The writer's designation or department should be shown immediately beneath the name. In the following examples, note that the title 'Mr' is never shown when the writer is a man, but 'Mrs/Miss/Ms' must always be added in brackets after a woman's name.

Examples

Yours faithfully

GEORGE RAINE
Chairman

Yours sincerely

KATIE ENGLAND (Miss)
General Manager

It is not necessary to type a line of underscores on which the writer may sign their name.

When signing on behalf of an employer it is usual to write 'for', 'pp' or 'per pro' in front of the letter, a mistake which is often made. 'Per pro' is an abbreviation of *per procurationem*, which simply means 'on behalf of'.

9 Enclosures

There are many different methods of indicating that an enclosure is being sent along with the letter:

- Affix a coloured 'enclosure' sticker usually in the bottom left-hand corner of the letter.
- Type three dots in the left-hand margin on the same line where the enclosure is indicated in the body of the letter.
- Type 'Enc' or 'Encs' at the foot of the letter 2 line spaces after the designation of the sender. This is acknowledged as the most common form of indicating enclosures.

10 Copies to be circulated

When a copy of a letter is to be sent to a third party (perhaps someone in the same organisation), it is usual to indicate this by typing 'cc' followed by two spaces and the name of the recipient of the copy. The usual position for this is at the foot of the letter after the designation or after any enclosure indicated.

Example

cc   Mrs Susan Jones, Accountant
Mr David Roberts, Company Secretary

If the writer does not wish the recipient of the letter to know that a third person is receiving a copy of the letter, then 'bcc' (blind copy circulated) must be typed. This should be shown only on *copies* of the letter and not on the original (top) copy.

Example

bcc   Mr Keith Lawson, Managing Director

Continuation pages

Some companies have printed continuation sheets which are used for second or subsequent pages of business letters. Such printed continuation sheets usually contain just the company's name and logo. If printed continuation sheets are not available, the second or subsequent pages should be typed on plain paper of a similar quality to that of the letterhead.

When it is necessary to take a letter to further pages, the following information should be shown at the top of the continuation sheet. These details are necessary as a reference in case the first and subsequent pages are separated in any way.

- Page number
- Date
- Addressee's name

When presenting a letter in indented (semi-blocked) format, it is usual to type all these details on the same line (see Fig. 1.3), but when typing in fully blocked format, such details must be blocked at the left margin to retain consistency (Fig. 1.4).

Mrs J Robinson	– 2 –	28 September 19--

Fig. 1.3 Continuation headings for indented layout.

2

28 September 19--

Mrs J Robinson

Fig. 1.4 Continuation headings for fully blocked layout.

Addressing envelopes

The envelope should always be prepared immediately after the letter by copying the information from the inside address section of the letter, including any 'attention' or 'confidential' indication. In order to ensure that the post office franking does not obscure the name and address on the envelope, type should begin half way down and one-third in from the left of the envelope, as shown in Fig. 1.5.

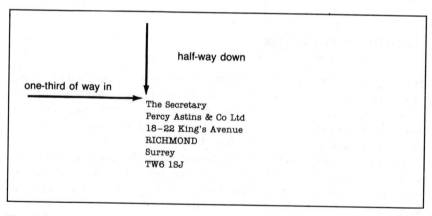

Fig. 1.5 Envelope addressing. Whether typing a letter in fully blocked layout (with open punctuation) or indented layout (with standard punctuation), it is now accepted practice to present envelopes in blocked layout.

Assignments on material in this chapter can be found on pp 344–5.

Chapter 2

Getting the message across

The body of your letter should contain the message you have to convey. It is important to convey this message accurately, briefly and concisely in plain English. Plain writing does not mean adopting a boring, dull style, but simply writing in an easy, natural way without becoming long-winded or too familiar. The secret of good business letter writing is to write in plain language as if one person is talking to another, like 'a conversation by post'.

Rules of good writing

1 Study your recipient's interests

It is a good idea to put yourself in the place of the recipient of your letter and try to imagine how they will take what you write and how you write it. Ask yourself 'How would I feel if I received this letter?'. Anticipate the recipient's needs, wishes, interests and problems, and consider how you can meet them.

2 Write clearly and to the point·

If you are quite clear about what you want to say in your letter, you should be able to say it clearly and in a langauge your recipient will understand – as though you were having a conversation with them. Keep your sentences short, and avoid overuse of conjuctions such as 'and', 'but', 'however'; these tend to make sentences too long.

3 Be courteous and considerate

Courtesy does not mean use of old-fashioned phrases such as 'your kind enquiry', 'your valued custom', etc. It means showing a consideration for your correspondent. Courtesy is a quality that enables a request to be refused without killing all hope of future business, or allows a refusal to perform a favour to be made without killing a friendship.

Courtesy means replying promptly to all letters – answer letters on the same day they are received if possible. If you cannot answer immediately, write and explain why. This will create a good impression and build goodwill.

Courtesy means understanding and respecting the recipient's point of view and resisting the temptation to reply as if they were wrong. If you feel your correspondent's comments are unfair, try to respond tactfully without giving offence. Try to resist the temptation to reply to a rude letter in the same tone. Instead answer courteously without lowering your dignity.

4 Adopt a tone suited to the occasion

For your letter to achieve its purpose, the tone must be correct as it reflects the spirit in which you project your message. It is possible to convey any message in a way that would not cause offence, even if it is a complaint or a reply to such a letter. Ignoring the tone could result in a message that sounds aggressive, tactless, curt, rude, sarcastic or offensive to your recipient.

Instead of	Say
We cannot do anything about your problem.	Unfortunately, we are unable to help you on this occasion.
This problem would not have happened if you had connected the wires properly.	The problem will be resolved by connecting the wires in accordance with the instructions provided.
Your television's guarantee is up, so you will have to pay for it to be fixed.	The guarantee for your television has expired so unfortunately you would have to bear the cost of any repairs.

5 Write naturally and sincerely

Try to take a genuine interest in the recipient and their problems. Your message should sound sincere, while written in your own words and in your own way. Write naturally as if you are having a conversation.

Instead of	Say
I have pleasure in informing you . . .	I am pleased to tell you . . .
We do not anticipate any increase in prices.	We do not expect prices to rise.
Please be good enough to advise us.	Please inform us. Please let us know.
Please favour us with a reply.	Please let us have your comments as soon as possible.

6 Avoid wordiness

Business people today have many letters to read. They welcome the letter which is direct and to the point.

Instead of	Say
We would like to express our regret at being unable to fulfil your requirements.	We are sorry we cannot meet your requirements.
I am sorry to have to point out that we do not have these goods in stock at the present moment in time.	We are presently out of stock of this item.
We are writing with reference to . . .	We are writing about . . .
This information is required in connection with . . .	This information is needed for/to . . .
We shall be in a position to . . .	We shall be able to . . .
In the course of the next few weeks . . .	During the next few weeks . . .
Payment of their account will be made by Watsons next month.	Watsons will pay their account next month.

7 Avoid commercial jargon

Do not use roundabout, old-fashioned phrases that add nothing to the sense of your message. They may have been used in business letters several decades ago, but they have no place in today's modern business language. A good business letter will use no more words than are necessary to convey a clear and accurate message. It will also be free of unnecessary long-winded jargon as shown in these examples.

Instead of	Say
The writer wishes to acknowledge . . . We are in receipt of . . . We beg to acknowledge receipt of . . . We beg to thank you for your letter of . . .	Thank you for your letter of . . .
The favour of your early reply will be appreciated. Awaiting the favour of your early reply. Assuring you of our best attention at all times.	Omit all these

At your earliest conveniece	. . . as soon as possible
Enclosed please find . . .	I/We enclose . . .
. . . only too pleased to . . .	. . . very glad to . . .
Please be good enough to advise us	please let us know
the same	your letter/the goods/etc.
under separate cover	separately (or by registered post, etc.)
your goodself	you
take into consideration . . .	consider . . .

8 Write simply and effectively

Plain, simple words will be more easily understood than long words. Single words should be used instead of elaborate phrases.

Instead of	Say
communication	letter
purchase	buy
terminate	end
utilise	use
in the near future	soon
at the present time	now/at present
come to a decision	decide

9 Check your letters

Before signing a letter, ask yourself the following questions:
(a) Will it be understood?
(b) Does it sound natural and sincere?
(c) Is the tone right?
(d) Are all the details accurate?
(e) Is all the essential information included?
(f) Is it clear, concise and courteous?
(g) Is all the spelling correct?
(h) Is it properly punctuated and grammatically correct?
(i) Is it organised logically?
(j) Is its appearance attractive, well-displayed and consistent?

If you can say 'Yes!' to all these questions, then you may safely sign and send it.

Assignments on material included in this chapter can be found on pp 345–6.

Chapter 3

Structuring the body of the letter

Many business letters are short and routine and can be written or dictated without any special preparation. Those that are not so routine require thought and careful planning.

If you are replying to a letter, it is useful to underscore or highlight each part of the letter that asks for information or which requires comment. Then arrange your reply in a relevant order by planning which point you will mention first, second, etc.

Some letters are very short and may consist of one or two paragraphs only. As a general rule, however, the body of the text should flow logically from beginning to end, and many letters fall naturally into a four-point framework:

Opening or introduction

The first paragraph will acknowledge any previous corrrespondence or provide an introduction to the matter being discussed.

Examples

- Thank you for your letter of . . .
- We wish to hold our annual conference at your hotel on Wednesday 22 October.
- A colleague recommended that I should contact you regarding . . .
- We have received your order number . . .
- The above consignment was received by us today . . .

Caution: If you begin a letter with 'Further to your letter of . . .' or 'With reference to . . .' do not forget such expressions need to be followed by a comma and continued, otherwise the sentences will be incomplete.

Middle section (details)

This section will be the main part of the letter. This is where you give all the information which has been requested, or which the recipient needs to know.

Alternatively, you could be requesting information/advice. All the facts should be stated in this central section, arranged logically in separate paragraphs where appropriate.

Future action (or response)

After all the details have been provided, it is logical to state the response required from the recipient, or what action you wish them to take. Alternatively, you may state what action you will take as a result.

Examples

- If payment is not made within seven days, we will have no alternative but to place this matter in the hands of our solicitor.

- Please complete the enclosed reply form and return it to us immediately for a full colour catalogue and price list.

- Please let us know the costs involved, and also send us some specimen menus.

Closing section

A simple one-line close will usually be all that is required to finish off your letter.

Examples

- I look forward to hearing from you soon.
- A prompt reply would be appreciated.
- We apologise again for any inconvenience.
- If you require any further information, please let me know.

Caution: Avoid the closing which begins with a participle, for instance, 'Thanking you in anticipation' or 'Looking forward to hearing from you'. Such expressions are not full sentences and should not be used in modern business letter writing.

Instead of	Say
Hoping to hear from you soon.	I/We hope to hear from you soon.
Trusting this information meets with your requirements.	I trust this information meets with your requirements.
Looking forward to our next meeting.	I look forward to our next meeting.

This four-point plan for structuring the body of your letters is illustrated in Fig. 3.1.

Assignments on material included in this chapter can be found on pp 346–8.

INSTITUTE OF SECRETARIES
Wilson House
West Street
London
SW1 2AR
Telephone 081-987-2432
Fax 081-987-2556

JT/SAT

12 May 19--

Mrs J L Price
15 Knight Road
Manchester
M2 9GJ

Dear Janice

19-- SECRETARIES' CONFERENCE
TUESDAY/WEDNESDAY 8/9 OCTOBER 19 - -

I have pleasure in inviting you to attend our special
conference to be held at the Clifton Hotel, London, on   [Opening]
8/9 October.

This is an intensive, practical conference for
professional secretaries, with the aim of increasing
their managerial and office productivity, and bringing
them up-to-date with the latest technology and
techniques.

The seminar is power-packed with a distinguished   [Details]
panel of professional speakers, giving expert advice on
many useful topics. A detailed programme is enclosed
giving full information of this not-to-be-missed
conference.

If you decide to join us, please complete the enclosed
registration form and return it to me before 30 June   [Action]
with your fee of £50 per person.

I am sure you will not want to miss this opportunity
of attending our conference, and look forward to   [Close]
meeting you there.

Yours sincerely

JEREMY TAN
Conference Secretary

Enc

Fig. 3.1 Four-point plan for paragraphing letters. This letter illustrates how to
structure a letter logically with (a) the opening or introduction, (b) the main body
or details, (c) the action or response section and (d) the closing section.

Unit 2
Routine business letters

Chapter 4

Enquiries and replies

Enquiries for information about goods or services are sent and received in business all the time. In a routine letter of enquiry, observe the following procedures:

1 State clearly and concisely what you want – general information, a catalogue, price list, sample, quotation, etc.
2 If there is a limit to the price at which you are prepared to buy, do not mention this, otherwise the supplier may raise the quotation to the limit you mention.
3 Most suppliers state their terms of payment when replying, so there is no need for you to ask for them unless you are seeking special rates.
4 Keep your enquiry brief and concise.

Enquiries mean potential business, so they must be acknowledged promptly. If it is from an established customer, say how much you appreciate it; if it is from a prospective customer, say you are glad to receive it and express the hope of a lasting and friendly business relationship.

Requests for catalogues and price lists

4.1 Routine requests where formal reply is unnecessary

Suppliers receive many *routine requests*[1] for catalogues and price lists. Unless the writer requests information not already included a written reply is often not necessary, and a *'With Compliments' slip*[2] may be sent instead. In the following enquiries, written replies are not necessary. The items requested may be sent under cover of a 'With Compliments' slip:

Example 1

Dear Sir/Madam

Will you please send me a copy of your catalogue and price list of portable disc players, together with copies of any descriptive leaflets that I could pass to prospective customers[3].

Yours faithfully

Example 2

Dear Sir/Madam

I have seen one of your safes in the office of a local firm, and they passed on your address to me.

Please send me a copy of your current catalogue. I am particularly interested in safes suitable for a small office.

Yours faithfully

4.2 Potentially large business

Where an enquiry suggests that large or regular orders are possible, a 'With Compliments' slip is not enough. Instead, write a letter and take the opportunity to promote your products.

(a) Enquiry

Dear Sir/Madam

I have a large hardware store in Southampton and am interested in the electric heaters you are now advertising in the West Country Gazette.

Please send me your illustrated catalogue and a price list.

Yours faithfully

(b) Reply

Dear Ms Johnson

We were very pleased to receive your letter enquiring about electric heaters and are pleased to enclose a copy of our latest illustrated catalogue.

We feel you may be particularly interested in our Model F heater, our newest model. Without any increase in fuel consumption, it gives out 15% more heat than earlier models. You will find details of our terms in the price list printed on the inside front cover of the catalogue.

Perhaps you would consider placing a trial order, to provide an opportunity to test its efficiency. At the same time, this would enable you to see for yourself the high quality of material and finish put into this model.

Yours sincerely

4.3 Requests for advice

A written reply is also necessary when the enquiry suggests that the writer would welcome advice or guidance.

(a) Enquiry

Dear Sir/Madam

Will you please send me a copy of your current typewriter catalogue and price list. I am particularly interested in purchasing an electronic typewriter with a memory and single-line display.

Yours faithfully

(b) Reply

Dear Mr Freeman

I have pleasure in enclosing the catalogue of typewriters which you requested in your letter of 8 February. This includes details of a number of electronic typewriters by various manufacturers.

As you mention your requirement for a memory, have you considered a dedicated word processor? You will find details on pages 15-25, and will see from the price list that prices of the smaller models compare very reasonably with electronic typewriters.

If you would like demonstrations on any of the models in the catalogue, I would be happy to arrange for our representative to call on you whenever convenient.

Yours sincerely

4.4 Enquiries through recommendations

When writing to a supplier who has been recommended, it may be to your advantage to mention the fact.

(a) Enquiry

Dear Sir/Madam

My neighbour, Mr W Stevens of 29 High Street, Derby, recently bought an electric lawnmower from you. He is delighted with the machine and has recommended that I contact you.

I need a similar machine, but smaller, and should be glad if you would send me a copy of your catalogue and any other information that may help me to make the best choice for my purpose.

Yours faithfully

(b) Reply

Dear Ms Garson

I enclose a catalogue and price list of our lawnmowers, as requested in your letter of 18 May.

The machine bought by your friend was a 38 cm RANSOME. This is an excellent machine, and you will find details of the smaller size of 30 cm shown on page 15 of the catalogue. Alternatively, smaller than this is the PANTHER JUNIOR shown on page 17.

We have both these models in stock and should be glad to show them to you if you would care to call at our showroom.

Yours sincerely

4.5 Requests for samples

A request for a sample of goods provides the supplier with an excellent opportunity to present products to advantage. A reply should be convincing, giving confidence in the products.

(a) Enquiry

Dear Sirs

We have received a number of enquiries for floor coverings suitable for use on the rough floors that seem to be a feature of much of the new building taking place here.

It would be helpful if you could send us samples showing your range of suitable coverings and, if one is available, a pattern-card of the designs in which they are supplied.

Yours faithfully

(b) Reply

Dear Mrs King

Thank you for your enquiry for samples and a pattern-card of our floor coverings.

We have today sent to you by rail <u>a range</u>[4] of samples, specially selected for their hard-wearing qualities, but regret we have no pattern-card we can send you.

For the purpose you mention, we recommend quality number 5, which is specially suitable for rough and uneven surfaces.

We encourage you to test the samples provided. Once you have done this, if you feel it would help to discuss the matter, we will arrange for our technical representative to call you for an appointment.

In the meantime, our price list is enclosed which also shows details of our conditions and terms of trading. We hope these will be of use when you wish to place an order.

Yours sincerely

General enquiries and replies

When writing a general letter of enquiry, be sure to be specific in the details required, e.g. prices, delivery details, terms of payment. When replying, be sure you have answered every query in the enquiry letter.

4.6 An enquiry for office equipment

(a) Enquiry

Dear Sir/Madam

We would be pleased to receive details of fax machines supplied by you, together with prices.

We need a model suitable for sending diagrams and printed messages mostly within the UK.

Yours faithfully

(b) Reply

Dear Mrs Rawson

Further to your enquiry, I have pleasure in enclosing details of our latest fax machines.

All the models illustrated can be supplied from stock at competitive prices, shown on the price list inside the catalogue.

May I suggest a visit to our showrooms. It would then be possible to demonstrate the various machines and at the same time show you our wide range of office equipment.

Yours sincerely

(c) Request for demonstration

Dear Mr Jenkinson

I have studied with interest the literature you sent me with your letter of 28 April.

Our Administration Manager, Mr Gordon Tan, would like to attend your showrooms to see a demonstration and report on which machine would be most suitable for our purposes. Would it be convenient to arrange this for next Friday 6 May at 3.30 pm.

Yours sincerely

(d) Reply confirming demonstration

Dear Mrs Rawson

Further to your letter of 2 May, I am pleased to confirm arrangements for a demonstration of our fax machines on Friday 6 May at 3.30 pm.

When Mr Tan arrives, he should ask for me.

Yours sincerely

4.7 An enumerated enquiry

When you have many points on which information is required, it may be useful to enumerate your enquiry.

(a) Enquiry

Dear Sir/Madam

During a recent visit to the Ideal Home Exhibition I saw a sample of your plastic tile flooring. This type of flooring would, I think, be suitable for the ground floor of my house, but I have not been able to find anyone who is familiar with it.

Would you please give me the following information:

1 What special preparation would be necessary for the underflooring?

2 In what colours and designs can the tiles be supplied?

3 Are the tiles likely to be affected by rising damp?

4 Would it be necessary to employ a specialist to lay the floor? If so, can you recommend one?

I shall appreciate your advice on these matters.

Yours faithfully

(b) Reply

Dear Mr Wilson

Thank you for your enquiry of 18 August regarding our plastic tile flooring. A copy of our brochure is enclosed showing the designs and range of colours in which the tiles are supplied.

Bottomline, 22 The Square, Rugby, is a very reliable firm and do all our work in your area. I have asked the company to get in touch with you to inspect your floors. Their consultant will be able to advise you on what preparation is necessary and whether dampness is likely to cause a problem.

Our plastic tile flooring is hard-wearing and if the tiles are laid professionally[5], I am sure the work will give you lasting satisfaction.

Yours sincerely

4.8 First enquiries

When your enquiry is to a supplier whom you have not dealt with previously, say how you obtained their name and give some details about your own business.

A reply to a first enquiry should be given special attention in order to create goodwill.

(a) Enquiry

Dear Sir/Madam

Dekkers of Sheffield inform us that you are manufacturers of polyester cotton bedsheets and pillow cases.

We are large dealers in textiles and believe there is a promising market in our area for moderately priced goods of this kind.

We would like you to send us details of your various ranges, including sizes, colours and prices, together with samples of the different qualities of material used.

Please also state your terms of payment and discounts allowed on purchases of quantities of not less than 500 of individual items. Prices quoted should include delivery to the above address.

Your prompt reply would be appreciated.

Yours faithfully

(b) Reply

Dear Ms Harrison

I was very pleased to receive your enquiry of 15 January and enclose our illustrated catalogue and price list giving the details requested.

A full range of samples has also been forwarded by separate post. When you have had an opportunity to examine them, I feel confident you will agree that the goods are both excellent in quality and very reasonably priced.

On regular purchases of quantities of not less than 500 individual items, we would allow a trade discount of 33%. In addition, for payment within 10 days from receipt of invoice, a special discount of 5% of net price would be allowed.

Polyester cotton products are rapidly becoming popular because they are strong, warm and light. After studying our prices you will not be surprised to learn that we are finding it difficult to meet the demand. However, if you place your order not later than the end of this month, we guarantee delivery within 14 days of receipt.

I am sure you will also be interested to see details of our other products which are shown in our catalogue; if further details are required on any of these please contact me.

I look forward to receiving your first order.

Yours sincerely

4.9 First enquiry from foreign importers

This letter is from a foreign importer so a friendly and helpful reply is necessary in order to create a good impression.

(a) Enquiry

Dear Sir/Madam

We learn from Spett, Mancienne Fratelli of Rome that you are producing for export handmade gloves in a variety of natural leathers. There is a steady demand in this country for gloves of high quality, and although sales are not particularly high, good prices are obtained.

Will you please send me a copy of your glove catalogue, with details of your prices and payment terms. I should find it most helpful if you could also supply samples of the various skins in which the gloves are supplied.

Thank you for your prompt attention.

Yours faithfully

(b) Reply

Dear Mr Fratelli

Thank you for the interest shown in our products in your letter of 22 August.

A copy of our illustrated catalogue is enclosed, together with samples of some of the skins we regularly use in our manufactures. Unfortunately, we cannot send you immediately a full range of samples, but you may rest assured that such leathers as chamois and doeskin, not represented in the parcel, are of the same high quality.

Mr Frank North, our Overseas Director, will be visiting Rome early next month. He will be pleased to visit you and bring with him a wide range of our goods. When you see them we think you will agree that the quality of materials used and the high standard of the craftsmanship[6] will appeal to the most selective buyer.

We also manufacture a wide range of handmade leather handbags in which you may be interested. They are fully illustrated in the catalogue and are of the same high quality as our gloves. Mr North will be able to show you samples when he calls.

We look forward to the pleasure of receiving an order from you soon.

Yours sincerely

Requests for goods on approval

Customers often ask for goods to be sent *on approval*[7]. They must be returned within the time stated, otherwise the customer is presumed to have bought them and cannot return them afterwards.

4.10 Customer requests goods on approval

(a) Request

Dear Sir/Madam

Several of my customers have recently expressed an interest in your waterproof garments, and have enquired about their quality.

Provided quality and price are satisfactory, there are prospects of good sales here. However, before placing a firm order I should be glad if you would send me a selection of men's and children's waterproof raincoats and leggings, on 14 days' approval. Any of the items unsold at the end of this period, and which I decide not to keep as stock, would be returned at my own expense.

I look forward to your reply.

Yours faithfully

(b) Reply

In this reply the supplier seeks protection by asking for references. Alternatively, some suppliers request a returnable deposit or a third-party guarantee. While safeguarding oneself, it is important not to offend customers by implying lack of trust.

Dear Mrs Grimethorpe

I was very pleased to receive your request of 12 March for waterproof garments on approval.

As we have not previously done business together, you will appreciate that I must request either the usual <u>trade references</u>[8], or the name of a bank to which we may refer. As soon as these enquiries are satisfactorily settled, we shall be happy to send you a good selection of the items mentioned in your letter.

I sincerely hope that our first transaction together will be the beginning of a long and pleasant business association.

Yours sincerely

(c) Despatch of goods

Having received satisfactory references, the supplier sends a confident, direct and helpful letter. The reason for the low prices is given in order to *dispel any suspicion*[9] the customer may have that the goods are poor quality.

Dear Mrs Grimethorpe

Having received satisfactory references, I am pleased to be able to send you a generous selection of our waterproof garments as requested in your letter of 12 March.

This selection includes several new and attractive models in which the water-resistant qualities have been improved by a special process. Thanks to economies in our methods of manufacture, it has also been possible to reduce our prices, which are now lower than those for imported waterproof garments of similar quality.

When you have had an opportunity to inspect the garments, please let us know which you have decided to keep and arrange to return the remainder.

I hope this first selection will meet your requirements. If you require a further selection, please do not hesitate to contact me.

Yours sincerely

(d) Customer returns surplus

In this letter the customer informs the supplier of the goods to be kept, and encloses payment.

Dear Mrs Robinson

A few weeks ago you were good enough to send me a selection of waterproof garments on approval.

Quality and prices are both satisfactory and I have arranged to keep the items shown on the attached statement. My cheque for £456 is enclosed in settlement.

Thank you for the prompt and considerate way in which you have handled this transaction.

Yours sincerely

Visits by travellers

Customers often form their opinions of a company from the impressions created by its representatives. This stresses the need for careful selection and proper training of sales staff. Apart from being specialists in the art of persuasion, such travellers must also fulfil the following requirements:

- They should have an excellent knowledge of the goods to be sold, and the uses to which they can be put.
- They should know the customer's needs.
- With knowledge of both the above, they should be able to give sound advice and guidance to customers.

4.11 Request for representative to call

(a) Enquiry

Dear Sir/Madam

I read with interest your advertisement for plastic kitchenware in the current issue of the House Furnishing Review.

I would appreciate it if you could arrange for your representative to call when next in this district. It would be helpful if a good selection of items from your product range could be brought along.

This is a rapidly developing district and, provided prices are right, your goods should find a ready sale.

Yours faithfully

(b) Supplier's offer of visit

This reply contains a number of good points:

- It is helpful and friendly.
- It presents the case from the buyer's viewpoint.
- It arouses interest by referring to successes.
- It gives reasons why an order should be placed without delay.
- It does not sound like a routine reply, and has a personal note.

Dear Mr Kennings

Thank you for your enquiry of 1 November.

Our representative, Ms Jane Whitelaw, will be in your area next week, and she will be calling on you. In the meantime, we are enclosing an illustrated catalogue of our plastic goods, and also details of our terms and conditions of sale.

Plastic kitchenware has long been a popular feature of the modern kitchen. Its bright and attractive colours have strong appeal, and wherever dealers have arranged them in special window displays, good sales are reported.

When you have inspected the samples Ms Whitelaw will bring with her, you will understand why we have a large demand for these products. Therefore, if you wish to have a stock of these goods before Christmas, we advise you to place your order by the end of this month.

Yours sincerely

Requests for concessions

Customers sometimes ask for goods that are no longer available, or special terms which cannot be granted. Such requests need to be handled with care to avoid giving offence or losing business.

4.12 Request for <u>sole distribution rights</u>[10]

(a) Enquiry

Dear Sir/Madam

We have recently extended our radio and television department and are now thinking of adding new ranges to our present stocks. We are particularly interested in your BELLTONE radio and television models and should be glad if you would send us your trade catalogue and terms of sale and payment.

Your products are not yet offered by any other dealer in this town, and if we decide to introduce them we should like to request sole distribution rights in this area.

We look forward to a favourable reply.

Yours faithfully

(b) Request declined

In this reply the supplier tactfully refuses the request. The refusal is not stated in so many words, but is implied in the third paragraph.

Dear Mr Sanderson

Thank you for your letter of 8 April enquiring about our BELLTONE radio and television products.

This range has now been discontinued and replaced by the CLAIRTONE. You will see from the enclosed catalogue that the new models are attractively designed and include the latest technical improvements. Although rather more expensive than their predecessors, the CLAIRTONE models have already been well received and good sales are regularly being reported from other areas.

As part of our efforts to keep down manufacturing costs, I am sure you will understand that we must increase sales by distributing through as many outlets as possible. Dealers in other areas appear to be well satisfied with their sales under this arrangement, and it appears to be working very well.

I hope we may look forward to receiving your own orders soon, and also your permission to include your name in our list of approved dealers.

Yours sincerely

4.13 Request for special terms

(a) Enquiry

Dear Sir or Madam

Will you please send us your current catalogue and price list for bicycles. We are interested in machines for both men and women, and also for children.

We are the leading bicycle dealers in this city, where cycling is popular, and have branches in five neighbouring towns. If the quality of your products is satisfactory and the prices are reasonable, we expect to place regular orders for fairly large numbers.

In the circumstances, will you please indicate whether you are able to allow us a special discount. This would enable us to maintain the low selling prices which have been an important reason for the growth of our business. In return, we would be prepared to place orders for a guaranteed annual minimum number of bicycles, the figure to be mutually agreed.

We look forward to hearing from you soon.

Yours faithfully

(b) Reply

In this reply the manufacturer is cautious, offering allowances on a *sliding-scale basis*[11].

Dear Ms Denning

We were glad to learn from your letter of 18 July of your interest in our products. As requested, our catalogue and price list is enclosed, together with details of our conditions of sale and terms of payment.

We have examined your proposal to place orders for a guaranteed minimum number of machines in return for a special allowance. However, after careful consideration, we feel it would be better to offer you a special allowance on the following sliding scale basis:

On purchase exceeding an annual total of:

£1,000 but not exceeding £2,500	3%
£2,500 but not exceeding £5,000	4%
£5,000 and above	5%

No special allowance could be given on annual total purchases below
£1,000.

We feel that an arrangement on these lines would be more satisfactory
to both of us.

We shall be pleased to learn that you accept our proposal and, subject
to the usual trade references, look forward to receiving your orders.

Yours sincerely

4.14 Letter declining special terms

In this letter, a supplier tactfully refuses a request to reduce prices. Instead,
a counter-suggestion is made.

Dear Mr Ellis

We have carefully considered your letter of 18 December.

As our firms have done business with each other for many years, we
should like to grant your request to lower the prices of our sportswear.
However, our own overheads[12] have risen sharply in the past 12
months, and to reduce prices by the 15% you mention could not be
done without considerably lowering our standards of quality. This is
something we are not prepared to do.

Instead of a 15% reduction on sportswear, we suggest a reduction of
5% on all our products for orders of £300 or more. On orders of this
size we could make such a reduction without lowering our standards.

We hope you will agree to our counter-suggestion and look forward to
receiving regular orders from you as in the past.

Yours sincerely

Useful expressions

Requests

Openings

1 We are interested in . . . and should be pleased if you would send us . . .
2 We have received an enquiry for . . . and should be grateful
if you would send us . . .

3 We have seen your advertisement in . . .
4 I understand you are manufacturers of (dealers in) . . . and should like to receive your current catalogue.

Closes

1 An early reply would be appreciated.
2 When replying, please also include delivery details.
3 Please also state whether you could supply the goods from stock, as we need them urgently.
4 If you can supply suitable goods, we may place regular orders for large quantities.

Replies to requests

Openings

1 Many thanks for your letter of . . . . As requested, we enclose . . .
2 In reply to your enquiry of . . . we are sending by separate post . . .
3 I was pleased to learn from your letter of . . . that you are interested in our . . .
4 We were pleased to receive your enquiry of . . . for . . .

Closes

1 We look forward to receiving a trial order from you soon.
2 We shall be pleased to send you any further information you may need.
3 I hope the samples reach you safely and look forward to receiving your order.
4 Any orders you may place with us will have our prompt attention.

Glossary

1 **routine requests** requests of an everyday nature
2 **with compliments slip** a small printed note containing the company's name, address, contact numbers and the wording 'With compliments'
3 **prospective customers** people who may be expected to buy
4 **a range** a representative collection
5 **laid professionally** put down by an expert
6 **craftsmanship** expert skill in making something
7 **on approval** for inspection, and return if not wanted
8 **trade references** names of traders who may be referred to
9 **dispel any suspicion** remove doubt
10 **sole distribution rights** the right to be the only distributor in a given area for certain products
11 **sliding scale basis** varying with the quantity bought
12 **overheads** regular standing charges such as rent, lighting, administration costs, etc.

Assignments on material included in this chapter can be found on pp 348–50

Chapter 5

Quotations, estimates and tenders

A quotation is a promise to supply goods on the terms stated. The prospective buyer is under no obligation to buy the goods for which a quotation is requested, and suppliers will not normally risk their reputations by quoting for goods they cannot or do not intend to supply. A satisfactory quotation will include the following:

- An expression of thanks for the enquiry
- Details of prices, discounts and terms of payment
- Clear indication of what the prices cover, e.g. packing, carriage, insurance
- An undertaking as to date of delivery
- The period for which the quotation is valid[1]
- An expression of hope that the quotation will be accepted.

Terminology

When requesting a quotation, the buyer must be careful to establish clearly whether the prices are to include such additional charges as carriage and insurance. Failure to do this may, if not specified in the supplier's quotation, lead to serious disagreement, especially where such charges are heavy, as in foreign trade dealings. Some terminology associated with quotations is shown here:

- Carriage paid. The quoted price includes delivery to the buyer's premises.
- Carriage forward. The buyer pays the delivery charges.
- Loco, ex works, ex factory, ex warehouse. The buyer pays all expenses of handling from the time the goods leave the factory or warehouse.
- for (free on rail). The quotation covers the cost of transport to the nearest railway station and of loading on to truck.
- fas (free alongside ship). The quotation covers the cost of using lighters or barges to bring the goods to the ship, but not the expense of lifting the goods on board.
- fob (free on board). The quotation covers the cost of loading the goods on to the ship, after which the buyer becomes responsible for all charges.
- ex ship. The quoted price includes delivery over the side of the ship, either into lighters or barges or, if the ship is near enough, on to the quay.

Routine quotations

5.1 Request for quotations for printing paper

(a) Request

This request complies with the requirements of a satisfactory letter of enquiry.

- It states clearly and concisely what is required.
- It explains what the paper is for, and thus helps the supplier to quote for paper of the right quality.
- It states the amount required, which is important because of the effect of quantity upon price.
- It states when delivery is required, an important condition in any contract for the purchase of goods.
- It states what the price is to cover, in this case 'delivery at our works'.

Dear Sir or Madam

We shall shortly be requiring 50 reams of good quality white poster paper suitable for auction bills and poster work generally. We require paper which will retain its white appearance after pasting on walls and hoardings.

Please let us have a quotation, including delivery at our works within 4 weeks of our order, together with some samples.

Yours faithfully

(b) Quotation

This reply by the supplier should be sent promptly, and it should be equally businesslike, ensuring all the points from the enquiry are answered.

Dear Mr Keenan

We thank you for your enquiry of yesterday and, as requested, enclose samples of different qualities of paper suitable for poster work.

We are pleased to quote as follows:

A1 quality Printing Paper	white	£1.21 per kg
A2 quality Printing Paper	white	£1.15 per kg
A3 quality Printing Paper	white	£1.10 per kg

These prices include delivery at your works.

All these papers are of good quality and quite suitable for poster work. We guarantee that they will not discolour when pasted.

We can promise delivery within one week from receiving your order, and hope you will find both samples and prices satisfactory.

Yours sincerely

5.2 Request for quotation for crockery

Here is another example of a satisfactory request for a quotation. It states exactly what is wanted and covers the important points of discounts, packing, delivery and terms of payment.

(a) Request

Dear Sir or Madam

You have previously supplied us with crockery and we should be glad if you would now quote for the items named below, manufactured by the Ridgeway Pottery Company of Hanley. The pattern we require is listed in your 19-- catalogue as 'number 59 Conway Spot (Green)'.

300 Teacups and Saucers
300 Tea Plates
 40 1-litre Teapots

Prices quoted should include packing and delivery to the above address.

When replying please also state discounts allowable, terms of payment and earliest possible date of delivery.

Yours faithfully

(b) Quotation

Dear Mr Clarke

CONWAY SPOT (GREEN) GILT RIMS

Thank you for your enquiry of 18 April for a further supply of our crockery. We are pleased to quote as follows:

Teacups   £43.75 per hundred

Tea Saucers	£36.00 per hundred
Tea Plates	£36.00 per hundred
Teapots, 1-litre	£2.20 each

These prices include packing and delivery, but crates are charged for, with an allowance for their return in good condition.

We can deliver from stock and will allow you a discount of 5%, but only on items ordered in quantities of 100 or more. In addition, there would be a cash discount of 2% on total cost of payment within one month from date of invoice.

We hope you will find these terms satisfactory and look forward to the pleasure of your order.

Yours sincerely

Quotations subject to conditions of acceptance

Very often a quotation is made subject to certain conditions of acceptance. These conditions vary with the circumstances and the type of business. They may relate to a stated time within which the quotation must be accepted, or to goods of which supplies are limited and cannot be repeated. The supplier must make it clear when quoting for goods in limited supply or subject to their being available when the order is received. Examples of qualifying statements are:

- This offer is made subject to the goods being available when the order is received.
- This offer is subject to acceptance within 7 days.
- The prices quoted will apply only to orders received on or before 31 March.
- Goods ordered from our 19-- catalogue can be supplied only while stocks last.
- For acceptance within 14 days.

5.3 Foreign buyer's request for quotation

(a) Enquiry

Dear Sir/Madam

We have recently received a number of requests for your lightweight raincoats and have good reason to believe that we could place regular orders with you provided your prices are competitive.

From the description in your catalogue we feel that your AQUATITE range would be most suitable for this region, and should be pleased to receive your quotation for men's and women's coats in both small and medium sizes, delivered cif Alexandria[2].

Provided prices are right, we should place a first order for 400 raincoats, namely 100 of each of the 4 qualities. Shipment would be required within 4 weeks of order.

Yours faithfully

(b) Quotation

The reply by the English manufacturer is a good example of the modern style in business letter writing. The tone is friendly and the language is simple and clear. The writer shows an awareness of the problems of the tropical resident (e.g. the reference to condensation) and gives information of the kind likely to bring about a sale (e.g. mention of 'repeat orders' and 'specially treated').

Another point of interest here is the statement of freight and insurance charges separately from the cost of the goods. This is convenient for calculating the trade discount, and also tells the buyer exactly what is to be paid for the goods themselves. Note also the statement 'For acceptance within one month'. Here the supplier promises to sell goods at the quoted price within a given period of time.

The supplier's attempt to interest the customer in other products is sound business technique.

Dear Ms Barden

AQUATITE RAINWEAR

We were pleased to learn from your letter of 15 June of the enquiries you have received for our raincoats.

Our AQUATITE range is particularly suitable for warm climates, and during the past year we have supplied this range to dealers in several tropical countries. We have already had repeat orders[3] from many of them. This range is popular not only because of its light weight, but also because the material used has been specially treated to prevent excessive condensation on the inside surface.

We are pleased to quote as follows:

100 AQUATITE coats	men's	medium	£7.50 ea	750.00
100 AQUATITE coats	men's	small	£6.80 ea	680.00
100 AQUATITE coats	women's medium		£6.00 ea	600.00
100 AQUATITE coats	women's small		£5.40 ea	540.00
				2,570.00
less 33⅓% trade discount				856.66
Net price				1,713.34
Freight (London to Alexandria)				86.00
Insurance				22.50
TOTAL				1,812.84

Terms: 2½% one month from date of invoice

Shipment: Within 3-4 weeks of receiving order

For acceptance within one month.

We feel you may be interested in some of our other products, and enclose descriptive booklets and a supply of sales literature for distribution among your customers.

We hope to receive your order soon.

Yours sincerely

Tabulated quotations

Many quotations are either tabulated or prepared on special forms. Such tabulated quotations are:

- Clear, since information is presented in a form which is readily understood
- Complete, since essential information is unlikely to be omitted

Tabulated quotations are particularly suitable where there are many items. Like quotations on specially prepared forms, they should be sent with a *covering letter*[4] which:

- Expresses thanks for the enquiry
- Makes favourable comments on the goods themselves
- Draws attention to other products likely to interest the buyer
- Expresses hope of receiving an order

Such treatment creates a favourable impression and helps to build goodwill.

5.4 Covering letter with quotation on specially prepared form

(a) Covering letter

Dear Mrs Greenway

We thank you for your enquiry of 15 August and are pleased to enclose our quotation for leather shoes and handbags. All items can be delivered from stock.

These items are made from very best quality leather and can be supplied in a range of designs and colours wide enough to meet the requirements of a fashionable trade such as yours.

We look forward to receiving your order, and meanwhile enclose a copy of our catalogue in which you will find details of our other products. These include leather purses and gloves, described and illustrated on pages 18-25. The catalogue will give all essential facts about our goods, but if you have any queries please do not hesitate to let us know.

Yours sincerely

(b) Quotation

In the quotation shown in Fig. 5.1, note the following points:

- It is given a serial number to assist future reference.
- Use of catalogue numbers identifies items with precision and avoids misunderstandings. Individual shapes and sizes are also given their own serial numbers, thus enabling customers' special wishes to be met with safety.
- 'For acceptance within 21 days' protects the supplier should the buyer order goods at a later date when prices may have risen.
- '4% one month' indicates a discount of 4% will be allowed on quoted prices if payment is made within one month; for payment made after one month but within two months, discount is reduced to 2%.

Estimates and specifications

Whereas a quotation is an offer to sell *goods* at a price and under stated conditions, an estimate is an offer to do *certain work* for a stated price, usually on the basis of a specification. Like a quotation, an estimate is not legally binding so the person making it is not bound to accept any order that may be placed against it.

CENTRAL LEATHERCRAFT LTD
85–87 Cheapside, London EC2V 6AA
Telephone 071-242-2177/8

Quotation no JBS/234 Date 20 August 19--

Messrs Smith Jenkins & Co
15 Holme Avenue
SHEFFIELD
S6 2LW

Catalogue Number	Item	Quantity	Unit Price
			£
S 25	Men's Box Calf Shoes (brown)	12 pairs	25.75
	Mens Box Calf Shoes (black)	36 pairs	25.50
S 27	Ladies' Glace Kid Tie Shoes (various colours)	48 pairs	24.80
S 42	Ladies' Calf Colt Court Shoes	24 pairs	24.35
H 212	Ladies' Handbags – Emperor	36	26.50
H 221	Ladies' Handbags – Paladin	36	28.75
H 229	Ladies' Handbags – Aristocrat	12	30.00
	FOR ACCEPTANCE WITHIN 21 DAYS		

Delivery ex works

Terms 4% one month; 2½% two months

(signed)

for Central Leathercraft Ltd

Fig. 5.1 A quotation form

5.5 Estimate for installation of central heating

(a) Enquiry

In this enquiry the writer encloses a specification giving a detailed description of the work to be done and materials to be used. This will provide the basis for the contractor's estimate. The plan would consist of a rough sketch to scale showing the required positions of the radiators.

Dear Sir/Madam

Would you please let me have an estimate for installing central heating in my new bungalow at 1 Margate Road, St Annes-on-Sea. A plan of the bungalow is attached showing required positions and sizes of radiators, together with a specification showing further details and materials to be used.

Cost is, of course, a matter of some importance. However, as you will note from the specification, I am interested only in first-class workmanship and in the use of best quality materials. Completion of the work is required by 31 August at the latest.

In your reply I shall be glad if you will give me a firm completion date so that I can make arrangements for our removal from London.

Yours faithfully

(b) Specification

SPECIFICATION FOR INSTALLING CENTRAL HEATING
at 1 MARGATE ROAD, ST ANNES-ON-SEA

1 Installation[5] of latest small-bored central heating, to be carried out with best quality copper piping of 15 mm bore, fitted with 'Ryajand' electric pump of fully adequate power and lagged under floor to prevent loss of heat.

2 Existing boiler to be replaced by a Glow-worm No 52 automatic gas-fired boiler, rated at 15.2 kW and complete with gas governor, flame-failure safety device and boiler water thermostat.

3 Installation of a Randall No 103 clock controller to give automatic operation of the central heating system at predetermined times.

4 Existing hot-water cylinder to be replaced by a calorifier-type cylinder[6] suitable for supplying domestic hot water separately from the central heating system.

5 Seven 'Dimplex' or similar flat-type radiators to be fitted under windows of five rooms, and in hall and kitchen, according to plan enclosed; also a towel rail in bathroom. Sizes of radiators and towel rail to be as specified in plan attached to my letter dated 5 July 19-- addressed to yourselves.

6 Each radiator to be separately controlled, swivelled for cleaning and painted pale cream with red-lead undercoating.

7 The system to be provided with the necessary fall for emptying and to prevent air-locks.

8 All work to be carried out from under floor to avoid cutting or lifting floor boards, which are tongued and grooved.

9 Insulation[7] of roof with 80 mm fibreglass.

J HARRIS

5 July 19--

(c) Contractor's estimate

The contractor can calculate costs from the information provided, and will send an estimate with a covering letter. The letter should provide the following information:

- A reference to satisfy work carried out elsewhere, which will give the customer confidence.
- A promised completion date.
- A market prices and wages adjustment clause, to protect the contractor from unforeseen increases that may raise costs and reduce profits.
- A hope that the estimate will be accepted.

In this letter, note that the contractor aims to inspire confidence by referring to work done elsewhere and the promise to arrange an inspection if required.

Dear Mr Harris

INSTALLATION OF CENTRAL HEATING AT
1 MARGATE ROAD, ST ANNES-ON-SEA

Thank you for your letter of 5 July enclosing specification and plan for a gas-fired central heating system at the above address.

We should be glad to carry out the work for a total of £1,062.50 with a 2½% discount for settlement within one month of the date of our account. We can promise to complete all work by 31 August if we receive your instructions by the end of this month. Please note that the price quoted is based on present costs of materials and labour. Should these costs rise we should have to add the increased costs to our price.

We have installed many similar heating systems in your area. Our reputation for high class work is well known, but if you would like to inspect one of our recent installations before making a firm decision, we will arrange this for you.

We hope you will be satisfied with the price quoted, and look forward to receiving your instructions soon.

Yours sincerely

Tenders

A tender is usually made in response to a published advertisement. It is an offer for the supply of specified goods or the performance of specified work at prices and under conditions set out in the tender. A tender becomes legally binding only when it is accepted, and up to that time it may be withdrawn.

It is usual for tenders to be made on the advertisers' own forms, which include a specification where necessary and set out the terms in full detail.

5.6 A public invitation to tender

THE COUNTY COUNCIL OF LANCASHIRE

COUNTY HALL, PRESTON PR1 2RL

Tenders are invited for the supply to the Council's power station at Bamford, during the year 19--, of approximately 2,000 tonnes of best quality furnace coke, delivered in quantities as required. Tenders must be submitted on the official form obtainable from County Hall to reach the Clerk of the Council not later than 12.00 noon on Friday 30 June.

The Council does not bind itself to accept the lowest, or any, of the tenders submitted.

B BRADEN
Clerk to the Council

5.7 Contractor's letter enclosing tender

After obtaining the official form and completing it accordingly, it should be returned with a formal covering letter.

CONFIDENTIAL

Clerk to the Council
County Hall
PRESTON
PR1 2RL

Dear Mr Braden

TENDER FOR FURNACE COKE

Having read the terms and conditions in the official form supplied by you, I enclose my tender for the supply of coke to the Bamford power station during 19--. I hope to learn that it has been accepted.

Yours sincerely

5.8 A closed invitation to tender

An invitation to tender restricted to members of a particular organisation or group is called a 'closed tender'. This example is taken from the *Baghdad Observer*.

STATE ORGANIZATION FOR ENGINEERING INDUSTRIES
P O BOX 3093 BAGHDAD IRAQ

TENDER NO 1977
FOR THE SUPPLY OF 16,145 TONNES
OF
ALUMINIUM AND ALUMINIUM ALLOY INGOTS,
BILLETS AND SLABS

1 The SOEI invites tenderers who are registered in the Chamber of Commerce and hold a Certificate of Income Tax of this year, as well as a certificate issued by the Registrar of Commercial Agencies confirming that he is licensed by the Director General of Registration and Supervision of Companies, to participate in the above tender. General terms and conditions together with specifications and quantities sheets can be obtained from the Planning and Financial Control Department at the 3rd floor of this Organisation against payment of one Iraqi Dinar for each copy.

2 All offers are to be put in the tender box of this Organisation, Commercial Affairs Department, 4th floor, marked with the name and number of the tender at or before 1200 hours on Saturday 31 January 19--.

3 Offers should be accompanied by preliminary guarantee issued by the Rafidain Bank, equal to not less than 5 per cent of the C & F value of the offer.

4 Any offer submitted after the closing date of the tender, or which does not comply with the above terms, will not be accepted.

5 This Organisation does not bind itself to accept the lowest or any other offer.

6 Foreign companies who have no local agents in Iraq shall be exempted from the conditions stated in item number 1 above.

ALI AL-HAMDANI (ENGINEER)
PRESIDENT

Quotations not accepted or amended

When a buyer rejects a quotation or other offer, it is courteous to write and thank the supplier for their trouble and explain the reason for rejection. The letter of rejection should:

- Thank the supplier for their offer
- Express regret at inability to accept
- State reasons for non-acceptance
- If appropriate, make a *counter-offer*[8]
- Suggest that there may be other opportunities to do business together

5.9 Buyer rejects supplier's quotation

Dear Ms Gore

Thank you for your quotation for strawboards dated 19 February.

I thank you for your trouble in this matter, but as your prices are very much higher than those I have been quoted by other dealers, I regret I cannot give you an immediate order.

I shall bear your firm in mind when I require other products in the future.

Yours sincerely

5.10 Supplier grants request for better terms

(a) Enquiry

Dear Ms Hansen

I write to thank you for your letter of 18 August and for the samples of cotton underwear you very kindly sent me.

I appreciate the good quality of these garments, but unfortunately your prices appear to be on the high side even for garments of this quality. To accept the prices you quote would leave me with only a small profit on my sales since this is an area in which the principal demand is for articles in the medium price range.

I like the quality of your goods and would welcome the opportunity to do business with you. May I suggest that you could perhaps make some allowance on your quoted prices which would help to introduce your goods to my customers. If you cannot do so, then I must regretfully decline your offer as it stands.

Yours sincerely

(b) Reply

Dear Mr Daniels

I am sorry to learn from your letter of 23 August that you find our prices too high. We do our best to keep prices as low as possible without sacrificing quality, and to this end are constantly enquiring into new methods of manufacture.

Considering the quality of the goods offered, we do not feel that the prices we quoted are at all excessive. However, bearing in mind the special character of your trade, we are prepared to offer you a special discount of 4% on a first order for £400. This allowance is made because we should like to do business with you if possible, but I must stress that it is the furthest we can go to help you.

I hope this revised offer will now enable you to place an order.

Yours sincerely

Follow-up letters

When a buyer has asked for a quotation but does not place an order or even acknowledge the quotation, it is natural for the supplier to wonder why. A keen supplier will arrange for a representative to call, or send a follow-up letter if the enquiry is from a distance.

5.11 Supplier's follow-up letter

Here is an effective follow-up letter, in a tone which shows the buyer genuinely wants to help, and in a style which is direct and straight to the point. It considers the buyer's convenience by offering a choice of action, and closes with a reassuring promise of service.

Dear Mrs Larkin

As we have not heard from you since we sent you our catalogue of filing systems, we wonder whether you require further information before deciding to place an order.

The modern system of lateral filing has important space-saving advantages wherever economy of space is important. However, if space is not one of your problems, our flat-top suspended system may suit you better. The neat and tidy appearance it gives to the filing drawers and the ease and speed with which wanted files are located are only two of its features which many users find attractive.

Would you like us to send our Mr Robinson to call and discuss your needs with you? He has advised on equipment for many large, modern offices and would be able to recommend the system most suited to your own requirements. There would, of course, be no obligation of any kind. Alternatively, perhaps you would prefer to pay a visit to our showroom and see for yourself how the different systems work.

You may be sure that whichever of these opportunities you decide to accept, you would receive personal attention and the best possible advice.

Yours sincerely

5.12 Letter to save a lost customer

No successful business can afford to lose its regular customers. Periodical checks must be carried out to identify those whose orders have tended to fall off, and suitable follow-up letters must be sent.

Dear Sir/Madam

We notice with regret that it is some considerable time since we last received an order from you. We hope this is in no way due to dissatisfaction with our service or with the quality of goods we have supplied.

In either of these situations we should be grateful to hear from you, as we are most anxious to ensure that customers obtain maximum satisfaction from their dealings with us. If the lack of orders from you is due to changes in the type of goods you handle, we may still be able to meet your needs if you will let us know in what directions your policy has changed.

Not having heard otherwise, we assume that you are selling the same range of sports goods, and so enclose a copy of our latest illustrated catalogue. We feel this compares favourably in range, quality and price with the catalogues of other manufacturers. At the same time, we take the opportunity to mention that our terms are now much easier than formerly, following the withdrawal of <u>exchange control</u>[9] and other official measures since we last did business together.

Yours faithfully

Useful expressions

Requests for quotations, estimates, etc.

Openings

1 Please quote for the supply of . . .
2 Please send me a quotation for the supply of . . .
3 We wish to have the following work carried out and should be glad if you would submit an estimate.

Closes

1 As the matter is urgent we should like this information by the end of this week.
2 If you can give us a competitive quotation, we expect to place a large order.
3 If your prices compare favourably with those of other suppliers, we shall send you an early order.

Replies to requests for quotations, etc.

Openings

1 Thank you for your letter of . . .
2 We thank you for your enquiry of . . . and are pleased to quote as follows:
3 With reference to your enquiry of . . ., we shall be glad to supply . . . at the price of . . .
4 We are sorry to learn that you find our quotation of . . . too high.

Closes

1 We trust you will find our quotation satisfactory and look forward to receiving your order.
2 We shall be pleased to receive your order, which will have our prompt and careful attention.
3 As the prices quoted are exceptionally low and likely to rise, we would advise you to place your order without delay.
4 As our stocks of these goods are limited, we suggest you place an order immediately.

Glossary

1 **valid** hold good
2 **cif Alexandria** price covers charges for insurance and transport to the port named
3 **repeat orders** successive orders for similar goods
4 **covering letter** a brief letter enclosing other documents
5 **installation** the act of putting equipment in position
6 **calorifier-type cylinder** a cylinder which keeps water hot
7 **insulation** a covering used to retain heat
8 **counter-offer** an alternative to another offer
9 **exchange control** official control in the foreign exchange market

Assignments on material included in this chapter can be found on p 350.

Chapter 6

Orders and their fulfilment

Placing orders

1 Printed order forms

Most companies have official printed order forms, of which the advantages are:

(a) such forms are prenumbered and therefore reference is easy;
(b) printed headings ensure that no information will be omitted.

Printed on the back of some forms are general conditions under which orders are placed. Reference to these conditions must be made on the front, otherwise the supplier will not be legally bound by them.

2 Letter orders

Smaller companies may not use printed forms but instead place orders in the form of a letter. When sending an order by letter, accuracy and clarity must be ensured, by including:

(a) an accurate and full description of goods required;
(b) catalogue numbers;
(c) quantities;
(d) prices;
(e) delivery requirements (place, date, mode of transport, whether the order will be carriage paid or *carriage forward*[1], etc.); and
(f) terms of payment agreed in *preliminary negotiations*[2].

3 Legal position of the parties

According to English law, the buyer's order is only an *offer* to buy. The arrangement is not legally binding until the supplier has accepted the offer. After that, both parties are legally bound to honour their agreement.

(a) The buyer's obligations

When a binding agreement comes into force, the buyer is required by law:

- To accept the goods supplied, provided they comply with the terms of the order.
- To pay for the goods at the time of delivery or within the period specified by the supplier.
- To check the goods as soon as possible (failure to give prompt notice of faults to the supplier will be taken as acceptance of the goods).

(b) The supplier's obligations

The supplier is required by law:

- To deliver the goods exactly as ordered, at the agreed time.
- To guarantee the goods to be free from faults of which the buyer could not be aware at the time of purchase.

If faulty goods are delivered, the buyer can demand either a reduction in price, a replacement of the goods, or cancellation of the order. Damages may possibly be claimed.

Routine orders

Routine orders may be short and formal, but they must include essential details describing the goods, as well as delivery and terms of payment. Where two or more items are included on an order, they should be listed separately for ease of reference.

6.1 Confirmation of telephone order

Dear

Please accept confirmation of the order we placed with you by telephone this morning for the following:

3 'Excelda Studio' electronic typewriters
   each with 12 pitch daisy wheel

Price: £490 each, less 40% trade discount
           carriage forward

These machines are urgently required and we understand that you are arranging for immediate delivery from stock.

Yours sincerely

6.2 Tabulated order

Dear Sir/Madam

Please accept our order for the following books on our usual discount terms of 25% off published prices:

NUMBER OF COPIES	TITLE	AUTHOR	PUBLISHED PRICE
50	Communication for Business	Taylor	£8.99
50	Modern Business Correspondence	Gartside	£8.99
25	PEI Guide to English for Business Communications	Collins	£5.99

We look forward to prompt delivery.

Yours faithfully

6.3 Order based on quotation

Dear

We thank you for your quotation of 4 June and shall be glad if you will supply, for delivery not later than the end of this month:

100 reams of A2 quality Printing Paper, white, at £1.15 per kg, including delivery

Yours sincerely

6.4 Covering letter with order form

When a covering letter is sent with an order form, all essential details will be shown on the form and any additional explanations in the covering letter.

Dear

We thank you for your quotation of 5 July and enclose our order
number 237 for 4 of the items.

All these items are urgently required by our customer, so we hope you
will send them immediately.

Yours sincerely

J B SIMPSON & CO LTD
18 Deansgate, Blackpool FY3 7YG
Telephone 234612

Order no 237   Date 7 July 19 – –

Nylon Fabrics Ltd
18 Brazenose Street
MANCHESTER
M60 8AS

Please supply:

Quantity	Item(s)	Catalogue Number	Price
25	Bed Sheets (106 cm) blue	75	£3.50 each
25	Bed Sheets (120 cm) primrose	82	£4.00 each
50	Pillow Cases blue	117	£1.90 each
50	Pillow Cases primrose	121	£1.90 each

(signed)

for J B Simpson & Co Ltd

Fig. 6.1 An order form

Acknowledging orders

An order should be acknowledged immediately if it cannot be fulfilled straight away. For small, routine orders a printed acknowledgement or a postcard may be enough, but a short letter stating when delivery may be expected is better and also helps to create good will. If the goods cannot be supplied at all, you should write explaining why and offer suitable substitutes if they are available.

6.5 Formal acknowledgement of routine order

Dear

Thank you for your order number 237 for bed coverings.

As all items were in stock, they have been despatched to you today by passenger train, carriage forward.

We hope you will find these goods satisfactory, and that we may have the pleasure of further orders from you.

Yours sincerely

6.6 Acknowledgement of a first order

First orders, i.e. orders from new customers, should most certainly be acknowledged by letter.

Dear

We were very pleased to receive your order of 18 June for cotton prints, and welcome you as one of our customers.

We confirm supply of the prints at the prices stated in your letter, and are arranging for despatch by our own delivery vehicles early next week. We feel confident that you will be completely satisfied with these goods and that you will find them of exceptional value for money.

As you may not be aware of the wide range of goods we have available, we are enclosing a copy of our catalogue. We hope that our handling of your first order with us will lead to further business between us and mark the beginning of a happy working relationship.

Yours sincerely

6.7 Acknowledgement of order pointing out delayed delivery

When goods ordered cannot be delivered immediately, a letter should apologise for the delay and give an explanation. Also state when delivery may be expected, if possible, and express the hope that the customer is not inconvenienced unduly.

(a) Reason for delay: Breakdown in production

Dear

We thank you for your order of 15 March for electric shavers, but regret that we cannot supply them immediately owing to a fire in our factory.

We are making every effort to resume production and fully expect to be able to deliver the shavers by the end of this month.

We apologise for the delay and trust it will not cause you serious inconvenience.

Yours sincerely

(b) Reason for delay: stocks not available

Dear

We were pleased to receive your order of 20 January.

Unfortunately we regret that we are at present out of stock of the make ordered. This is due to the prolonged cold weather which has increased demand considerably. The manufacturers have, however, promised us a further supply by the end of this month and if you could wait until then we would deliver your requirements promptly.

We are sorry not to be able to meet your present order immediately, but hope to hear from you soon that delivery at the beginning of next month will not inconvenience you unduly.

Yours sincerely

(c) Reason for delay: a transport strike

Dear

YOUR ORDER NUMBER 531

Much to our regret a strike of transport workers in Liverpool is causing some delay in the despatch of a number of our consignments. The goods in your order dated 25 June are among those held up.

To ensure the goods reached you on time we sent them by rail to Liverpool 3 days ahead of schedule, but now learn that they are still at the station awaiting transport to the docks.

We are making private arrangements to get them to the docks in time for shipment by SS Arabian Prince, which is due to sail for Alexandria on 2 August.

Meanwhile, we apologise for this delay and hope you will understand that it is due entirely to circumstances outside our control.

Yours sincerely

Declining orders

There may be times when a supplier will not accept a buyer's order:

1 He is not satisfied with the buyer's terms and conditions.
2 The buyer's credit is suspect.
3 The goods are not available.

Utmost care should be taken when writing to reject an order so that good will and future business are not affected.

6.8 Supplier refuses price reduction

When a supplier cannot grant a request for a lower price, reasons should be given.

Dear

We have carefully considered your counter-proposal[3] of 15 August to our offer of woollen underwear, but very much regret that we cannot accept it.

The prices quoted in our letter of 13 August leave us with only the smallest of margins, and are in fact lower than those of our competitors for goods of similar quality.

The wool used in the manufacture of our THERMALINE range undergoes a special patented process which prevents shrinkage and increases durability. The fact that we are the largest suppliers of woollen underwear in this country is in itself evidence of the good value of our products.

We hope you will give further thought to this matter, but if you then still feel you cannot accept our offer we hope it will not prevent you from approaching us on some future occasion. We shall always be happy to consider carefully any proposals likely to lead to business between us.

Yours sincerely

6.9 Supplier rejects buyer's delivery terms

When delivery terms cannot be met, the supplier should show a genuine desire to help customers in difficulty. In this letter, the suggestion that the customer should try another supplier, who is named, is bound to be appreciated and will help to build goodwill.

Dear Mr Johnson

YOUR ORDER NUMBER R345

We were pleased to receive your order of 2 November for 6 ATLANTIS television sets. However, since you state the firm condition of delivery before Christmas, we deeply regret that we cannot supply you on this occasion.

The manufacturers of these goods are finding it impossible to meet current demand[4] for this popular television set. We placed an order for 24 sets one month ago, but were informed that all orders were being met in strict rotation[5]. Our own order will not be met before the end of January.

I understand from our telephone conversation this morning that your customers are unwilling to consider other makes. In the circumstances I hope you will be able to meet your requirements from some other source. May I suggest that you try Television Services Ltd of Leicester. They usually carry large stocks and may be able to help you.

Yours sincerely

6.10 Supplier refuses to extend credit

If a previous account remains unpaid, the utmost tact is necessary when rejecting another order. Nothing is more likely to offend a customer than the suggestion that they may not be trustworthy. In this letter, the writer tactfully avoids suggestion of mistrust and instead gives internal difficulties as the reason for refusing further credit.

Dear

We were pleased to receive your order of 15 April for a further supply of transistor radio sets.

However, due to current difficult conditions we have had to try and ensure that our many customers keep their accounts within reasonable limits. Only in this way can we meet our own commitments[6].

At present the balance of your account stands at over £800, and we hope that you will be able to reduce it before we grant credit for further supplies.

In the circumstances, we should be grateful if you could send us your cheque for, say, half the amount owed. We could then arrange to supply the goods now requested and charge them to your account.

We hope to hear from you soon.

Yours faithfully

Suppliers' counter-offers

When a supplier receives an order which cannot be met for some reason, any of the following options are available:

1 Send a *substitute*[7]. Careful judgement will be required, however, since there is the risk that the customer may be annoyed to receive something different from what was ordered. It is only advisable to send a substitute if a customer is well known or if there is a clear need for urgency. Such substitutes should be sent 'on approval', with the supplier accepting responsibility for carriage charges both ways.

2 Make a counter-offer.

3 Decline the order.

6.11 Supplier sends a substitute article

Dear

We were pleased to receive your letter of 10 April together with your order for a number of items included in our qutoation reference RS980.

All the items ordered are in stock except for the 25 cushion covers in strawberry pink. Stocks of these have been sold out since we quoted for them, and the manufacturers inform us that it will be another 4 weeks before they can send replacements.

As you state that delivery of all items is a matter of urgency, we have substituted covers in a deep orange, identical in design and quality with those ordered. They are attractive and rich-looking, and very popular with our other customers. We hope you will find them satisfactory but, if not, please return them at our expense. We shall be glad either to exchange them or to arrange credit.

All items will be delivered by our own vehicles tomorrow. We hope you will be pleased with them.

Yours sincerely

6.12 Supplier makes a counter-offer

In making a counter-offer, the supplier must exercise a great deal of skill to bring about a sale. The buyer is, after all, being offered something that has not been asked for. Therefore, it is important that the suggested substitute provides an article which is at least as good as the one ordered.

Dear

Thank you for your letter of 12 May ordering 800 metres of 100 cm wide watered silk.

We regret to say that we can no longer supply this silk. Fashions constantly change and in recent years the demand for watered silks has fallen to such an extent that we have ceased to produce them.

In their place we can offer our new GOSSAMER brand of rayon[8]. This is a finely woven, hard-wearing, non-creasable material with a most attractive lustre[9]. The large number of repeat orders we regularly receive from leading distributors and dress manufacturers is clear evidence of the widespread popularity of this brand. At the low price of only £2.20 per metre, this rayon is much cheaper than silk and its appearance is just as attractive.

We also manufacture other cloths in which you may be interested, and are sending a complete range of patterns by parcel post. All these cloths are selling very well in many countries and can be supplied from stock. If, as we hope, you decide to place an order, we could meet it within one week.

We hope to hear from you soon.

Yours sincerely

Packing and despatch

When goods are despatched the buyer should be notified either by an advice note or by letter stating what has been sent, when it was sent and the means of transport used. The customer then knows that the goods are on the way and can make the necessary arrangements to receive them.

6.13 Request for forwarding instructions

Dear

We are pleased to confirm that the 12 Olivetti KX R193 electronic typewriters which you ordered on 15 October are now ready for despatch.

When placing your order you stressed the importance of prompt delivery, and I am glad to say that by making a special effort we have been able to improve by a few days on the delivery date agreed upon.

We now await your shipping instructions, and immediately we receive them will send you our advice of despatch.

Yours sincerely

6.14 Advice of goods ready for despatch

Dear

We are pleased to confirm that all the books which you ordered on 3 April are now packed and ready for despatch.

The consignment awaits collection at our warehouse and consists of two cases, each weighing about 100 kg.

Arrangements for shipment, cif Singapore, have already been made with W Watson & Co Ltd, our <u>forwarding agents</u>[10]. As soon as we receive their statement of charges, we will arrange for shipping documents to be sent to you through Barclays Bank against our draft for acceptance, as agreed.

We appreciate this opportunity to serve you, and look forward to further business with you.

Yours sincerely

6.15 Notification of goods despatched

Dear

ORDER NUMBER S 524

The mohair rugs you ordered on 5 January have been packed in four special waterproof-lined cases. They will be collected tomorrow by British Rail for consignment by passenger train, and should reach you by Friday.

We feel sure you will find the consignment supports our claim to sell the best rugs of their kind, and hope we may look forward to further orders from you.

Yours sincerely

6.16 Report of damage in transit

It is the legal duty of the buyer to collect any purchases from the supplier. Unless the terms of the sale include delivery, the railway or other carrier is considered the agent of the buyer. The buyer is, therefore, responsible for any loss, damage or delay which may affect the goods after the carrier has taken over.

Dear

ORDER NUMBER S 524

We regret to inform you that of the four cases of mohair rugs which were despatched on 28 January, one was delivered damaged. The waterproof lining was badly torn and it will be necessary to send seven of the rugs for cleaning before we can offer them for sale.

Will you therefore please arrange to send replacements immediately and charge them to our account.

We realise that the responsibility for damage is ours, and have already taken up the matter of compensation[11] with the railway authorities.

Yours sincerely

6.17 Report of non-delivery of goods

When goods do not arrive as promised, avoid the tendency to blame the supplier as it may not be their fault. Your letter should be restricted to a statement of the facts and a request for information.

Dear

ORDER NUMBER S 524

You wrote to us on 28 January informing us that the mohair rugs supplied to the above order were being despatched.

We expected these goods a week ago, and on the faith of your notification of despatch, promised immediate delivery to a number of our customers. As the goods have not yet reached us, we naturally feel our customers have been let down.

Delivery of the rugs is now a matter of urgency. Will you please find out from British Rail what has happened to the consignment, and let us know when we may expect delivery.

We are also, of course, making our own enquiries at this end.

Yours sincerely

6.18 Complaint to carrier concerning non-delivery

Upon receiving the foregoing letter the supplier should at once take up the matter with the carriers, either by telephone or by letter. If a letter is sent, it must contain no suggestion of the annoyance that is naturally felt, but should be confined to the facts and ask for an immediate enquiry into the circumstances.

Dear

We regret to report that a consignment of mohair rugs, addressed to W Hart & Co, 25–27 Gordon Avenue, Warrington, has not yet reached them.

These cases were collected by your carrier on 28 January for consignment by passenger train, and should have been delivered by 1 February. We hold your carrier's receipt number 3542.

As our customer is now urgently in need of these goods, we must ask you to make enquiries and let us know the cause of the delay and when delivery will be made.

Please treat this matter as one of extreme urgency.

Yours sincerely

Useful expressions

Placing orders

Openings

1 Thank you for your quotation of . . .
2 We have received your quotation of . . . and enclose our official order form.
3 Please supply the following items as quickly as possible and charge to our account:

Closes

1 Prompt delivery would be appreciated as the goods are needed urgently.
2 Please acknowledge receipt of this order and confirm that you will be able to deliver by . . .
3 We hope to receive your advice of delivery by return of post.

Acknowledging orders

Openings

1 Thank you for your order of . . .
2 We thank you for your order number . . . and will despatch the goods by . . .
3 We are sorry to inform you that the goods ordered on . . . cannot be supplied.

Closes

1 We hope the goods reach you safely and that you will be pleased with them.
2 We hope you will find the goods satisfactory, and look forward to receiving your further orders.

3 We are pleased to inform you that these goods have been despatched today (will be despatched in . . ./are now awaiting collection at . . .).

Glossary

1 **carriage forward** transportation costs paid by the buyer
2 **preliminary negotiations** earlier discussions regarding terms
3 **counter-proposal** an alternative to an earlier proposal
4 **current demand** requirements at the present time
5 **in strict rotation** in turn, as received
6 **commitments** obligations to be fulfilled
7 **substitute** goods which take the place of others
8 **rayon** artificial silk
9 **lustre** a shiny surface
10 **forwarding agents** agents who arrange for transportation of goods
11 **compensation** payment for loss

Assignments on material covered in this chapter can be found on p 351.

Chapter 7

Invoicing and settlement of accounts

Payment of the amount owing for goods supplied or services rendered is the final stage in a business transaction. In the retail trade, transactions are usually for cash, whereas it is customary to allow credit in wholesale and foreign trade.

Invoices and adjustments

When goods are supplied on credit, the supplier sends an invoice to the buyer to:

1 Inform the buyer of the amount due.
2 Enable the buyer to check the goods delivered.
3 Enable entry in the buyer's purchases day book.

When received, an invoice should be checked carefully, not only against the goods supplied, but also for the accuracy of both prices and calculations.

At home, invoices are sometimes sent with the goods, but they are more usually posted separately from the goods. Any buyer who is not a regular customer, will be expected to settle the account at once, but regular customers will be given credit, invoices being charged to their accounts. Payment will then be made later on the basis of a statement of account sent by the supplier monthly or at other periodic intervals.

An example of an invoice is shown in Fig 7.1.

Pro forma invoices

A pro forma invoice (meaning 'for form's sake') differs from an ordinary invoice only in it being marked 'Pro Forma'. It is used:

1 To cover goods sent 'on approval' or 'on consignment' (see pages 29 and 267).
2 To serve as a formal quotation.
3 To serve as a request for payment in advance for goods ordered by an unknown customer or a doubtful payer.
4 Where the value of goods exported is required for customs purposes.

Pro forma invoices are not entered in the books of account and are not charged to the accounts of the persons to whom they are sent.

7.1 Covering letter with invoice

It is not normally necessary to send a covering letter with an invoice, particularly when the invoice is sent with the goods. If the invoice is sent separately, a short but polite covering letter may be sent with it.

(a) Non-regular customer

Dear Sir/Madam

YOUR ORDER NUMBER AW25

We are pleased to enclose our invoice number B 832 for the polyester shirts ordered on 13 August.

The goods are available from stock and will be sent to you immediately we receive the amount due, namely £312.28.

Yours faithfully

(b) Regular customer

Dear Sir or Madam

YOUR ORDER NUMBER AW 25

Our invoice number B 832 is enclosed covering the polyester shirts ordered on 13 August.

These shirts have been packed ready for despatch and are being sent to you, carriage paid[1], by rail. They should reach you within a few days.

Yours faithfully

Debit and credit notes

If the supplier has undercharged the buyer, a debit note may be sent for the amount of the undercharge. A debit note is in the nature of a supplementary invoice.

JOHN G GARTSIDE & CO LTD
Albion Works, Thomas Street
Manchester M60 2QA
Telephone 061-980-2132

INVOICE

Messrs John Hughes & Co
112 Kingsway
LIVERPOOL
L20 6HJ

Your order no: AW 25

Date: 18 August 19--

Invoice no: B 832

Quantity	Item(s)	Unit Price	Total
			£
10	Polyester shirts, small	5.00	50.00
21	Polyester shirts, medium	6.00	126.00
12	Polyester shirts, large	7.25	87.00
			263.00
	VAT (@ 17.5%)		46.03
	One case (returnable)		3.25
			312.28
	Terms 2½% one month		

E & OE

Registered in England No 523807

Fig. 7.1 Invoice The invoice informs the buyer of the amount due for goods supplied on credit. **NB** VAT (Value Added Tax) was introduced in the United Kingdom in April 1973. A tax on goods and services, it is payable to HM Customs and Excise. The inclusion of E & OE (errors and omissions excepted) in invoices and statements reserves the supplier's right to correct any errors which may be contained in the document.

If the supplier has overcharged the buyer, then a credit note is sent. Credit notes are also issued to buyers when they return either goods (as where they are unsuitable) or packing materials on which there is a *rebate* [2]. Credit notes are usually printed in red to distinguish them from invoices and debit notes. Examples of credit and debit notes are shown in Figs 7.2 and 7.3.

JOHN G GARTSIDE & CO LTD
Albion Works, Thomas Street
Manchester M60 2QA
Telephone 061-980-2132

DEBIT NOTE

Messrs John Hughes & Co   Date 22 August 19--
112 Kingsway
L I V E R P O O L   Debit Note No. D.75
L20 6HJ

Date	Details		Price
			£
18.8.--	To 21 Polyester Shirts, medium charged on invoice number B 832 @ £6.00 each		
	Should be £6.70 each		
	Difference		14.70

Registered in England No 523807

Fig. 7.2 Debit note A debit note is sent by the supplier to a buyer who has been undercharged in the original invoice.

7.2 Supplier sends debit note

Dear Sir/Madam

I regret to have to inform you that an unfortunate error has been discovered in our invoice number B 832 of 18 August.

The correct charge for polyester shirts, medium, is £6.70 and not £6.00 as stated. We are, therefore, enclosing a debit note for the amount undercharged, namely £14.70.

This mistake is due to a typing error and we are sorry it was not noticed before the invoice was sent.

Yours faithfully

JOHN G GARTSIDE & CO LTD
Albion Works, Thomas Street
Manchester M60 2QA
Telephone 061-980-2132

CREDIT NOTE

Messrs John Hughes & Co
112 Kingsway
LIVERPOOL
L20 6HJ

Date 25 August 19- -

Credit Note No. C.521

Date	Details	Price
		£
18.8.- -	By One case returned charged to you on invoice number B 832	3.25

Registered in England No 523807

Fig. 7.3 Credit note A credit note is sent by the supplier to a buyer who has been overcharged in the original invoice, or to acknowledge and allow credit for goods returned by the buyer. It is usually printed in red.

7.3 Buyer requests credit note

When notifying an overcharge it is the practice of some customers to send a debit note to the supplier as a claim for the amount overcharged. If the supplier agrees to the claim, he will then issue a credit note to the customer.

(a) Returned packing case

Dear Sir or Madam

We have today returned to you by rail one empty packing case, charged on your invoice number B 832 of 18 August at £24.00.

A debit note for this amount is enclosed and we shall be glad to receive your credit note in return.

Yours faithfully

(b) Incorrect trade discount

Dear Sir or Madam

Your invoice number 2370 dated 10 September allows a trade discount of only 33⅓% instead of the 40% to which you agreed in your letter of 5 August because of the unusually large order.

Calculated on the invoice gross total of £1,500 the difference in discount is exactly £100 and if you will kindly adjust your charge we shall be glad to pass the invoice for immediate payment.

Yours faithfully

7.4 Supplier refuses request for credit note

(a) Retailer's request

Dear Sir or Madam

On 1 September we returned to you by parcel post one cassette tape recorder, Model EK76, Serial Number 048617, one of a consignment of 12 delivered on 5 August and charged on your invoice number 5624 dated 2 August.

The customer who bought this recorder complained about its performance. It was for this reason that we returned it to you after satisfying ourselves that the complaint was justified.

We have received no acknowledgement of the returned recorder or of the letter we sent to you on 1 September. It may be that you are trying to obtain a replacement for us. If this is the case, and a replacement is not immediately available, please send us a credit note for the invoiced cost of the returned recorder, namely, £175.

We hope to hear from you soon.

Yours faithfully

(b) Wholesaler's reply

Dear

We are sorry to learn from your letter of 16 September of the need to return one of the recorders supplied to you and charged on our invoice number 5624.

We received your letter of 1 September, but regret that we have no trace of the returned recorder. It would help if you could describe the kind of container in which it was packed and state exactly how it was addressed. As soon as we receive this information we will make a thorough investigation[3].

Meanwhile, I am sure you will understand that we cannot either provide a free replacement or grant the credit you request. If you could wait for about 10 days, we could replace the recorder, but would have to charge it to your account if our further enquiries should prove unsuccessful.

Yours sincerely

Statements of account

A statement (see Fig. 7.4) is a demand for payment. It is a summary of the transactions between buyer and supplier during the period it covers, usually one month. It starts with the balance owing at the beginning of the period, if any. Thereafter, amounts of invoices and debit notes issued are listed, and amounts of any credit notes issued and payments made by the buyer are deducted. The closing balance shows the amount owing at the date of the statement.

Statements, like invoices, are generally sent without a covering letter. If a covering letter is sent, it need only be very short and formal.

JOHN G GARTSIDE & CO LTD
Albion Works, Thomas Street
Manchester M60 2QA
Telephone 061-980-2132

STATEMENT

Messrs John Hughes & Co   Date 31 August 19--
112 Kingsway
LIVERPOOL
L20 6HJ

Date	Details	Debit	Credit	Balance
		£	£	£
1.8.--	Account rendered			115.53
18.8.--	Invoice B 832	312.28		427.81
20.8.--	Cheque received		100.00	327.81
22.8.--	Debit Note D 75	6.30		334.11
25.8.--	Credit Note C 52		3.25	330.86

E & OE   Registered in England No 523807

Fig. 7.4 Statement A statement is a demand for payment sent at stated periods by the supplier to buyers. It summarises all transactions over the period it covers, and enables the buyer to check the ledger against the particulars given. Any errors discovered and agreed will be adjusted either by debit or credit note.

7.5 Covering letter with statement

Dear Sir or Madam

We enclose our statement of account for all transactions during August. If payment is made within 14 days you may deduct the customary cash discount of 2½%.

Yours faithfully

7.6 Supplier reports underpaid statement

(a) Supplier's letter

Dear Sir or Madam

We are enclosing our September statement, totalling £820.57.

The opening balance brought forward is the amount left uncovered by the cheque received from you against our August statement, which totalled £560.27. The cheque received from you, however, was drawn for £500.27 only, leaving the unpaid balance of £60 now brought forward.

We should appreciate early settlement of the total amount now due.

Yours faithfully

(b) Buyer's reply

Dear Sir or Madam

We have received your letter of 15 October enclosing September's statement.

We apologise for the underpayment of £60 on your August statement. This was due to a misreading of the amount due. The final figure was not very clearly printed, and we mistakenly read it as £500.27 instead of £560.27.

Our cheque for the total amount on the September statement, of £820.57, is now enclosed.

Yours faithfully

7.7 Supplier reports errors in statement

(a) Buyer's notification

Dear Sir/Madam

On checking your statement for July we notice the following errors:

1 The sum of £4.10 for the return of empty packing cases, covered by your credit note number 521 dated 5 July, has not been entered.

2 Invoice Number W825 for £27.32 has been debited twice – once on 11 July and again on 21 July.

We are, therefore, deducting the sum of £31.42 from the balance shown on your statement, and enclose our cheque for £154.50 in full settlement.

Yours faithfully

(b) Supplier's acknowledgement

Dear Sir/Madam

Thank you for your letter of 10 August enclosing your cheque for £154.50 in full settlement of the amount due against our July statement.

We confirm your deduction of £31.42 and apologise for the errors in the statement. Please accept our apologies for the inconvenience caused.

Yours faithfully

Varying the terms of payment

When a customer is required to pay for goods as, or before, they are delivered, he is said to pay 'on invoice'. Customers known to be *creditworthy*[4] may be granted 'open account' terms, under which invoices are charged to their accounts, settlement being made on the basis of statements of account sent by the supplier.

When a customer finds it necessary to ask for time to pay, the reasons given must be strong enough to convince the supplier that the difficulties are purely temporary and that payment will be made later.

7.8 Customer requests time to pay (granted)

(a) Customer's request

Dear Sir/Madam

We have received your letter of 6 August reminding us that payment of the amount owing on your June statement is overdue.

We were under the impression that payment was not due until the end of August, when we would have had no difficulty in settling your account. However, it seems that we misunderstood your terms of payment.

In the circumstances we should be grateful if you could allow us to defer payment[5] for a further 3 weeks. Our present difficulty is purely temporary. Before the end of the month payments are due to us from a number of our regular customers who are notably prompt payers.

We very much regret having to make this request, but hope you will be able to grant it.

Yours faithfully

(b) Supplier's reply

Dear Sir/Madam

Having carefully considered your letter of 8 August, we have decided to allow you to defer payment of your account to the end of August.

We grant this request as an exceptional measure only because of the promptness with which you have settled your accounts in the past. We sincerely hope that in future dealings you will be able to keep to our terms of payment. As you do not seem to have been clear about them, we take this opportunity to remind you that they are as follows:

2½% discount for payment within 10 days
Net cash for payment within one month

Yours faithfully

7.9 Customer requests time to pay (not granted)

(a) Customer's request

Dear Sir/Madam

I am replying to you letter of 23 July asking for immediate payment of the £687 due on your invoice number AV54.

When we wrote promising to pay you in full by 15 July, we fully expected to be able to do so. However, we were unfortunately called upon to meet an unforeseen and unusually heavy demand earlier this month.

We are, therefore, enclosing a cheque for £200 on account[6], and ask you to be good enough to allow us a further few weeks in which to settle the balance. We fully expect to be able to settle your account in full by the end of August. If you could grant this deferment, we should be most grateful.

Yours faithfully

(b) Supplier's reply

In refusing requests of this kind, it is better for suppliers to stress the benefits the customer is likely to gain from making payments promptly rather than to stress their own difficulties in seeking prompt payment. The customer is, after all, more interested in problems closer to home.

Dear

Thank you for your letter of 25 July sending us a cheque for £200 on account and asking for an extension of time in which to pay the balance.

As your account is now more than 2 months overdue we find your present cheque quite insufficient. It is hardly reasonable to expect us to wait a further month for the balance, particularly as we invoiced the goods at a specially low price which was mentioned to you at the time.

We sympathise with your difficulties, but need hardly remind you that it is in our customers' long-term interests to pay their accounts promptly so as to qualify for discounts and at the same time build a reputation for financial reliability.

In the circumstances, we hope that in your own interests you will make arrangements to clear your account without further delay. We look forward to receiving your cheque for the balance on your account within the next few days.

Yours sincerely

7.10 Supplier questions partial payment

When making payment on a statement, the debtor should always state whether the payment is 'on account' or 'in full settlement', otherwise it may give rise to letters such as the following.

Dear

We thank you for your letter of 10 October sending us your cheque for £58.67. Our official receipt is enclosed.

As you do not say that the cheque is on account, we are wondering whether the amount of £58.67 was intended to be £88.67 – the balance on your account as shown in our September statement.

In any case, we look forward to receiving the uncleared balance of £30 within the next few days.

Yours sincerely

7.11 Supplier disallows discount deduction

Dear

We thank you for your letter of yesterday enclosing your cheque for £292.50 in full settlement of our May statement.

We regret that we cannot accept this payment as a full discharge of the £300 due on our statement. The terms of payment allow the 2½% cash discount only on accounts paid within 10 days of statement, whereas your present payment is more than a month overdue.

The balance still owing is £7.50 and to save you the trouble of making a separate payment we will include this amount in your next payment and will prepare our July statement accordingly.

Yours sincerely

Methods of payment

Various methods of payment may be used in settling accounts:

1 Cash (coins and notes).

2 Payments through the Post Office.
   (a) *Postal orders and money orders* (the latter for foreign payments only).
   British postal orders and money orders are issued and paid in many
   countries abroad. Payment is made in the currency of the country of
   payment at the current rate of exchange. Postal orders are used for small
   sums (up to £20 in the United Kingdom).

   Money orders (other than telegraph money orders) are no longer issued
   for payment in the United Kingdom, but are issued for amounts up
   to £50 for payment abroad. This method is used by senders who have
   no bank or giro (postal cheque) account. Upon payment of the charge
   for a telegram, money orders may be telegraphed. A person sending a
   money order should ask the payee for a receipt since there is no other
   evidence of payment.

   (b) *Giro transfers.* 'Giro' is a term commonly applied to the postal cheque
   system run by post offices in most Western European countries and
   Japan. In most of these countries, bank cheque facilities have not been
   developed to nearly the same extent as in the United Kingdom. Apart
   from cash transactions, giro transfer or postal cheque is the chief means
   of payment. Anyone can make a deposit or receive a payment, whether
   or not they hold a giro account.

   (c) *The COD system.* In the COD (cash on delivery) system, the buyer pays
   for the goods at the time they are handed over by the carrier (this includes
   the postal system). In this way the supplier makes certain of receiving
   payment for goods supplied to unknown customers.

3 Payments through banks.
   (a) Home trade relies on cheques, credit transfers (bank giro), banker's draft
   and letters of credit.
   • *Cheques*: A bank cheque is always payable on demand. It is by far
   the commonest form of payment used to settle credit transactions in
   the home trade of countries where the bank cheque system has been
   developed. It may also be used to pay debts abroad. A receipt is the
   best, but not the only, evidence of payment and cheques which have
   been paid by a banker and later returned to customers may be produced
   as receipts. When payment is made by cheque a separate receipt is
   therefore unnecessary, though the payer may legally demand a receipt
   if required.
   • *Credit transfers*: The system of credit transfers operated by banks is
   in many ways similar to the postal cheque (giro) system and is now
   commonly referred to as a bank giro. The payer completes a credit
   transfer or giro transfer slip for each separate payment and enters it on

a list, which is passed (in duplicate) to the banker together with the slips and a cheque for the total amount. The banker then distributes the slips to the banks of the payees concerned, whose accounts are then credited. Payees receive the transfer slips from their bankers. A separate advice of payment by the payer is therefore unnecessary, though some payers make it their practice to send one.

    ● *Banker's drafts*: A banker's draft is a document bought from a bank. It orders the branch bank, or the agent on whom it is drawn, to pay the stated sum of money on demand to the person named (the payee) in the draft. In foreign transactions, the payee receives payment in the local curency at the current rate of exchange. Banker's drafts are convenient for paying large sums of money in circumstances where a creditor would hesitate to take a cheque in payment. Like cheques, they may be crossed for added safety.

(b) Foreign trade may use bankers' transfers (mail, telegraphic and telex); bills of exchange and promissory notes; bank commercial credits (documentary credits if a documentary bill is used); banker's drafts; and letters of credit.

The form of payment to be used is a matter for arrangement between the parties concerned.

7.12 Supplier asks customer to select terms of payment

Dear

Thank you for your letter of 3 April, but you do not say whether you wish this transaction to be for cash or on credit.

When we wrote to you on 20 March we explained our willingness to offer easy credit terms to customers who do not wish to pay cash, and also that we allow generous discounts to cash customers.

We may not have made it clear that when placing orders, customers should state whether cash or credit terms are required.

Please be good enough to state which you prefer so that we can arrange your account accordingly.

Yours sincerely

7.13 Form letter enclosing payment (and acknowledgement)

Every business has a good deal of purely routine correspondence. Letters enclosing or acknowledging payments are of this kind. They often take a standard form suitable for all occasions and are therefore known as 'form letters'.

In this case, a supply of preprinted letters is prepared with blank spaces for the inclusion of variable types of information (reference numbers, correspondents' names and addresses, dates, sums of money, etc.).

Of course the personal touch which personalised letters provide is lost with such form letters. However, many companies now use mail merge facilities on word processors to produce personalised form letters which look like individual originals.

(a) Sender's form letter

Dear Sir or Madam

We have pleasure in enclosing our cheque (bill/draft/etc.) for £. . . in full settlement (part settlement) of your statement (invoice) dated . . . .

Please send us your official receipt.

Yours faithfully

(b) Form letter acknowledging payment

Dear

Thank you for your letter of . . . enclosing cheque (bill/draft/etc.) for £. . . in full settlement (part payment) of our statement of account (invoice) dated . . . .

We are pleased to enclose our official receipt.

Yours sincerely

7.14 Letter informing supplier of payment by credit transfer (bank giro)

Dear Sir or Madam

I am pleased to inform you that a credit transfer has been made to your account at the Barminster Bank, Church Street, Dover, in payment of the amount due for the goods supplied on 2 May and charged on your invoice number 1524.

Yours faithfully

7.15 Letter informing supplier of payment by banker's draft

Dear Sir or Madam

I have pleasure in enclosing a banker's draft, drawn on the Midminster Bank, Benghazi, for £672.72 and crossed 'Account Payee only'.

The draft is sent in full settlement of your account dated 31 May.

Please acknowledge its safe receipt.

Yours faithfully

7.16 Supplier sends goods COD

Dear Sir or Madam

Thank you for your order for one of our Model 50 cameras. This model is an improved version of our famous Model 40, which has already established itself firmly in public favour. We feel sure you will be delighted with it. At the price of £59.25 we believe it represents the best value on the market for cameras of this type.

Your camera will be sent to you today by compensation-fee parcel post, for delivery against payment of our trade charge of £60. This charge includes packing and postal registration and COD charges.

Under our guarantee you are entitled to a refund of your payment in full if you are not completely satisfied, but you must return the camera by compensation-fee parcel post within 7 days.

Yours faithfully

Useful expressions

Payments Due

Openings

1 Enclosed is our statement for the quarter ended . . . .
2 We enclose our statement to 31 . . . showing a balance of £. . . .
3 We are sorry it was necessary to return our invoice number . . . for correction.
4 We very much regret having to ask for an extension of credit on your January statement.

Closes

1 Please let us have your credit note for the amount of this overcharge.
2 If you will make the necessary adjustment, we will settle the account immediately.
3 We apologise again for this error and enclose our credit note for the overcharge.

Payments made

Openings

1 We enclose our cheque for £. . . in payment for goods supplied on . . . .
2 We have pleasure in enclosing our cheque for . . . in payment of your invoice number . . . .
3 We acknowledge with thanks your cheque for £. . . .
4 We thank you for your cheque for £. . . in part payment of your account.

Closes

1 We hope to receive the amount due by the end of this month.
2 We should be obliged if you will send us your cheque immediately.
3 As the amount owing is considerably overdue, we must now ask you to send us your cheque by return.

Glossary

1 **carriage paid** sender pays for transport
2 **rebate** a refund or allowance
3 **investigation** a detailed enquiry
4 **creditworthy** believed to be financially sound
5 **defer payment** pay at a later date
6 **on account** in part payment

Assignments on material included in this chapter can be found on p 351.

Chapter 8

Letters requesting payment

Tone

Whatever the cause of a customer's failure to pay promptly, it is always annoying to the supplier, but no suggestion of annoyance must be allowed to creep into the correspondence. It may be better not to write at all and, instead, call on the customer if possible, or telephone to tactfully persuade at least part payment to be made on account. In difficult cases it may even be good policy to accept a part payment rather than resort to legal action, which would be both expensive and time-consuming.

There may be several good reasons why a customer fails to pay on time, some of them deserving sympathy. There is, of course, always the customer who is only too ready to invent excuses and who needs to be watched. Each case must be treated on its merits, the style and tone of any letters depending on such factors as the age of the debt, whether later payment is *habitual*[1], and how important the customer is. However, no letter must ever be less than polite, and even the final letter threatening legal action must be written 'with regret'.

Late payments

When there is a need to write explaining difficulties in paying an account by the due date and to ask to defer payment, the following plan is useful:

- Refer to the account which cannot be paid immediately.
- Regret inability to pay, giving reasons.
- Suggest extension of period for payment.
- Hope suggestion will be accepted.

8.1 Customer explains inability to pay

This letter is from a regular and reliable customer. It makes a reasonable request and a supplier refusing it would run the risk of driving that customer away. If the supplier refuses, the customer might pay the outstanding amount, but could then start buying from a competitor. In the process, the supplier would lose many valuable future orders.

Dear Sir/Madam

Your invoice number 527 dated 20 July for £516 is due for payment at the end of this month.

Most unfortunately a fire broke out in our Despatch Department last week and destroyed a large part of a valuable consignment due for delivery to a cash customer. Our claim is now with the insurance company, but it is unlikely to be met for another 3 or 4 weeks and until then we are faced with a difficult financial problem.

I am therefore writing for permission to <u>defer payment</u>[2] of your invoice until the end of September.

As you are aware, my accounts with you have always been settled promptly, and it is with regret that I am now forced to make this request. I hope, however, that you will find it possible to grant it.

Yours faithfully

8.2 Customer explains late payment

Dear

Further to your letter of 4 July, I now enclose a cheque for £182.57 in full settlement of your invoice number W 563, with my apologies for late payment.

This is due to my absence from the office through illness and my failure to leave instructions for your account to be paid. I did not discover the <u>oversight</u>[3] until I returned to the office yesterday.

I would not like you to think that failure to settle your account on time was in any way intentional, and apologise for this delay.

Yours sincerely

Collection letters

The preliminary steps in debt collection are as follows:

1 A first end-of-month statement of account.
2 A second end-of-month statement of account, with added comment.
3 A first letter, worded formally.
4 Second and third letters.

5 A final letter notifying that legal action will be taken unless the amount is paid within a stipulated period of time.

A customer whose account is only slightly *overdue*[4] would understandably be offended to receive a personal letter concerning this. This is why the first 2 reminders usually take the form of end-of-the-month statements of account. Even where the second of these statements is marked with such comments as 'Second application', 'Account overdue – please *remit*[5]' or 'Immediate attention is requested', this is unlikely to give offence.

1 First applications for payment

It is not wise to write a letter until a customer has been given the opportunity to pay on these impersonal statements. Letters requesting payment of overdue accounts are termed 'collection letters'. They aim to:

(a) persuade the customer to settle the account;
(b) retain custom and goodwill.

It would be easy to give offence, so any letters must be written with tact and restraint. It may also be the case that the supplier is at fault, as in the case where a payment received has not been recorded, or goods sent or service given is not satisfactory.

8.3 A printed collection letter

A first collection letter may be printed as a 'form letter' as in this example where the individual details are typed in appropriately. Alternatively, the details may be stored on a word processor so that the letter may be personalised.

Dear Sir or Madam

ACCOUNT NUMBER . . .

According to our records, the above account dated . . . , has not been settled.

The enclosed statement shows the amount owing to be £. . . .

We hope to receive an early settlement[6] of this account.

Yours faithfully

8.4 Personalised collection letters

There may be circumstances where an individual letter rather than a form letter is more appropriate. It should then be addressed to a senior official and marked 'Confidential'.

(a) To a regular payee

Dear Sir/Madam

ACCOUNT NUMBER 6251

As you are usually very prompt in settling your accounts, we wonder whether there is any special reason why we have not received payment of the above account, already a month overdue.

We think you may not have received the statement of account sent on 31 May showing a balance owing of £105.67. A copy is enclosed, which we hope will receive your early attention.

Yours faithfully

(b) To a new customer

Dear Sir/Madam

ACCOUNT NUMBER 5768

We regret having to remind you that we have not received payment of the balance of £105.67 due on our statement for December, sent to you on 2 January, a copy of which is enclosed.

We would remind you that unusually low prices were quoted to you on the understanding of an early settlement.

It may well be that non-payment is due to an oversight, and we now ask you to be good enough to send us your cheque within the next few days.

Yours faithfully

(c) To a customer who has sent a part-payment

Dear

Thank you for your letter of 8 March enclosing a cheque for £100 in part-payment of the balance due on our February statement.

Your payment leaves an unpaid balance of £225.62 and, as our policy is to work on small profit margins, we regret that we cannot grant long term credit facilities.

We hope you will not think it is unreasonable for us to ask for immediate payment of this balance.

Yours sincerely

8.5 Reminder to customer who has already paid

The need for a cautious approach is always necessary since the customer may not be at fault, as where the payment has *gone astray*[7], or where the supplier has received it but failed to record it.

(a) Request for payment

Dear Sir/Madam

ACCOUNT NUMBER S542

According to our records our account for cutlery supplied to you on 21 October has not been paid.

We enclose a detailed statement showing the amount owing to be £105.62 and hope you can now make an early settlement.

Yours faithfully

(b) Customer's reply

Dear

YOUR ACCOUNT NUMBER S542

We were surprised to receive your letter of 8 December stating that you had not received payment of the above account.

In fact, our cheque (number 065821, drawn on Barclays Bank, Blackpool) for £105.62 was posted to you on 3 November. As this cheque appears to have gone astray, I have instructed the bank not to pay on it and now enclose a replacement cheque for the same amount.

Yours sincerely

2 Second application letters

If a reply to the first application is not received, a second application should be sent after about 10 days. This should be firmer in tone, but still polite. Nothing must be said to cause annoyance or ill will. Co-operation is required, and this will not be achieved by annoying the customer.

Addressed to a senior official under 'Confidential' cover, such letters should be planned as follows:

(a) refer to previous application;
(b) assume that something unusual accounts for the delay in payment;
(c) suggest that an explanation would be welcome;
(d) ask for payment to be sent.

8.6 Specimen second application letters

(a) Second letter, following 8.4(a)

Dear Sir/Madam

ACCOUNT NUMBER 6251

As we have not received a reply to our letter of 5 July requesting settlement of the above account, we are writing again to remind you that the amount still owing is £105.67.

No doubt there is some special reason for the delay in payment, and we should welcome an explanation together with your remittance.

Yours faithfully

(b) Second letter, following 8.4(b)

Dear Sir or Madam

On 18 February we wrote reminding you that our December statement sent on 2 January showed a balance of £105.67 outstanding and due for payment by 31 January.

As settlement of this account is now more than a month overdue, we must ask you either to send us your remittance within the next few days, or at least to offer an explanation of the delay in payment.

Yours faithfully

(c) Second letter, following 8.4(c)

Dear Sir/Madam

We have not heard from you since we wrote on 10 March about the unpaid balance of £225.62 on your account. In view of your past good record, we have not previously pressed for a settlement.

To regular customers such as yourself our terms of payment are 3% one month[8], and we hope you will not withhold payment any longer, in which case it would be necessary for us to revise these terms.

In the circumstances we look forward to receiving your cheque for the above amount within the next few days.

Yours faithfully

3 Third application letters

If payment is still not made and if no explanation has been received, a third letter becomes necessary. Such a letter should show that steps will be taken to enforce payment if necessary, such steps depending on individual circumstances. Third letters should follow this plan:

(a) Review earlier efforts to collect payment.
(b) Give a final opportunity to pay by stating a reasonable *deadline date*[9].
(c) State that you wish to be fair and reasonable.
(d) State action to be taken if this third request is ignored.
(e) Regret the necessity for the letter.

8.7 Specimen third application letters

(a) Third letter, following 8.6(a)

Dear Sir/Madam

ACCOUNT NUMBER 6251

We do not appear to have received replies to our two previous requests of 5 and 16 July for payment of the sum of £105.67 still owing on the above account.

It is with the utmost regret that we have now reached the state when we must press for immediate payment. We have no wish to be unreasonable, but failing payment by 7 August I am afraid you will leave us no choice but to place the matter in other hands. We sincerely hope this will not become necessary.

Yours faithfully

(b) Third letter, following 8.6(b)

Dear Sir/Madam

It is very difficult to understand why we have not heard from you in reply to our two letters of 18 February and 2 March about the sum of £105.67 due on our December statement. We had hoped that you would at least explain why the account continues to remain unpaid.

I am sure you will agree that we have shown every consideration in the circumstances. However, failing any reply to our earlier requests for payment, I am afraid we shall have no choice but to take other steps to recover the amount due.

We are most anxious to avoid doing anything through which your credit and reputation might suffer, and even at this late stage are prepared to give you a further opportunity to put matters right. Therefore, we propose to give you until the end of this month to clear your acount[10].

Yours faithfully

(c) Third letter, following 8.6(c)

Dear Sir/Madam

We are both surprised and disappointed not to have heard from you in answer to our two letters of 10 and 23 March reminding you of the balance of £225.62 still owing on our February statement.

This failure either to clear your account or even to offer an explanation is all the more disappointing because of our past satisfactory dealings over many years.

In the circumstances, we cannot be blamed for saying now that unless we hear from you within 10 days we shall have to consider seriously the further steps we ought to take to obtain payment.

Yours faithfully

4 Final collection letters

If all three applications are ignored, it is reasonable to assume that the customer either cannot, or will not, settle the account. A brief notification of the action that is to be taken must then be sent as a final warning.

8.8 Specimen final collection letters

(a) Final letter, following 8.7(a)

Dear Sir/Madam

We are surprised and very much regret that we have received no reply to the further letter we sent to you on 28 July regarding the long overdue payment of £105.67 on your account.

Our relations in the past have always been good. Even so, we cannot allow the amount to remain unpaid indefinitely, and we are reluctantly compelled to put this matter in the hands of our solicitors unless the amount due is paid or a satisfactory explanation received by the end of this month.

Yours faithfully

(b) Final letter, following 8.7(b)

Dear Sir/Madam

We are disappointed not to have received any word from you in answer to our letter of 16 March concerning non-payment of the balance of £105.67 outstanding on our December statement.

As our business relations in the past have always been pleasant and friendly, we are now making a final request for payment in the hope that it will not be necessary to turn the matter over to an agent for collection.

We have, therefore, decided to defer this step for 7 days to give you the opportunity either to pay or at least to send us an explanation.

Yours faithfully

(c) Final letter, following 8.7(c)

Dear Sir/Madam

We are quite unable to understand why we have received no reply to our letter of 7 April, the third we have sent requesting payment of the balance of £225.62 still owing on your account with us.

We feel that we have shown reasonable patience and treated you with every consideration, but the time has now come when we must regretfully take steps to recover payment at law, and the matter will now be placed in the hands of our solicitors.

Yours faithfully

Useful expressions

First applications

Openings

1 We notice that your account, which was due for payment on . . . , is still outstanding.
2 We wish to draw your attention to our invoice number . . . for £. . . which remains unpaid.
3 We are writing to remind you that we have not yet received the balance of our . . . statement amounting to £. . . , payment of which is now more than a month overdue.

Closes

1 We hope to receive your cheque by return.
2 We look forward to your remittance within the next few days.
3 As our statement may have gone astray, we now enclose a copy and shall be glad if you will pass it immediately for payment.

Second applications

Openings

1 We do not appear to have had any reply to our request of . . . for settlement of £. . . due on our invoice . . . dated . . . .
2 We regret not having received a reply to our letter of . . . reminding you that your account had not been settled.
3 We are at a loss to understand why we have received no reply to our letter of . . . requesting settlement of our . . . statement in the sum of £. . . .

Closes

1 We trust you will now attend to this matter without further delay.
2 We must now ask you to settle this account by return.
3 We regret that we must now press for immediate payment of the amount outstanding.

Third applications

Openings

1 We wrote to you on . . . and again on . . . concerning the amount owing on our invoice number . . . .
2 As we have had no reply to our previous requests for payment of our . . . statement, we must now ask you to remit the amount due (£. . .) by the end of this month.
3 We note with surprise and disappointment that we have had no replies to our two previous applications for payment of your outstanding account.

Closes

1 Unless we receive your cheque in full settlement by . . . we shall have no alternative but to instruct our solicitors to recover the amount due.
2 Unless we receive your cheque in full settlement by the end of this month, we shall be compelled to take further steps to enforce payment.
3 We still hope you will discharge this account without further delay and thus save yourself the inconvenience and considerable costs of legal action.

Glossary

1 **habitual** customary, usual
2 **defer payment** pay later
3 **oversight** unintentional omission
4 **overdue** remaining unpaid
5 **remit** send money, pay
6 **settlement** completion by payment
7 **gone astray** been lost in transit
8 **3% one month** subject to a 3 per cent discount if paid within one month
9 **deadline date** final date for payment
10 **clear your account** pay the total balance owing

Assignments on material included in this chapter can be found on p 355.

Chapter 9

Complaints and adjustments

Handling complaints

The utmost tact must be exercised when making a complaint, or when dealing with one. Complaints may be made because:

- the wrong goods have been sent
- poor service has been received
- the quality of the goods is not satisfactory
- the goods have been delivered damaged or late
- the prices charged are not as agreed

1 Making a complaint

When you have a genuine complaint you will feel angry, but you must show *restraint*[1] in your letter, if only because the supplier may not be to blame. The following points need to be considered:

(a) Do not delay, as this will weaken your position and the supplier may have difficulty in investigating the cause.
(b) Do not assume that the supplier is automatically to blame; there may be a perfectly good defence.
(c) Confine your complaint to a statement of the facts, followed by either an enquiry as to what the supplier proposes to do about it, or a suggestion of how the matter can be rectified.
(d) Avoid rudeness; this would create ill-feeling and cause the supplier to be unwilling to resolve matters.

2 Dealing with a complaint

Most suppliers naturally wish to hear if customers have cause to complain. This is better than custom being lost and trade taken elsewhere. It also provides an opportunity to investigate, to explain, and to put things right. In this way, goodwill may be preserved. Receiving such complaints may also suggest ways in which the supplier's products or services could be improved.

When dealing with dissatisfied customers, remember the following rules:

(a) It is often said that the customer *is always right*. This may not always be the case, but it is sound practice to assume that *he may be right*.

(b) Acknowledge a complaint promptly. If you are unable to reply fully, explain that it is being investigated and a full reply will be sent later.

(c) If the complaint is unreasonable, point this out politely and in a way that will not offend.

(d) If you are to blame, admit it readily, express regret and promise to put matters right.

(e) Never blame any of your staff; in the end, you are responsible for their actions.

(f) Thank the customer for informing you about the matter.

Complaints concerning goods

9.1 Complaint concerning wrong goods

If goods are received which are not of the kind or quality ordered, then you are entitled to return them at the supplier's expense.

(a) Complaint

Dear Sir/Madam

On 12 August I ordered 12 copies of <u>Background Music</u> by H Lowery under my order number FT567.   [Order number and date]

On opening the parcel received this morning I found that it contained 12 copies of <u>History of Music</u> by the same author. I regret that I cannot keep these books as I have an adequate stock already. I am therefore returning the books by parcel post for immediate replacement, as I have several customers waiting for them.   [Reason for dissatisfaction]

I trust you will credit my account with the invoiced value of the returned copies, including <u>reimbursement</u>[2] for the postage cost of £7.90.   [Action requested]

Yours faithfully

(b) Reply

Dear Mr Ramsay

We are sorry to learn from your letter of 18 August that a
mistake should have occurred in dealing with your order.

[Express regret]

This mistake is entirely our own, and we apologise for the
inconvenience it is causing you. This occurred due to staff
shortage during this unusually busy season, and also the
fact that these 2 books by Lowery have identical bindings.

[Explain how
the mistake
occurred]

Twelve copies of the correct title have been despatched by
parcel post today.

[Action taken to
rectify the
matter]

Your account will be credited with the invoiced value of
the books and cost of return postage. Our credit note is
enclosed.

We apologise again for this mistake.

Yours sincerely

9.2 Complaint concerning quality

A buyer is entitled to *reject*[3] goods which are not of the quality or description
ordered. However, later deliveries, even of the correct goods, may also not
be accepted.

(a) Complaint

Dear Sir/Madam

We have recently received several complaints from
customers about your fountain pens. The pens are clearly
not giving satisfaction, and in some cases we have had to
refund the purchase price.

[Reason for
complaint]

The pens complained about are part of the batch of 500
supplied against our order number 8562 dated 28 March.
This order was placed on the basis of a sample pen left by
your representative. We have ourselves compared the
performance of this sample with that of a number of the
pens from this batch, and there is little doubt that many
of them are faulty – some of them leak and others blot
when writing.

[Further details]

The complaints we have received relate only to pens from
the batch mentioned above. Pens supplied before these
have always been satisfactory.

We therefore wish you to accept return of the unsold   [Action
balance, amounting to 377 pens, and replace them with   required[
pens of the quality our earlier dealings with you have led
us to expect. Please let us know what arrangements you
wish us to make for their return.

Yours faithfully

(b) Reply (accepting complaint)

Dear

Thank you for your letter dated 10 May pointing out faults in the pens
supplied to your order number 8562. This has caused us a good deal of
concern and we are glad that you brought this matter to our notice.

We have now tested a number of pens from the production batch you
mention, and agree that they are not perfect. The defects have been
traced to a fault in one of the machines, which has now been rectified.

Please arrange to return to us your unsold balance of 377 pens,
carriage forward. We have already arranged for 400 pens to be sent to
replace this unsold balance. The extra 23 pens are sent without charge,
and will enable you to provide free replacement of any further pens
about which you may receive complaints.

We apologise for the inconvenience this has caused you.

Yours sincerely

(c) Alternative reply (rejecting complaint)

If circumstances show that a complaint must be rejected, you must show an
understanding of the customer's position and carefully explain why a rejection
is necessary.

Dear

We are sorry to learn from your letter of 10 May of the difficulties you
are having with the pens supplied to your order number 8562.

All our pens are manufactured to be identical in design and
performance, and we cannot understand why some of them should
have given trouble to your customers. It is normal practice for each

pen to be individually examined by our Inspection Department before being passed into store. However, from what you say, it would seem that a number of the pens included in the latest batch escaped the usual examination.

We sympathise with your problem, but regret that we cannot accept your suggestion to take back all the unsold stock from the batch concerned. Indeed, there should be no need for this since it is unlikely that the number of faulty pens can be very large. We will, of course, gladly replace any pen found to be unsatisfactory, and on this particular batch are prepared to allow you a special discount of 5% to compensate for your inconvenience.

We trust you will accept this as being a fair and reasonable solution of this matter.

Yours sincerely

9.3 Complaint concerning quantity

(a) Surplus goods delivered

When a supplier delivers more than the quantity ordered, the buyer is legally entitled to reject either all the goods or only the excess quantity. Alternatively, all the goods may be accepted and the excess paid for at the same rate. In this letter the buyer rejects the surplus goods but is not obliged to return them; it is the supplier's responsibility to arrange for their collection.

Dear Sir/Madam

Thank you for your promptness in delivering the coffee we ordered on 30 July. However, 160 bags were delivered this morning instead of 120 as stated on our order.

Unfortunately, our present needs are completely covered and we cannot make use of the 40 bags sent in excess of our order. These bags will, therefore, be held in our warehouse until we receive your instructions.

Yours faithfully

(b) Shortage in delivery

When a supplier delivers less than the quantity ordered, the customer cannot be compelled to accept delivery by instalments, and may request immediate delivery of the balance.

Dear Sir/Madam

OUR ORDER NUMBER 861

We thank you for so promptly delivering the gas coke ordered on 20 March. However, although we ordered 5 tonnes in 50-kg bags, only 80 bags were delivered. Your carrier was unable to explain the shortage, and we have not received any explanation from you.

We still need the full quantity ordered and shall be glad if you will arrange to deliver the remaining 20 bags as soon as possible.

Yours faithfully

9.4 Complaint to manufacturer

(a) Customer's complaint

In this letter the buyer was informed by the supplier to write directly to the manufacturer regarding faulty goods.

Dear Sir/Madam

On 15 September I bought one of your 'Big Ben' alarm clocks (mains operated) from Stansfield Jewellers in this town. Unfortunately, I have been unable to get the alarm system to work and am very disappointed with my purchase.

On the advice of Stansfield's manager I am returning the clock to you with this letter for correction of the fault.

Please arrange for the clock to be put in full working order and return it to me as soon as possible.

Yours faithfully

(b) Manufacturer's reply

Here, the manufacturer shows genuine interest in the complaint and does everything possible to ensure customer satisfaction. The considerate manner in which the complaint is treated helps to build a reputation for reliability and fair dealing.

Dear Mrs Wood

Thank you for your letter of 20 September enclosing the defective 'Big Ben' alarm clock.

Your comments on the performance of the clock are very interesting, and we have passed it to our engineers for inspection.

Meanwhile, we are arranging to replace your clock with a new one which has been tested thoroughly to ensure that it is in perfect working order. This will be despatched within the next few days.

We are sorry for the trouble and inconvenience this matter has caused you, but are confident that the replacement clock will prove satisfactory and give you the service you are entitled to expect from our products.

Yours sincerely

Complaints concerning delivery

No supplier likes to be accused of negligence or carelessness, which is often what a complaint about packaging amounts to. Such complaints must be carefully worded so as not to give offence. Nothing is to be gained by being sarcastic or insulting – you are much more likely to get what you want by being courteous. Show that you regret having to complain, but explain that the trouble is too serious not to be reported.

9.5 Complaint concerning damaged goods

(a) Complaint

The writer of this letter points out damage which was discovered after checking the consignment. Any suggestion that the damage to the goods is due to faulty packing is tactfully avoided.

Dear Sir/Madam

OUR ORDER NUMBER R569

We ordered 36 compact discs on 3 January and they were delivered yesterday. Unfortunately, I regret that 8 of them were badly scratched.

The package containing these goods appeared to be in perfect condition and I accepted and signed for it without question[4]. It was on unpacking the compact discs when the damage was discovered, and I can only assume that this was due to 'careless handling at some stage prior to packing.

I am enclosing a list of the damaged goods and shall be glad if you will replace them. They have been kept aside in case you need them to support a claim on your suppliers for compensation.

I hope to hear from you soon.

Yours faithfully

(b) Reply

The supplier's reply promptly complies with the customer's request and shows a desire to improve the service to customers.

Dear

YOUR ORDER NUMBER R569

We were sorry to learn from your letter of 10 January that some of the compact discs supplied to the above order were damaged when they reached you.

Replacements for the damaged goods have been sent by parcel post this morning. It will not be necessary for you to return the damaged goods, and they may be destroyed.

Despite the care we take in packing goods sent by carrier, there have recently been several reports of damage. To avoid further inconvenience and annoyance to customers, as well as expense to ourselves, we are now seeking the advice of a packaging consultant in the hope of improving our methods of handling.

We regret the need for you to write to us and hope the steps we are taking will ensure the safe arrival of all your orders in future.

Yours sincerely

9.6 Complaint regarding bad packing

(a) Complaint

Dear Sir/Madam

The carpet supplied to our order number C395 of 3 July was delivered by your carriers this morning.

We noticed that one of the outer edges of the wrapping has been worn through, presumably as a result of friction in transit, and when we took off the wrapping it was not surprising to find that the carpet itself was soiled and slightly frayed at the edge.

This is the second time in 3 weeks that we have had cause to write to you about the same matter, and we find it hard to understand why precautions could not be taken to prevent a repetition of the earlier damage.

Although other carpets have been delivered in good condition, this second experience within such a short time suggests the need for special precautions against friction when carpets are packed onto your delivery vehicles. We hope that you will bear this in mind in handling our future orders.

In view of the condition of the present carpet, we cannot offer it for sale at the normal price and propose to reduce our selling price by 10%. We suggest that you make us an allowance of 10% on the invoice cost. If you cannot do this, then I am afraid we shall have to return the carpet for replacement.

We hope to receive a prompt reply.

Yours faithfully

(b) Reply

Dear

We were very sorry to learn from your letter of 15 August that the carpet supplied to your order number C395 was damaged on delivery.

Our head packer informs us that the carpet was first wrapped in heavy oiled waterproof paper and then in a double thickness of jut canvas. Under normal conditions this should have been enough protection. However, on this occasion our delivery van contained a full load of carpets for delivery to other customers on the same day, and it is obvious that special packing precautions are necessary in such cases. In all future consignments, we are arranging for specially reinforced end-packings which will hopefully prevent any future damage.

We realise the need to reduce your selling price for the damaged carpet, and readily agree to the special allowance of 10% which you suggest.

Yours sincerely

9.7 Complaint regarding non-delivery

(a) Complaint

Dear Sir/Madam

On 25 September we placed our order number RT56 for printed headed notepaper and invoice forms. You acknowledged the order on 30 September, but as this is now some 3 weeks ago and we have not yet received advice of delivery, we are wondering if the order has since been overlooked.

Your representative promised an early delivery and this was an important factor in persuading us to place this order with you.

The delay in delivery is now causing inconvenience, and we must ask you to complete the order immediately, otherwise we shall be obliged to cancel it and obtain the stationery elsewhere.

Your prompt reply will be appreciated.

Yours faithfully

(b) Reply

Only a very *diplomatic*[5] reply can keep the goodwill of the above customer, who is obviously feeling very let down. With such an understanding and helpful reply from the printer as that below, the customer cannot continue to feel annoyed.

Dear Mr Sargeant

We thank you for your letter of 18 October and quite understand your annoyance at not yet having received the stationery ordered on 25 September.

Orders for printed stationery are at present taking from 3 to 4 weeks for delivery, and our representatives have been instructed to make this clear to customers. Apparently you were not told that it would take so long, and we regret this.

However, on receiving your letter we put your order in hand at once. The stationery will be sent from here tomorrow by express parcel post, and it should reach you within 24 hours of your receiving this letter.

It is very unfortunate that there should have been any misunderstanding, but we hope you will forgive the delay which has been caused.

Yours sincerely

9.8 Complaint regarding frequent late deliveries

This correspondence shows how important it is when sending letters of complaint to write with restraint and not to assume that the supplier is at fault.

(a) Complaint

Dear Sir/Madam

We ordered 6 filing cabinets from you on 2 July on the understanding that they would be delivered within one week. However, these were not received until this morning.

Unfortunately, there have been similar delays on several previous occasions, and their increasing frequency in recent months compels us to say that business between us cannot continue in conditions such as these.

We have felt it necessary to make our feelings known since we cannot give reliable delivery dates to our customers unless we can count on undertakings given by our suppliers.

We hope you will understand our position in this matter, and trust that from now on we can rely on punctual delivery of our orders.

Yours faithfully

(b) Reply

Dear

Your letter of 18 July regarding delays in delivery came as a surprise, as the absence of any earlier complaints led us to believe that goods supplied to your orders were reaching you promptly.

It is our usual practice to deliver goods well in advance of the promised delivery dates, and the filing cabinets to which you refer left here on 5 July. We are very concerned that our efforts to give punctual delivery should be frustrated by delays in transit. It is very possible that other customers are also affected, and we are taking up this whole question with our carriers.

We thank you for drawing our attention to a situation of which we had been quite unaware until you wrote to us. Please accept our apologies for the inconvenience you have been caused.

Yours sincerely

9.9 Complaint regarding uncompleted work

This correspondence relates to a builder's failure to complete work on a new bungalow within the agreed contract time. The buyer's letter is firm but reasonably worded. The builder's reply shows understanding and is convincing, business-like and helpful.

(a) Complaint

Dear Sir/Madam

BUNGALOW AT 1 CRESCENT ROAD, CHINGFORD

When I signed the contract for the building of this property, you estimated that the work would be completed and the bungalow ready for occupation 'in about 6 months'. This is now over 8 months ago and the work is still only half finished.

The delay is causing inconvenience not only to me but also to the buyer of my present home, which I cannot transfer until the bungalow is finished.

I would like to ask you to press forward with this work without any further delay, and wish to know when you expect it to be completed.

Yours faithfully

(b) Reply

Dear Mr Watson

BUNGALOW AT 1 CRESCENT ROAD, CHINGFORD

Thank you for your letter of 18 June. We are of course aware that the estimated period for completion of your bungalow has already been exceeded and wish to say at once that we realise what inconvenience the delay must be causing you.

We would, however, ask you to remember first that we have had an exceptionally severe winter and during several prolonged periods of heavy snow, work on the site has been quite impossible. Secondly, there has been a nationwide shortage of building materials, especially bricks and timber, from which the trade is only just recovering. Without these 2 difficulties, which could not be foreseen, the estimated completion period of 6 months would have been observed.

In the improved weather conditions, work on the bungalow is now proceeding satisfactorily and, unless we have other unforeseen hold-ups[6], we can safely promise that the bungalow will be ready for you by the end of August.

Yours sincerely

9.10 Complaint regarding delivery charges

Some customers are only too ready to complain if things do not suit them. Others who are dissatisfied do not complain, but instead they quietly withdraw their custom and transfer it to some other supplier. This correspondence relates to such a case.

(a) Supplier's enquiry

Dear Sir/Madam

We are sorry to notice that we have had no orders from you since last April. As you have at no time notified us of defects in our products or about the quality of our service, we can only assume that we have given you no cause to be dissatisfied. If we have, then we should be glad to know of it.

If the cause of your discontinued orders is the present depressed state of the market, you may be interested in our latest price list showing a reduction of 7½% on all grocery items, a copy of which is enclosed.

Should there be any matter in which we may have given you cause to be dissatisfied, we hope you will give us the opportunity to put it right so that our custom can be renewed.

Yours faithfully

(b) Customer's reply (complaint)

Dear

Thank you for your letter of 5 July. As you wish to know why we have placed no orders with you recently, we are willing to raise a matter which caused us some annoyance.

On 21 April last year we sent you two orders, one for £74 and one for £42. Your terms at the time provided for free delivery of all orders for £100 or more, but although you delivered these two orders together we were charged with the cost of carriage.

As the orders were submitted on different forms, we grant that you had a perfect right to treat them as separate orders. However, for all practical purposes they could very well have been treated as one, since they were placed on the same day and delivered at the same time. The fact that you did not do this seemed to us to be a particularly ungenerous[7] way of treating a regular customer of many years' standing.

Having now given you our explanation, we should welcome your comments.

Yours sincerely

(c) Supplier's reply

Dear

Thank you for your letter of 8 July. Your explanation gives us the opportunity to explain a most regrettable misunderstanding.

Our charge for carriage on your last two orders arose because they were for goods dealt with by two separate departments, neither of which was aware that a separate order was being handled by another.

At that time, these departments were each responsible for their own packing and despatch arrangements. However, since then this work has been taken over by a centralised packing and despatch department so a repetition of the same kind of misunderstanding is now unlikely.

We trust you will accept our word that the charge we made was quite unintentional[8], and hope that having received our explanation, you will feel able to renew your former custom.

Yours sincerely

9.11 Complaint regarding poor service

This correspondence relates to circumstances where a customer does not receive proper attention. In answer to their telephone enquiry regarding a damaged tape recorder, the supplier suggests that the goods be sent for inspection in order to obtain a quotation for its repair. The customer does so, but hears no more.

(a) Customer's initial letter

The customer writes to the supplier on 28 June after the telephone conversation with Mr Jackson. The customer's letter is addressed 'For the attention of

Mr K J Jackson' as this was the representative who dealt with the telephone enquiry. Note that the correct salutation 'Dear Sirs' is used.

FOR THE ATTENTION OF MR K J JACKSON

Dear Sirs

STEREO CASSETTE RECORDER, MODEL NUMBER 660

Further to my telephone call this morning, I am sending with this letter the above tape recorder. I understand that arrangements can be made for it to be inspected and also a quotation for its repair.

The following faults will be found:

1 The recorder does not reproduce clearly on the right-hand speaker.

2 Distortion suggests that the recording head may need replacing.

3 The winding mechanism appears to be faulty.

It is possible that inspection may reveal other faults.

It would help to speed matters if you could let me have the quotation by telephone as I want this work to be carried out and the recorder returned as quickly as possible.

I hope to hear from you soon.

Yours faithfully

(b) Supplier's acknowledgement

On 5 July, the supplier sent a printed form number WE69376 acknowledging receipt of both the recorder and the customer's letter of 28 June, but did not quote as promised. Two weeks later, on 18 July, the customer wrote to the supplier again. Note that rather than suggest that the quotation has not been sent, the letter states more tactfully that it has not yet been received.

FOR THE ATTENTION OF MR K J JACKSON

Dear Sirs

STEREO CASSETTE RECORDER, MODEL NUMBER 660

On 28 June I sent the above recorder to you by parcel post for inspection and a quotation for servicing. As the matter was of some urgency I suggested a quotation by telephone.

On 5 July, your form number WE69376 acknowledged receipt of the recorder and my letter, but to date I have not received a quotation.

If a quotation has not already been sent, I should be grateful if you could now do so to enable work on the recorder to be put in hand without further delay.

Yours sincerely

(c) Quotation is received and customer sends remittance

On 25 July, a service card headed 'Job Reference WE69376' was received by the customer requesting payment of £60.85 before the service could be carried out. On 28 July the customer sends a cheque for this amount with a covering letter.

Dear Mr Jackson

STEREO CASSETTE RECORDER, MODEL NUMBER 660

I am returning your service card WE69376 with a cheque for £60.85 to cover the cost of servicing the above recorder.

This recorder has now been with you for over 4 weeks and I am greatly inconvenienced without it. I hope you can arrange for its immediate repair and that it can be returned within the next few days.

Yours sincerely

(d) Customer receives a further payment request

No acknowledgement of receipt of the customer's cheque was received. On 14 August the customer received a printed note stating that work on the recorder had now been completed and requesting payment of the amount due.

(e) Customer writes to the Manager

Delay in returning the recorder, and now a request for payment of an amount already paid, understandably angered the customer. The immediate reaction was to write a 'strong' letter to the Manager. Instead, the result was in terms more likely to gain co-operation in rectifying what was probably quite an innocent mistake.

Dear Sir

SEREO CASSETTE RECORDER, MODEL NUMBER 660

I am sorry to have to write to you personally regarding delay in the
return of the above recorder sent in for repair on 28 June. The facts
are as follows:

1 On 28 June I spoke to your Mr K J Jackson regarding my faulty
   tape recorder, and as a result sent my letter dated 28 June together
   with the recorder, requesting a quotation.

2 On 5 July your Service Department acknowledged receipt of the
   recorder and my letter.

3 Not having received the quotation I sent a reminder on 18 July, and
   on 25 July received a service card (reference WE69376) quoting a
   charge of £60.85 for servicing.

4 This card was returned on 28 July with my cheque for this amount
   and my letter asking for the service to be carried out and the
   recorder returned as a matter of urgency.

I heard nothing more until this morning, when I was surprised to
receive a printed form stating that the work had been completed and
asking for payment of the amount due.

I am sure you will appreciate my concern at the length of time involved
in this matter. As it is now 2 full months since I sent it to you, I hope
you will arrange to return it immediately.

Yours faithfully

(f) Manager's apology

In the reply, the Manager admits fault. Sincerity in this matter will help to
restore customer confidence and goodwill.

Dear Mr Richards

STEREO CASSETTE RECORDER, MODEL NUMBER 660

I was very sorry to learn from your letter of 14 August of the problems
experienced in the repair and return of your tape recorder.

I have investigated this matter personally, and regret that the delay is
due to the absence through illness of the assistant who was dealing
with your order initially.

Please accept my apologies for the inconvenience which has been caused. The recorder has now been sent to you by express parcel post, and I hope it will reach you quickly and in good condition.

Please do not hesitate to contact me if I can be of further assistance.

Yours sincerely

(g) Customer thanks Manager

The correspondence could have ended with the Manager's letter, but the customer rightly felt that it would be a matter of courtesy to thank the manager for such prompt intervention.

Dear Mrs Stansfield

STEREO CASSETTE RECORDER, MODEL NUMBER 660

Thank you for your letter of 3 September and for dealing so promptly with this matter. I can appreciate the circumstances which led to the delay which was experienced.

My tape recorder has now been delivered and appears to be in good working order.

Yours sincerely

Cancelling orders

A buyer is legally entitled to cancel his order:

1 At any time before it has been accepted by the supplier.
2 If the goods delivered are of the wrong type or quality (as where they do not conform to sample).
3 If the goods are not delivered by the stated time (or within a reasonable time if no delivery date has been fixed).
4 If more, or less, than the quantity ordered is delivered.
5 If the goods arrive damaged (but only where transportation is the supplier's responsibility).

Unless the contract provides otherwise, it is the buyer's legal duty to collect and transport the goods from the supplier's premises. This would be so where the goods are sold *loco*, ex works or similar terms. The buyer is then liable for any loss or damage occurring during transport. Similarly under an fob or a cif contract, the customer is liable from the time the goods are loaded onto the ship.

9.12 Buyer seeks to cancel order due to adequate stocks

(a) Customer's letter

Dear Sir/Madam

On 2 March I ordered 100 tennis rackets to be delivered at the end of this month.

Persistent bad weather has seriously affected sales and I now find that my present stock will probably satisfy demand in the present season. I am therefore writing to ask you to cancel part of my order and to deliver only 50 of these rackets instead of the 100 ordered.

I am sorry to make this request so late, but hope that you will be able to agree to it in view of our long-standing business association. Should sales improve I would get in touch with you again and take a further delivery.

I look forward to a favourable reply.

Yours faithfully

(b) Supplier agrees to cancel order

A supplier will often agree to cancel or modify the buyer's order, for a number of reasons:

- A wish to oblige a good customer.
- The loss of profit involved may be minimal.
- It helps to create customer good will.
- There may be a ready market for the goods elsewhere.
- The customer's financial position may be doubtful.
- Legal proceedings are costly.

Dear

We have received your letter of 2 May asking us to cancel part of the order you placed on 2 March for tennis rackets.

We are naturally disappointed that there should be any need for this request. However, we always like to oblige our regular customers and in the circumstances are prepared to reduce the number of rackets from 100 to 50 as requested.

We do hope, however, that your sales will improve sufficiently to enable you to take up the balance of your order later on, and in this respect we hope to hear from you again soon.

Yours sincerely

(c) Supplier declines to cancel order

The supplier will sometimes decline to cancel an order for various reasons:

- A wish to retain a sale.
- The manufacture of goods that cannot easily be sold elsewhere may have begun.
- A keen entrepreneur may be unwilling to forgo their legal rights.

The letter refusing a request for cancellation must be carefully and considerately worded if it is not to cause offence and drive a customer away for good. Such a letter must show that you understand the buyer's problems, but tactfully explain the difficulties that cancellation would create for the supplier. The reasons given must be convincing, otherwise the supplier is liable to lose the customer's good will.

Dear

We have received your letter of 2 May asking us to cancel part of your order of 2 March for tennis rackets.

We are sorry you find it necessary to make this request, especially at this late stage. To be able to meet our customers' needs promptly we have to place our orders with manufacturers well in advance of the season and in estimating quantities we rely very largely upon the orders we have received.

We always dislike refusing requests of any kind from regular customers, but regret that on this occasion we have no choice but to do so. All orders, including your own, have already been made up and are now awaiting delivery.

I hope you will understand why we must hold you to your order. Had we received your request earlier we should have been glad to help you.

Yours sincerely

9.13 Cancellation of order through delay in delivery

Dear

In our order number 8546 dated 18 August, we stressed the importance of delivery by 4 October at the very latest.

We have already written to you twice reminding you of the importance of prompt delivery, but as you have failed to make delivery on time we are left with no choice but to cancel the order.

We take this action with regret, but as the goods were required for shipment abroad, and as the boat by which they were to be sent sails tomorrow, we now have no means of getting them to our client in time for the exhibition for which they were required.

We have informed our client of the action we have taken and should be glad if you would acknowledge the cancellation.

Yours sincerely

Useful expressions

Letters of complaint

Openings

1 The goods we ordered from you on . . . have not yet been delivered.
2 Delivery of the goods ordered on . . . is now considerably overdue.
3 We regret having to report that we have not yet received the goods ordered on . . . .
4 We regret to report that one of the cases of your consignment was badly damaged when delivered on . . . .
5 When we examined the goods despatched by you on . . . we found that . . . .
6 We have received a number of complaints from several customers regarding the . . . supplied by you on . . . .

Closes

1 Please look into this matter at once and let us know the reason for this delay.
2 We hope to hear from you soon that the goods will be sent immediately.
3 We feel there must be some explanation for this delay and await your prompt reply.
4 We hope to learn that you are prepared to make some allowance in the circumstances.

Replies to complaints

Openings

1 We are concerned to learn from your letter of . . . that the goods sent under your order number . . . did not reach you until . . . .
2 We are sorry that you have experienced delays in the delivery of . . . .
3 We note with regret that you are not satisfied with the goods supplied to your order of . . . .

4 Thank you for your letter of . . . which has given us the opportunity to rectify a most unfortunate mistake.
5 We wish to apologise for the unfortunate mistake pointed out in your letter of . . . .

Closes

1 We assure you that we are doing all we can to speed delivery and offer our apologies for the inconvenience this delay is causing you.
2 We hope you will be satisfied with the arrangements we have made, and apologise for the inconvenience caused.
3 We trust these arrangements will be satisfactory and look forward to receiving your future orders.
4 We regret the inconvenience which has been caused in this matter.
5 We apologise once again for the unfortunate mistake and can assure you that a similar incident will not occur again.

Glossary

1 **restraint** an effort to hold back an emotion
2 **reimbursement** a refund of money
3 **reject** refuse
4 **without question** without raising any objection
5 **diplomatic** tactful and considerate
6 **hold-ups** delays
7 **ungenerous** mean, selfish
8 **unintentional** not done purposely

Assignments on material included in this chapter can be found on pp 352–3.

Chapter 10

Credit and status enquiries

Reasons for credit

The main reason for buying on credit is for convenience.

1 It enables a retailer to hold stocks and to pay for them out of the proceeds of later sales. This increases the working capital and thus helps to finance the business.
2 It enables the buying public to enjoy the use of goods before they have saved the money needed to buy them.
3 It avoids the inconvenience of separate payments each time a purchase is made.

The main reason for selling on credit is to increase profits. Credit sales not only attract new customers but also keep old customers, since people who run accounts tend to shop at the place where the account is kept, whereas cash customers are free to shop anywhere.

Disadvantages of credit

There are a number of disadvantages in dealing on credit, both for the supplier and for the customer:

1 It increases the cost of doing business since it involves extra work in keeping records and collecting payments.
2 It exposes the supplier to the risk of bad debts.
3 The buyer pays more for the goods since the supplier must raise prices to cover the higher costs.

Requests for credit

A buyer who makes regular purchases from the same supplier will usually wish to avoid the inconvenience of paying for each transaction separately, and will ask for 'open account'[1] terms under which purchases will be paid for monthly or quarterly, or at some other agreed period. In other words, the goods are to be supplied on credit.

10.1 Customer requests open-account terms

(a) Request

Dear

We have been well satisfied with your handling of our past orders and, as our business is growing, expect to place even larger orders with you in the future.

As our dealings have now extended over a period of nearly 2 years, we should be glad if you would grant us open-account facilities with, say, quarterly settlements. This arrangement would save us the inconvenience of making separate payments on invoice[2].

Banker's and trade references can be provided on request.

We hope to receive your favourable reply soon.

Yours sincerely

(b) Reply

Dear

Thank you for your letter of 18 November requesting the transfer of your business from payment on invoice to open-account terms.

As our business relations with you over the past 2 years have been entirely satisfactory, we are quite willing to make the transfer, based on a 90-day settlement period. We note that you will supply references if necessary, but in your case this will not be necessary.

We are pleased that you have been satisfied with our past service and that expansion of your business is likely to lead to increased orders. You may rely upon our continued efforts to give you the same high standard of service as in the past.

Yours sincerely

10.2 Customer requests extension of credit

(a) Cash flow problem

Dear

We regret you have had to remind us that we have not settled your account due for payment on 30 October.

We had intended to settle this account before now, but because of the present depressed state of business our own customers have not been meeting their obligations as promptly as usual. This has adverslely affected[3] our cash flow.

Investment income due in less than a month's time will enable us to clear your account by the end of next month. We should, therefore, be grateful if you would accept the enclosed cheque for £200 as a payment on account[4]. The balance will be cleared as soon as possible.

Yours sincerely

(b) Lending restrictions and bad trade

Dear

STATEMENT OF ACCOUNT FOR AUGUST 19--

We have just received your letter of 8 October requesting settlement of our outstanding balance of £1685.00.

We are sorry not to have been able to clear this balance with our usual promptness, but the present depressed state of business and the current restrictions on bank lending have created difficulties for us. These difficulties are purely temporary as payments from customers are due to us early in the New Year on a number of recently completed contracts.

Our resources[5] are quite sufficient to meet all our obligations, but as you will appreciate we have no wish to realise on our assets[6] at the moment. We should therefore be grateful if you would grant us a 3 months' extension of credit, when we will settle your account in full.

Yours sincerely

(c) Bankruptcy of customer

Dear

We have received and checked your statement for the quarter ended 30 September and agree with the balance of £785.72 shown to be due.

Until now we have had no difficulty in meeting our commitments and have always settled our accounts with you promptly. We could have done so now but for the <u>bankruptcy</u>[7] of an important customer whose affairs are not likely to be settled for some time.

We should therefore be most grateful if you would allow us to defer payment of your present account to the end of next month. This would enable us to meet a temporarily difficult situation forced upon us by events that could not be foreseen.

During the next few weeks we shall be receiving payments under a number of large contracts and if you grant our request, we shall have no difficulty in settling with you in full when the time comes.

We hope to receive a favourable reply.

Yours sincerely

10.3 Supplier replies to request for extension of credit

(a) Request granted

Dear

We have received your letter of 10 October asking for an extension of time for payment of the amount due on our 30 September statement.

In the special circumstances you mention, and because of the promptness with which you have always settled with us in the past, we are willing to grant this extension.

We look forward to receiving your cheque in full settlement by 30 November.

Yours sincerely

(b) *Request refused*

Dear

I am sorry to learn from your letter of 10 October of the difficulty in which the bankruptcy of an important customer has placed you.

I should like to say at once that we fully understand your wish for an extension of time and would very much like to help you. Unfortunately, this is impossible because of commitments we ourselves must meet by the end of this month.

Your request is not at all unreasonable and if it had been at all possible we would have been pleased to grant it. In the circumstances, however, we must ask you to settle with us on the terms of payment originally agreed.

Yours sincerely

Business references

When goods are sold for cash there is no need for the supplier to enquire into the financial standing of the buyer. Where they are sold on credit, however, the ability to pay will be important. Then the supplier will want to know what the buyer's reputation is like, the extent of their business, and in particular whether accounts are paid promptly. It is on this information that the supplier will decide whether to allow credit and, if so, how much.

This information can be obtained from:

- trade references supplied by the customer
- the customer's banker
- various trade associations
- credit enquiry agencies

When a customer places an order with a new supplier, it is customary to supply trade references, that is the names of persons or firms to whom the supplier may refer for information. Alternatively, or in addition, the customer may give the name and address of the banker. References of this kind, supplied as they are by customers themsleves, must be accepted with caution since naturally only those who are likely to report favourably will be named as referees. Even a bank reference can be misleading – a customer may have a satisfactory banking account and yet have business dealings which would not bear looking into.

10.4 Supplier requests references

When a new customer places an order but fails to provide references, the supplier will naturally want some evidence of the customer's creditworthiness, especially if the order is a large one. The supplier's letter asking for references must avoid any suggestion that the customer is not to be trusted.

(a) Supplier's request for references by letter

Dear

We were pleased to receive your first order with us dated 19 May.

When opening new accounts it is our practice to ask customers for trade references. Perhaps you will be good enough to send us the names and addresses of two other suppliers with whom you have dealings.

We hope to receive this information by return, and meanwhile have put your order in hand for despatch immediately we hear further from you.

Yours sincerely

(b) Supplier's request for completion of credit application form

---

Dear

We thank you for your order number 526 of 15 June for polyester bedspreads and pillow cases.

As your name does not appear on our books and as we should like you to take advantage of our usual credit terms, we are enclosing our usual credit application form for your completion and return to us as soon as possible.

We should be able to deliver your present order in about 2 weeks' time, and look forward to receiving your further orders. We hope that this first transaction will mark the beginning of a pleasant business connection.

Yours sincerely

10.5 Customer returns completed credit application form (reply to 10.4(b))

Dear

Thank you for your letter of 18 June. As we fully expect to place further orders, we should obviously like to take advantage of your offer of credit facilities.

We quite understand the need for references and have completed and now return your credit application form giving the relevant information.

We look forward to receiving delivery of our first order by the end of this month, and to our future business dealings with you.

Yours sincerely

10.6 Customer supplies trade references

Dear Sir/Madam

Thank you for the catalogue and price list received earlier this month.

We now have pleasure in sending you our first order, number ST6868, for 6 Olivetti portable electronic typewriters, elite type, at your list price of £155 less 25% on your usual monthly terms.

These machines are needed for early delivery to customers and, as we understand you have the machines in stock, we should be glad if you would send them to reach us by the end of next week. We hope this will leave enough time for you to take up references with the following firms, with which we have had dealings over many years:

B Kisby & Co Ltd, 28–30 Lythan Square, Liverpool
The Atlas Manufacturing Co Ltd, Century House, Bristol

We look forward to doing further business with you in the future.

Yours faithfully

10.7 Customer supplies a banker's reference

Dear Sir/Madam

I am pleased to enclose a cheque for £2513 in full settlement of your invoice number 826 for the stereo tape recorders supplied earlier this month.

My directors have good reason to believe that these particular products will be a popular selling line in this part of the country. As we expect to place further orders with you from time to time, we should be glad if you would arrange to provide open-account facilities on a quarterly basis.

For information concerning our credit standing[8] we refer you to Barclays Bank Ltd, 25–27 The Arcade, Southampton.

I look forward to your early reply.

Yours faithfully

Status enquiries

Letters taking up trade references are written in formal, polite terms, and usually conform to the following plan:

- Request general information about the prospective customer's *standing*[9]
- Request an opinion on the wisdom of granting credit within a stated limit
- Give an assurance that the information will be treated confidentially
- Enclose a stamped, addressed envelope, or an international postal reply coupon if the correspondent lives abroad

Some large firms make their enquiries on a specially printed form containing the questions they would like answering. Use of such forms makes easier the task of the firms approached, and helps to ensure prompt replies.

When the supplier receives the information requested, it is courteous to send a suitable letter of acknowledgement and thanks.

Letters taking up references should be addressed to a senior official and marked 'Confidential'.

10.8 Supplier takes up trade references

(a) Example 1

Dear Sir/Madam

Watson & Jones of Newcastle wish to open an account with us and have given your name as a reference.

We should be grateful if you would supply us with any information about the firm's general standing and give us your opinion on whether they are likely to be reliable for credit up to £1,000 and to settle their accounts promptly.

We enclose a stamped, addressed envelope for your reply, which will of course be treated in strict confidence.

Yours faithfully

(b) Example 2

Dear Sir/Madam

We have received a request from Messrs Pierre Rocheford et Cie of Rabat for supplies of our products on open-account terms. They state that they have regularly traded with you over the past 2 years and have given us your name as a reference.

We should be obliged if you would kindly tell us in confidence whether you have found this company to be thoroughly reliable in their dealings with you and prompt in settling their accounts.

We understand their requirements may amount to approximately £2,000 a quarter, and should be glad to know if you feel they are able to meet commitments of this size. Any other information you can provide would be very welcome.

Your reply, for which we enclose an international postal reply coupon, will of course be treated in strict confidence.

Yours faithfully

10.9 Supplier requests his banker to take up bank reference

In view of the highly confidential relationship between bankers and their customers, a banker will not normally reply direct to private enquiries about the standing of a client. This information is, however, given willingly to fellow bankers. When taking up a bank reference, therefore, the supplier must do so through their own banker.

Dear Sir/Madam

The Colston Engineering Co Ltd, Oyo, have asked for a standing credit of £3,000, but as our knowledge of this company is limited to a few months' trading on a cash-on-invoice basis, we should like some information about their financial standing before dealing with their request.

The only reference they give us is that of their bankers – the National Bank of Nigeria, Ibadan. We shall be most grateful for any information you can obtain for us.

Yours faithfully

10.10 Supplier refers to credit enquiry agency

A supplier who wants an independent reference concerning a customer's business standing, may refer either to a trade association or to one of the numerous credit enquiry agencies. These agencies make it their business to supply information on the financial standing of both trading firms and professional and private individuals. They have a remarkable store of information, which they keep up-to-date from a variety of sources, including their own local agents. Where the information requested is not immediately available from their records, they will set up enquiries and can usually supply it within a few days.

Dear Sirs

We have been asked by A Griffiths & Co, Cardiff, to supply goods to the value of £1,750 against their first order on open-account terms.

We have no information about this firm but as there are prospects of further large orders from them, we should like to meet the present order on the terms sought if it is safe to do so.

Would you please let us have a report on the reputation and financial standing of the firm and, more particularly, your advice on whether it would be advisable to grant credit for this first order. We should also like your advice on the maximum amount for which it would be safe to grant credit on a quarterly account.

Yours faithfully

Replies to status enquiries

Where the credit of the firm enquired about is satisfactory, the reply to the enquiry presents no problem. However, where the firm's credit is uncertain, the reply calls for the utmost care. It is usual to phrase such replies in a manner that leaves the enquirer to 'read between the lines', i.e. to gather for themselves the true meaning.

Replies to letters taking up references should be marked 'Confidential' and follow the following plan:

- A statement of the facts and an honest expression of opinion.
- A hope that the information supplied will be useful.
- A tactful reminder that the information is confidential and that no responsibility for it can be accepted.

10.11 Trader's replies to credit information enquiry

(a) Favourable reply to 10.8(a)

Dear

We are pleased to state that the firm referred to in your letter of 25 May are a small but well-known and highly respectable firm who have been established in this town for more than 25 years.

We have now been doing business with this company for over 7 years on quarterly-account terms and although they have not usually taken advantage of cash discounts, they have always paid their account promptly on the net dates. The credit we have allowed this company has at times been well over the £1,000 you mention.

We hope this information will be helpful and that it will be treated as confidential.

Yours faithfully

(b) Discouraging reply to 10.8(b)

Dear

The company mentioned in your letter of 25 May has placed regular orders with us for several years. We believe the company to be trustworthy and reliable, although we are bound to say that they have not always settled their accounts with us by the due date.

Their account with us is on quarterly settlement terms, but we have never allowed it to reach the sum mentioned in your letter. This to us seems to be a case in which caution is necessary.

We are glad to be of help, but ask you to ensure that the information provided is treated as strictly confidential.

Yours faithfully

10.12 Banker's replies to credit information enquiry

(a) Favourable reply to 10.9

Dear

We have now received from the National Bank of Nigeria the information requested in your letter of 18 September.

The company you mention is a private company run as a family concern by three brothers, and was founded 15 years ago. It enjoys a good reputation. Our information shows that the company is punctually meeting its commitments and a credit in the sum you mention would seem to be safe.

This information is strictly confidential and is given without any responsibility on our part.

Yours sincerely

(b) Unfavourable reply to 10.9

Dear

We have now received from the National Bank of Nigeria information concerning the company referred to in your letter of 18 September.

This is a private company run as a family concern and operating on a small scale.

More detailed information we have received suggests that this is a case in which we would advise caution. You will of course treat this advice as strictly confidential.

Yours sincerely

10.13 Agency's replies to credit information enquiry

(a) Favourable reply to 10.10

Dear

We have now completed our enquiries relating to the firm mentioned in your letter of 10 February and are pleased to report favourably.

They are a well-founded and highly reputable firm. There are four partners and the capital at their command is estimated to be at least £100,000. They do a splendid trade and are regarded as one of the safest accounts in Cardiff.

From the information we have gathered we are of the opinion that you need not hesitate to allow the initial credit of £1,750 requested, and that on a quarterly account you could safely allow at least £5,000.

Yours sincerely

(b) Unfavourable reply to 10.10

Dear Sirs

We have completed our enquiries concerning the firm mentioned in your letter of 10 February and regret that we must advise caution in their request for credit.

About a year ago an action was brought against this company by one of its suppliers for recovery of sums due, though payment was later recovered in full.

Our enquiries reveal nothing to suggest that the firm is not straightforward. On the contrary, the firm's difficulties would seem to be due to bad management and in particular to overtrading[10]. Consequently, most of the firm's suppliers either give only very short credit for limited sums, or make deliveries on a cash basis.

This information is of course supplied in the strictest confidence.

Yours sincerely

Useful expressions

Suppliers' requests for references

Openings

1 Subject to satisfactory references we shall be glad to provide the open account facilities requested in your letter of . . . .
2 We were pleased to receive your order of . . . and shall be glad to consider open-account terms if you will kindly supply the usual trade references.

Closes

1 Subject to satisfactory references being received, we shall be glad to offer you open-account terms.
2 It is our usual practice to request references from new customers, and we hope to receive these soon.

Customers supply references

Openings

1 Thank you for your letter of . . . in reply to our request for open-account terms.
2 We have completed and now return the credit application form received with your letter of . . . .

Closes

1 We would refer you to the following firms who will be pleased to answer your enquiries . . . .
2 For the information required, please refer to our bankers, who are . . . .

Suppliers take up references

Openings

1 . . . of . . . has supplied your name as a reference in connection with his (her, their) application for open-account terms.
2 We have received a large order from . . . and should be grateful for any information you can provide regarding their reliability.
3 We should be grateful if you would obtain reliable information for us concerning . . . .

Closes

1 Any information you can provide will be appreciated.
2 Any information provided will, of course, be treated in strictest confidence.
3 Please accept our thanks in advance for any help you can give us.

Replies to references taken up

Openings

1 We welcome the opportunity to report favourably on . . . .
2 In reply to your letter of . . . we can thoroughly recommend the firm you enquire about.
3 The firm mentioned in your letter of . . . is not well known to us.

Closes

1 This information is given on the clear understanding that it will be treated confidentially.
2 We ourselves would not hesitate to grant credit up to £. . . .
3 This information is given to you in confidence and without any responsibility on our part.

Glossary

1 **open account** credit terms with periodic settlements
2 **payments on invoice** payment due on presentation of invoice
3 **adversely affected** made worse
4 **payment on account** part payment
5 **resources** financial position
6 **realise on our assets** sell assets in order to raise cash
7 **bankruptcy** inability to pay one's debts
8 **credit standing** financial position
9 **standing** status, reputation
10 **overtrading** trading beyond one's means

Assignments on material included in this chapter can be found on pp 356–7.

Chapter 11

A typical business transaction (correspondence and documents)

Letters of the kind considered in this unit are handled in business every day. This chapter illustrates their use in a typical transaction in the home trade.

G Wood & Sons have recently opened an electrical goods store in Bristol and place an order with Electrical Supplies Ltd, Birmingham, for the supply of goods on credit. The transaction opens with a request by G Wood & Sons for information regarding prices and terms for credit.

11.1 Request for quotation

G WOOD & SONS
36 Castle Street, Bristol BS1 2BQ
Telephone 54967

GW/ST

15 November 19--

Mr H Thomas
Electrical Supplies Ltd
29-31 Broad Street
Birmingham
B1 2HE

Dear Mr Thomas

We have recently opened an electrical goods store at the above address and have received a number of enquiries for the following domestic appliances, of which at present we do not hold stocks:

Swanson Electric Kettles, 2 litre
Cosiwarm Electric Blankets, single-bed size
Regency Electric Toasters
Marlborough Kitchen Wall Clocks

When I phoned you this morning you informed me that all these items are available in stock for immediate delivery. I should be glad if you would quote your prices and terms for payment 2 months from date of invoicing. Provided prices and terms are satisfactory, we would place with you a first order for 10 of each of these items.

The matter is of some urgency and we would appreciate an early reply.

Yours faithfully

G WOOD
Manager

11.2 Supplier's quotation

ELECTRICAL SUPPLIES LTD
29-31 Broad Street, Birmingham B1 2HE
Tel: 021-542 6614

HT/JH

17 November 19--

Mr G Wood
Messrs G Wood & Sons
36 Castle Street
Bristol
BS1 2BQ

Dear Mr Wood

QUOTATION NUMBER E542

We welcome your enquiry of 15 November and are pleased to quote as follows:

	£
Swanson Electric Kettles, 2 litre	25.00 each
Cosiwarm Electric Blankets, single-bed size	24.50 each
Regency Electric Toasters	25.50 each
Marlborough Kitchen Wall Clocks	27.50 each

The above are current catalogue prices from which we would allow you a trade discount of 33⅓%. Prices include packing and delivery to your premises.

It is our practice to ask all new customers for trade references. Will you therefore please submit the names and addresses of two suppliers with whom you have had regular dealings. Subject to satisfactory replies, we shall be glad to supply the goods and to allow you the 2 months' credit requested.

As there may be other items in which you are interested, we enclose copies of our current catalogue and price list, and look forwrd to the opportunity of doing business with you.

Yours sincerely

H Thomas
Secretary

11.3 Request for permissiion to quote company as reference

A buyer should obtain consent from the suppliers whose names may be submitted as references. Consent may be obtained verbally if there is urgency, but otherwise the buyer should make this request in writing. In this case, a letter was sent to J Williamson & Co, Southey House, Coventry, CV1 5RU, as well as the addressee of the following letter.

GW/ST

19 November 19--

R Johnson Bros
The Hayes
Cardiff
CF1 1JW

Dear Sirs

I wish to place an order with Electrical Supplies Ltd, Birmingham, with facilities on credit. As mine is a first order they have asked me to supply trade references.

I have been a regular customer of yours for the past 4 years and should be grateful if you would allow me to submit the name of your firm as one of my references.

I shall very much appreciate your consent to stand as referee, and hope to hear from you soon.

Yours faithfully

G Wood
Manager

11.4 Permission granted

R JOHNSON BROS
The Hayes, Cardiff CF1 1JW
Telephone 572382

RH/KI

22 November 19--

Mr G Wood
G Wood & Sons
36 Castle Street
Bristol
BS1 2BQ

Dear Mr Wood

We refer to your request of 19 November requesting permission to use our name as a reference in your transaction with Electrical Supplies Ltd.

During the time we have done business together you have been a very reliable customer. If your suppliers decide to approach us for a reference we shall be very happy to support your request for credit facilities.

Yours sincerely

R Harris
Financial Controller

11.5 Order

(a) Covering letter

GW/ST

24 November 19--

Mr H Thomas
Electrical Supplies Ltd
29-31 Broad Street
Birmingham
B1 2HE

Dear Mr Thomas

ORDER NUMBER 3241

Thank you for your letter of 17 November, quoting for domestic appliances and enclosing copies of your current catalogue and price list.

We give below the names of two suppliers with both of whom we have had regular dealings over the past 4 or 5 years:

R Johnson Bros, The Hayes, Cardiff CF1 1JW
J Williamson & Co, Southey House, Coventry CV1 5RU

We now enclose our order number 3241 for the goods mentioned in our original enquiry. They are urgently needed and, as they are available from stock, we trust you will make prompt delivery.

We place this order on the understanding that 2 months will be allowed for payment.

Yours sincerely

G Wood
Manager

Enc

(b) Order form

G WOOD & SONS
Electrical Supplies
36 Castle Street
Bristol BS1 2BQ
Telephone 54967

ORDER NO 3241   Date 24 November 19– –

Electrical Supplies Ltd
29–31 Broad Street
BIRMINGHAM
B1 2HE

Please supply

Quantity	Item(s)	Price
		£
10	Swanson Electric Kettles (2 litre)	25.00 each
10	Cosiwarm Electric Blankets (single-bed size)	24.50 each
10	Regency Electric Toasters	25.50 each
10	Marlborough Kitchen Wall Clocks	27.50 each

Terms   33⅓% trade discount

for G Wood & Sons

Fig. 11.1 Order form

11.6 Supplier's acknowledgement

It is good business practice to acknowledge and thank buyers for the order, particularly a first order, and trade reference information. The supplier will then take up the references and, having received favourable replies, will put the order in hand.

HT/JH

1 December 19--

Mr G Wood
G Wood & Sons
36 Castle Street
Bristol
BS1 2BQ

Dear Mr Wood

YOUR ORDER NUMBER 3241

Thank you for your letter of 24 November. We were very pleased to receive your order, and confirm supply of the goods at the prices and on the terms stated.

Your order has been passed to our warehouse for immediate despatch of the goods from stock, and we hope you will be pleased with them.

We look forward to doing further business with you.

Yours sincerely

H Thomas
Secretary

11.7 Advice note

Documents dealing with the despatch and delivery of goods include packing notes, advice of despatch notes, consignment notes and delivery notes. These documents are really copies of the invoice and are often prepared in sets, with the use of NCR (no carbon required) paper, at the same time as the invoice, but without information as to pricing.

The advice or despatch note informs the buyer that the goods are on the way and enables a check to be made when they arrive. It is often dispensed with and replaced either by an invoice sent on or before the day the goods are despatched, or sometimes by a letter notifying despatch.

For small items sent by post a packing note, which is simply a copy of the advice note, would be the only document used. Some suppliers, especially those using their own transport, also dispense with the advice note and instead use either a packing note or a delivery note.

For our present transaction the advice note would be prepared in some such form as shown in Fig. 11.2.

11.8 Consignment note

When goods are sent by rail the supplier is required to complete a consignment note, which represents the contract of carriage with the railway. It gives particulars of the quantity, weight, type and destination of the goods and states whether they are being sent carriage paid (i.e. paid by the sender) or carriage forward (i.e. paid by the buyer). In most cases the printed forms supplied by the railway are used, but a trader will someties prefer to use their own.

The completed consignment note is handed to the carrier when the goods are collected, and it travels with them. When the goods are delivered to the buyer the note must be signed as proof of delivery.

11.9 Delivery note

Sometimes two copies of the delivery note are prepared, one to be retained by the buyer, the other to be given back to the carrier signed as evidence that the goods have been delivered. Alternatively, the carrier may ask the buyer to sign a Delivery Book or a Delivery Sheet recording the calls a carrier has to make.

Where it is not possible for the buyer to inspect the goods before signing them, the signature should be qualified with some such comment as 'not examined' or 'goods unexamined', as a precaution.

11.10 Invoice

Invoice practice varies. Sometimes the invoice is enclosed with the goods and sometimes it is sent separately, either in advance of the goods, in which case it also serves as an advice note, or after the goods. It will be sent separately where the goods are baled, or supplied loose or in bulk.

ELECTRICAL SUPPLIES LTD
29–31 Broad Street
Birmingham B1 2HE
Telephone 021-542-6614

ADVICE NOTE

Messrs G Wood & Sons   Your Order No 3241
36 Castle Street
BRISTOL
BS1 2BQ   Date 3 December 19– –

Delivery details: Despatched today by rail in 3 cases (78, 79, 80)

Quantity	Item(s)
10	Swanson Electric Kettles (2 litre)
10	Cosiwarm Electric Blankets (single-bed size)
10	Regency Electric Toasters
10	Marlborough Kitchen Wall Clocks
	Despatched by rail, packed in three cases (numbers 78–80) on 3 December 19– –
	Carriage paid

Registered in England No 726549

Fig. 11.2   Advice note

(a) Covering letter

It is not always necessary to send a covering letter with an invoice, but if a letter is sent it need only be very short and formal.

HT/JH

3 December 19--

G Wood & Sons
36 Castle Street
Bristol
BS1 2BQ

Dear Sirs

YOUR ORDER NUMBER 3241

We enclose our invoice number 6740 for the domestic electrical appliances supplied to your order dated 24 November.

The goods have been packed in three cases, numbers 78, 79 and 80, and sent to you today by rail, carriage paid. We hope they will reach you promptly and in good condition.

If you settle the account within 2 months we will allow you to deduct from the amount due a special cash discount of 1½%.

Yours faithfully

H Thomas
Secretary

Enc

Notes

1 For reference purposes the invoice is given a serial number. The order number is also quoted.
2 The terms of payment indicate an allowable cash discount for payment within 2 months from date of invoice. This discount is deducted at the time of payment.
3 'E & O E' means 'errors and omissions excepted'. It reserves the right for the seller to correct any error in or omissions from the invoice.
4 When G Wood & Sons receive the invoice they will check it with the packing note or delivery note received with the goods to ensure all goods invoiced have been received. They will check the invoice for trade discounts and arithmetical accuracy before recording it in their books of account.

(b) Invoice

ELECTRICAL SUPPLIES LTD
29–31 Broad Street
Birmingham B1 2HE
Telephone 021-542-6614

INVOICE

G Wood & Sons   Your order no 3241
36 Castle Street
BRISTOL
BS1 2BQ   Date 3 December 19--

Invoice No 6740

Quantity	Item(s)	Unit Price	Total Price
		£	£
10	Swanson Electric Kettles (2 litre)	25.00	250.00
10	Cosiwarm Electric Blankets (single-bed size)	24.50	245.00
10	Regency Electric Toasters	25.50	255.00
10	Marlborough Kitchen Wall Clocks	27.50	275.00
			1025.00
	Less 33⅓% trade discount		341.66
			683.34
	VAT @ 17.5%		119.58
			802.92
	3 packing cases (returnable)		15.00
			817.92
	Terms: 1½% two months		

E & OE   Registered in England No 726549

Fig. 11.3 Invoice

5 As a rule the invoice is not used as a demand for payment, but as a record
of the transaction and statement of the indebtedness to which it gives rise.
The supplier will then later send a statement of account to the buyer.

11.11 Debit and credit notes

For the purposes served by these two documents, refer to pages 70–5.

(a) Buyer requests credit note

In our specimen transaction, G Wood & Sons will return the three packing
cases charged on the invoice. They will then write to the suppliers requesting
them to issue a credit note for the invoiced value of the cases. Depending on
their practice, G Wood & Sons may or may not prepare and send a debit note
when making the request.

GW/ST

10 December 19--

The Secretary
Electrical Supplies Ltd
29-31 Broad Street
Birmingham
B1 2HE

Dear Sir

INVOICE NUMBER 6740

We have today returned to you by rail the three packing cases charged
on the above invoice at a cost of £15.00.

We enclose a debit note for this amount and shall be glad to receive
your credit note.

All the goods supplied and invoiced reached us in good condition We
thank you for the promptness with which you dealt with our first
order.

Yours faithfully

G Wood
Manager

Enc

G WOOD & SONS
36 Castle Street
Bristol BS1 2BQ
Telephone 54967

DEBIT NOTE

Electrical Supplies Ltd   Date 10 December 19−−
29−31 Broad Street
BIRMINGHAM
B1 2HE   Debit Note No D 841

Date	Details	Total
		£
10.12.−−	To 3 packing cases charged on your	
	invoice number 6740 and returned	15.00

Fig. 11.4 Debit note

(b) Seller issues credit note

When Electrical Supplies Ltd receive the debit note (see Fig. 11.4) they will check return of the cases. They will then prepare the credit note requested and send it to G Wood & Sons, with or without a covering letter. Any letter sent need only be short and formal, but as this is the buyer's first transaction, the supplier would be wise to add a short note to encourage future business.

HT/JH

14 December 19--

G Wood & Sons
36 Castle Street
Bristol
BS1 2BQ

Dear Sirs

As requested in your letter of 10 December enclosing debit note
number D841, we confirm receipt of the three packing cases returned

to you. We are pleased to enclose our credit note number C672 for the sum of £15.00.

We hope we may look forward to receiving further orders from you.

Yours faithfully

H Thomas
Secretary

Enc

ELECTRICAL SUPPLIES LTD
29—31 Broad Street
Birmingham B1 2HE
Telephone 021-524-6614

CREDIT NOTE

G Wood & Sons   Date 14 December 19--
36 Castle Street
BRISTOL
BS1 2BQ   Credit Note No C 672

Date	Details	Total
		£
10.12.--	By 3 packing cases charged on invoice no 6740 and now returned	15.00

Fig. 11.5 Credit note

11.12 Statement of account

Statement of accounts are sent to customers at periodic intervals, normally monthly. Besides serving as a request for payment, the statement enables the buyer to compare the account kept by the supplier with that kept in the buyer's own books. Statements, like invoices, are often sent without a covering letter (see Fig. 11.6).

ELECTRICAL SUPPLIES LTD
29–31 Broad Street
Birmingham B1 2HE
Telephone 021-524-6614

STATEMENT

G Wood & Sons   Date 31 January 19--
36 Castle Street
BRISTOL
BS1 2BQ

Date	Details	Debit	Credit	Balance
		£	£	£
3.12.--	Invoice 6740	817.92		817.92
14.12.--	Credit note C 672		15.00	802.92
	(2½% seven days)			

E & OE   Registered in England No 726549

Fig. 11.6   Statement

11.13   Payment

Invoices and statements usually bear an indication of the terms of payment.
For example:

Prompt Cash: a somewhat elastic term, but generally taken to mean payment
within 15 days from date of invoice or statement.
2½% 30 days: this means that the debtor is entitled to deduct 2½% from the
amount due if payment is made within 30 days of the invoice or statement,
otherwise the full amount becomes payable.
Net 30 days: this means that the debtor must pay in full within 30 days.

Payments in business are usually made by cheque or, if they are numerous,
by credit transfer (bank giro). In this transaction, the buyer settles the account
by sending a cheque to the supplier.

GW/ST

4 February 19--

The Secretary
Electrical Supplies Ltd
29-31 Broad Street
Birmingham
B1 2HE

Dear Sir/Madam

We are in receipt of your statement of account dated 31 January 19--.

From the total amount due on the statement I have deducted the allowable cash discount of 2½% and enclose a cheque for £810.89 in full settlement.

Yours faithfully

G Wood
Manager

Enc

11.14   Receipt

A cheque paid by the banker on whom it is drawn supplies all the evidence of payment necessary. Consequently, it is not usual practice for formal receipts to be issued. This does not, however, affect the payer's legal right to request a receipt if one is required. In this case, the supplier's formal receipt or the buyer's cheque after it has been paid by the bank serve equally well as evidence of the payment made.

Unit 3
Special business letters

Chapter 12

Goodwill letters

One of the most important functions of business letters is to create good business relations. Business executives take the opportunity to send good wishes, congratulations or sympathy on such occasions as the award of an honour, a promotion, a wedding or a death. Such letters are very much appreciated by customers and colleagues and are very good for business.

General goodwill letters

The following letters are examples of ways in which goodwill can be built into the everyday business letter. The tone of the letters is courteous and friendly, and the added touches of personal interest are certain to make a good impression.

12.1 Letter with short personal greeting

A personal touch may sometimes take the form of a short final paragraph conveying a personal greeting.

Dear Mr Ellis

I am sorry not to have replied sooner to your letter of 25 October regarding the book <u>English and Commercial Correspondence</u>. My Export Director is in Lebanon and Syria on business and as I am dealing with his work as well as my own, I am afraid my correspondence has fallen behind.

Whether this book should be published in hardback or paperback is a decision I must leave to my Editorial Director, to whom I have passed on your letter. No doubt she will be writing to you very soon.

I trust you are keeping well.

With best wishes

Yours sincerely

12.2 Letter with extended personal greeting

An even more personal note may be introduced in the form of a final paragraph.

Dear Ms Jenner

I have now had an opportunity to review the book you sent to me recently.

This book presents a concise and very clear account of the new import regulations, with good examples of how they are likely to be applied.

More detailed comments are made on my written review which is attached.

I remember that you will be spending your approaching summer holiday in the south of France, and wish you good weather and an enjoyable time.

Yours sincerely

12.3 Letter explaining delayed reply

A favourable impression is created when a letter is answered on the day it is received. If this is not possible, the letter should be acknowledged immediately giving an explanation of the delay.

Dear Mrs Jones

I am sorry we cannot send you immediately the catalogue and price list requested in your letter of 13 March, as we are presently out of stock.

Supplies are expected from our printers in 2 weeks' time and as soon as they are received, we will send a copy to you.

Yours sincerely

12.4 Supplier's letter with friendly tone

Customers always look for a spirit of friendliness in those with whom they seek to do business. In this letter, the writer is both helpful and friendly. The aim is to interest the prospective customer, to create a feeling of confidence and to win their consideration, friendship – and, ultimately, their custom.

Dear Mr Jackson

We are pleased to enclose our catalogue and price list as requested in your letter of 12 October.

In this latest catalogue we have taken trouble to ensure it is both attractive and informative, and particulars of our trade discounts are shown inside the front cover.

May we suggest that next time you are in Bristol you should allow us to show you our factory, where you could see for yourself the high quality of materials and workmanship put into our products. This would also enable you to see at first hand the latest fancy leather goods, and to return with interesting and useful information for your customers.

If we can be of service in any way, please do not hesitate to let us know.

Yours sincerely

12.5 Letter welcoming a visitor from abroad

When customers from overseas visit your country, it is sound business practice to extend hospitality and to give any help and advice you can. The tone of such letters must sound sincere and friendly, giving the impression that the writer is genuinely anxious to be of service.

Dear Mr Brandon

It was a pleasure to receive your letter of 24 April and to learn that your colleague, Mr John Gelling, is making plans to visit England in July. We shall be very pleased to welcome him and to do all we can to make his visit enjoyable and successful.

I understand this will be Mr Gelling's first visit to England, and am sure he will wish to see some of our principal places of interest. A suitable programme is something we can discuss when he arrives. I would also be pleased to introduce him to several firms with whom he may like to do business.

When the date of Mr Gelling's visit is settled, please let me know his arrival details. I will arrange to meet him at the airport and drive him to his hotel. He may be assured of a warm welcome.

Yours sincerely

Letters in which tone is particularly important

In business it is sometimes necessary to refuse requests, to increase prices, explain an unfortunate oversight, apologise for mistakes, etc. In such letters, tone has to be the writer's main concern. Without due consideration, offence could be caused, bad feeling created and maybe business lost.

12.6 Letter conveying unwelcome news

It is sometimes necessary to refuse a request or to convey unwelcome news. When this is necessary, think of the reader, prepare the way for their disappointment by a suitable opening paragraph, and use an appropriate tone.

Dear Mr Foster

It was good of you to let me see your manuscript on <u>English for Business Studies</u>. I read it with interest and was impressed by the care and thoroughness with which you have treated the subject. I particularly like the clear and concise style of writing.

Had we not quite recently published <u>Practical English</u> by Freda Leonard, a book that covers very similar ground, I would have been very happy to accept your manuscript for publication. In the circumstances, however, I am unable to do so and am returning your manuscript with this letter.

I am sorry to have to disappoint you.

Yours sincerely

12.7 Letter disclaiming liability for loss

Here is another letter in which the opening paragraph is used to prepare the recipient for the rejection of his insurance claim.

Dear Sir/Madam

When we received your letter of 23 November, we sent a representative to inspect and report on the damage caused by the recent fire in your warehouse.

She has now submitted her report, which confirms your claim that the damage is extensive. However, she states that a large proportion of the stock damaged or destroyed was very old and some of it obsolete.

We regret, therefore, that we cannot accept your figure of £15,000 as a fair estimate of the loss, since it appears to be based on the original cost of the goods.

Yours sincerely

12.8 Letter refusing a request for credit

A letter refusing a request for credit without causing offence is one of the most difficult to write. Refusal will be prompted by doubts about the would-be creditor's standing, but the letter must contain no suggestion of this. Other reasons for the refusal must be found and tactfully explained.

   This letter is a wholesaler's reply to a trader who has started a new business which appears to be doing well. However, the business has not been established long enough to inspire confidence in the owner's financial standing.

Dear Miss Wardle

We were glad you approached us with a view to placing an order, and to learn of the good start of your new business.

The question of granting credit for newly-established businesses is never an easy one. Not a few get into difficulties because they overcommit themselves before they are thoroughly established. Although we believe that your own business promises very well, we feel it would be better for you to make your purchases on a cash basis at present. If this is not possible for the full amount, we suggest that you cut the size of your order, say by half. Should you be willing to do this we will allow you a special cash discount of 4% in addition to our usual trade terms. If this suggestion is acceptable to you, the goods could be delivered to you within 3 days.

We hope you will not look upon this letter as a refusal, but rather as a mark of our genuine wish to enter into business with you on terms that will bring lasting satisfaction to us both. When your business is firmly established, we will be very happy to welcome you as one of our credit customers.

Yours sincerely

12.9 Letter regretting an oversight

If you have made a mistake, or are in any way at fault, it should be admitted freely and without excuses. A letter written in an apologetic tone is likely to create goodwill, and it will be difficult for the recipient to continue to feel a grudge against you.

Dear Mrs Wright

I was very concerned when I received your letter of yesterday stating that the central heating system in your new house has not been completed by the date promised.

On referring to our earlier correspondence, I find that I had mistaken the date for completion. The fault is entirely mine and I deeply regret that it should have occurred.

I realise the inconvenience which my oversight must be causing you, and will do everything possible to avoid any further delay.

I have already given instructions for this work to take first priority, and our engineers will be placed on overtime to complete the work. These arrangements should ensure that the work is completed by next weekend.

My apologies once again for the inconvenience caused.

Yours sincerely

12.10 Letter regretting price increase

Customers will naturally resent increases in prices of goods, especially if they feel the increases are not justified. Goodwill can be preserved by explaining clearly and convincingly the reasons for the increases.

Dear Customer

Steadily rising prices over the past few years have been a matter of common experience and it will come as no surprise to you that our own costs have continued to rise with this general trend.

Increasing world demand has been an important factor in raising the prices of our imported raw materials. A recent national wage award has added to our labour costs, which have been increased still further by constantly increasing overheads.

Until now we have been able to absorb rising costs by economies in other areas. We now find that we can no longer do so, and therefore increases in our prices are unavoidable. The new prices will take effect from 1 October, and revised price lists are now being prepared. These should be ready within the next 2 weeks and copies will be sent to you.

We are sorry that these increases have been made necessary, but can assure you that they will not amount to an average of more than about 5%. As general prices have risen by nearly 10% since our previous price list, we hope you will not feel that our own increases are unreasonable.

Yours faithfully

Letters of thanks

Business executives have many opportunities for writing letters expressing appreciation and creating goodwill. Such 'thank you' letters can be as brief and as simple as you like, but they must express your appreciation with warmth and sincerity, making the reader feel that you really mean what you say – and that you enjoy saying it.

In letters of appreciation, do not include specific sales matters, or it may be thought that your thanks are merely an exuse for promoting business.

12.11 Letter of thanks for a first order

Dear Mr Martin

You will already have received our formal acknowledgement of your order number 456 dated 12 July. However, as this is your first order with us, I felt I must write to say how pleased we were to receive it and to thank you for the opportunity given to us to supply the goods you need.

I hope our handling of your order will lead to further business between us, and to a happy and mutually beneficial association.

Yours sincerely

12.12 Letter of thanks for a large order

Dear Ms Usher

I understand that you placed an unusually large order with us yesterday, and I wanted to write personally to say how very much your continued confidence in us is appreciated.

The happy working relationship between us for many years has always been valued, and we shall do our best to maintain it.

Yours sincerely

12.13 Letter of thanks for prompt settlement of accounts

Dear Mr Watts

I am writing to say how much we appreciate the promptness with which you have settled your accounts with us during the past year, especially as a number of them have been for very large amounts.

This has been of great help to us at a time when we have been faced with heavy commitments connected with the expansion of our business.

I hope our business relationship will continue in the future.

Yours sincerely

12.14 Letter of thanks for a service performed

Dear Miss Armstrong

Thank you for your letter of 30 March returning the draft of the catalogue we propose to send to our customers.

I am very grateful for all the trouble you have taken to examine the draft and comment on it in such detail. Your suggestions will prove most helpful.

I realise the value of time to a busy person like you, and this makes me all the more appreciative of the time you have so generously given me.

Yours sincerely

12.15 Letter of thanks for information received

Dear Mrs Webster

Thank you for your letter enclosing an account of the organisation and work of your local trade association.

I am very grateful for the interest you have shown in our proposal to include details of your association in the next issue of the Trade Association Year Book, and for your trouble in providing such an interesting account of your activities. Your account is sure to inspire and encourage associations in other areas.

Yours sincerely

Letters of congratulation

One of the best ways to promote goodwill is to write a letter of congratulation. The occasion may be a promotion, a new appointment, the award of an honour, the establishment of a new business, success in an examination, even a marriage or a birthday. Your letter may be short and formal, or conversational and informal, depending on the circumstances and the relationship between you and the recipient.

12.16 Formal letter of congratulation on the award of a public honour

Letters of congratulation sent to mark the award of a public honour need only be short and formal. To show a sign of personal interest, the salutation and complimentary close could be handwritten.

I was delighted to learn that your work at the South Down College of Commerce has been recognised in the New Year Honours List.

At a time when commercial education is so much in the public eye, it gives us all at the Ministry great pleasure to learn of your OBE.

12.17 Informal letter of congratulation on the award of a public honour

---

On looking through the Camford Times this morning I came across your name in the New Years Honours List, and I would like to add my congratulations to the many you will be receiving.

The award will give much pleasure to a wide circle of people who know you and your work. Your services to local industry and commerce over many years have been quite outstanding, and it is very gratifying to know that they have now been so suitably rewarded.

With very best wishes

12.18 Formal letter of congratulation on a promotion

Dear Dr Roberts

I would like to convey my warm congratulations on your appointment to the Board of Electrical Industries Ltd.

My fellow directors and I are delighted that the many years of service you have given to your company should at last have been rewarded in this way. We all join in sending you our very best wishes for the future.

Yours sincerely

12.19 Letter acknowledging congratulations

Courtesy requires that letters of congratulation should be acknowledged. In most cases a short, formal acknowledgement is all that is necessary.

This letter would be a suitable reply to the letter of congratulation in 12.16. The writer very properly takes the opportunity to acknowledge her debt to colleagues who have supported her in her work.

Dear Mrs Fleming

Thank you for your letter conveying congratulations on the award of my OBE.

I am, of course, very happy that anything I may have been able to do for commercial education in my limited field should have been rewarded by a public honour. At the same time I regard the award as being less of a tribute to me personally than to the work of my college as a whole – work in which I have always enjoyed the willing help and support of many colleagues.

Thank you again for your good wishes.

Yours sincerely

Letters of condolence and sympathy

Letters of condolence are not easy to write. There can be no set pattern to such letters since a lot depends on what kind of relationship the writer has with the recipient. As a general rule, however, such letters should usually be short, and written with sincerity. To show special consideration, letters of this kind should be handwritten.

Your letter should be written as soon as you learn the news. Express your sympathy in simple words which are warm and convincing, and say what you feel sincerely.

12.20 Letter of condolence to a neighbour

Dear Mrs McDermott

It was not until late last night that my wife and I learned of your husband's tragic death. Coming as it did without warning, it must have been a great shock to you. I want you to know how very sorry we both are, and to send our sincere sympathy.

If there is any way in which we can be of any help, either now or later, do please let us know. We shall be only too glad to do anything we can.

Yours sincerely

Peter Brand.

12.21 Letter of condolence to a customer

Dear Mr Kerr

I have just learned with deep regret of the death of your wife.

There is not much one can say at a time like this, but all of us at Simpsons who have dealt with you would like to extend our sincere sympathy in your loss.

Please count us among those who share your sorrow at this sad time.

Yours sincerely

12.22 Letter of condolence to a business associate

Dear Mrs Anderson

We were distressed to read in <u>The Times</u> this morning that your Chairman had died and I am writing at once to express our deep sympathy.

I had the privilege of knowing Sir James for many years and always regarded him as a personal friend. By his untimely passing, our industry has lost one of its best leaders. He will be greatly missed by all who knew him and had dealings with him.

Please convey our sympathy to Lady Langley and her family.

Yours sincerely

12.23 Letter of condolence to an employee

Dear Maxine

I was deeply sorry to learn of your father's death. I remember your father very well from the years he served in our Company's Accounts Department until his retirement 2 years ago. I well recall his love for his family, and the great sense of pride with which he always spoke of his daughters.

He has been greatly missed at Wilson's since his retirement, and I know that we all join in expressing our sympathy to you and your family at this very sad time.

Yours sincerely

12.24 Letter of condolence to a friend

Dear Henry

I felt I must write to say how deeply sorry we were at the news of Margaret's passing

She was a very dear friend and we shall greatly miss her cheerful outlook on life, her generous nature and her warmth of feeling for anyone in need of help. Above all, we will miss her for her wonderful sense of fun.

Tom and I send you our love and our assurance of continued friendship, now and always. If there is any help we can provide at any time, just let us know.

Yours

Alice

12.25 Letter of sympathy to a business associate

Dear Bill

When I called at your office yesterday I was very sorry to learn that you had been in a car accident on your way home from work recently. However, I was equally relieved to learn that you are now making good progress and are likely to be back at work again in a few weeks' time.

I had a long talk with Susan Carson and was glad to learn of your rising export orders. I expect to be in Leicester again at the end of next month, and shall take the opportunity to call on you.

In the meantime, I wish you a speedy recovery.

Yours sincerely

12.26 Acknowledgements of sympathy or condolence

You will naturally wish to acknowledge letters of the kind illustrated in this section. Such acknowledgements need only be short, but they show that you are genuinely moved by the warm expressions of sympathy you have received.

(a) Personal acknowledgement

To relatives and close friends, acknowledgements should be made to each one personally.

Dear Ms Hughes

My mother and family join me in thanking you for your very kind letter on the occasion of my father's death.

We have all been greatly comforted by the kindness and sympathy of our relatives and friends. Both at home and in the hospital, where my father spent 2 weeks prior to his passing, the kindness and sympathy shown by everyone has been almost overwhelming.

Yours sincerely

Laura Darabi

(b) Printed acknowledgement

When many letters of condolence have been received, it will be sufficient to prepare a printed general acknowledgement.

Mr and Mrs Ashton and family thank you most sincerely for your kind expression of sympathy in their sad loss. The kindness of so many friends and the many proofs of affection and esteem in which Margaret was held will always remain a proud and cherished memory.

97 Lake Rise
Romford
Essex
RM1 4EF

Assignments on material included in this chapter can be found on pp 357–8.

Chapter 13

Circular letters

Circular letters are used to send the same information to a number of people. They are extensively used in sales campaigns (see Chapter 14) and for announcing important developments in business, such as extensions, reorganisations, changes of address, etc.

A circular letter is prepared once only and it may then be duplicated for distribution to the various recipients. Names, addresses and individual salutations may be inserted after duplication in order to personalise the letter.

Word processing, with its mail-merge facilities, makes it possible for each letter to be an original, with the 'variable' details (i.e. inside address, salutation, etc.) being merged with the letter during printing.

Although circulars are being sent to many people, it is important to suggest an interest in the recipient by giving them a personal touch. Remember the following rules:

1 Be brief – people will not read a long-winded circular.
2 Make the letter as personal as possible by addressing each letter to a particular person, by name if you know it. Use *Dear Mr Smith* instead of *Dear Reader*, *Dear Subscriber* or *Dear Customer* instead of *Dear Sir or Madam*. Never use the plural form for the salutation – remember, one recipient will read each individual letter.
3 Create the impression of personal interest by using *you*, never *our customers*, *all customers*, *our clients*, *everyone*.

Instead of	*Say*
Our customers will appreciate . . .	You will appreciate . . .
We are pleased to inform all our clients . . .	We are pleased to inform you . . .
Everyone will be interested to learn . . .	You will be interested to learn . . .
Anyone visiting our new showroom will see . . .	If you visit our new showroom you will see . . .

Circulars announcing changes in business organisation

Changes in a firm's business arrangements may be announced by circular letters such as those which follow. Where the salutation has been left blank, it has been presumed that the letter would be word processed and individual names, addresses and salutations would be merged to add a personal touch.

13.1 Expansion of existing business

Dear Customer

To meet the growing demand for a hardware and general store in this area we have decided to extend our business by opening a new department.

Our new department will carry an extensive range of hardware and other domestic goods at prices which compare very favourably with those charged by other suppliers.

We would like the opportunity to demonstrate our new merchandise to you, and are therefore arranging a special window display during the week beginning 24 June. The official opening of our new department will take place on the following Monday, 1 July.

We hope you will visit our new department during opening week and give us the opportunity to show you that it maintains the reputation enjoyed by our other departments for giving sound value for money.

Yours sincerely

13.2 Opening of a new business

Dear Householder

We are pleased to announce the opening of our new retail grocery store at the above address on Monday 1 September.

Mrs Victoria Chadwick has been appointed Manager, and with her 15 years' experience of the trade we are sure that the goods supplied will be of <u>sound</u>[1] quality and reasonably priced.

Our new store will open at 8 am on Monday 1 September, and as a special celebration offer a discount of 10% will be allowed on all purchases made by the first 50 customers. We hope we may look forward to your being one of them.

Yours sincerely

13.3 Establishment of a new branch

Dear

Owing to the large increase in the volume of our trade with the Kingdom of Jordan, we have decided to open a branch in Amman, with Mr Faisal Shamlan as Manager.

Although we hope we have provided you with an efficient service in the past, this new branch in your country will result in your orders and enquiries being dealt with more promptly.

This new branch will open on 1 May, and from that date all orders and enquiries should be sent to

Mr Faisal Shamlan
Manager
Tyler & Co Ltd
18 Hussein Avenue
Amman

We take this opportunity to express our thanks for your custom in the past, and hope these new arrangements will lead to even higher standards in the service we provide.

Yours sincerely

13.4 Removal to new premises

Dear

The steady growth of our business has made necessary an early move to new and larger premises. We have been fortunate in acquiring[2] a particularly good site on the new industrial estate at Chorley, and from 1 July our new address will be as follows:

Unit 15
Chorley Industrial Estate
Grange Road
Chorley
Lincs CH2 4TH

Telephone 456453 Fax 456324

This new site is served by excellent transport facilities, both by road and rail, enabling deliveries to be made promptly. It also provides scope[3] for better methods of production which will increase output and also improve even further the quality of our goods.

We have very much appreciated your custom in the past and confidently expect to be able to offer you improvements in service when the new factory moves into full production.

We look forward to a continuing good business relationship with you.

Yours sincerely

13.5 Reorganisation of a store's departments

Dear

In order to provide you with even better service, we have recently extended and <u>relocated</u>[4] a number of departments in our store.

On the ground floor we now have a wide selection of greetings cards, including both boxed and individual Christmas cards.

In the Children's and Babywear Department on the first floor there is now a new 'Ladybird' section.

Our Fashion Fabrics and Soft Furnishings Departments are now together on the second floor. Light Fittings and Electrical Goods are relocated on the third floor.

The basement displays a good collection of wallpapers, most of which we are able to supply within 24 hours.

We take this opportunity to thank you for your past custom, and trust we may continue to be of service to you.

Yours sincerely

Circulars announcing changes in business partnerships

When a change takes place in the membership of a partnership, suppliers and customers should be notified by letter. For a retiring partner this is particularly important since they remain liable not only for debts contracted by the firm during membership, but also for debts contracted with old creditors in retirement.

The correct signature on such letters is that of the name of the firm, without the addition of any partner's name.

13.6 Retirement of a partner

Dear

We regret to inform you that our senior partner, Mr Harold West, has decided to retire on 31 May due to recent extended ill-health.

The withdrawal of Mr West's capital will be made good by contributions from the remaining partners, and the amount of the firm's captial will therefore remain unchanged. We will continue to trade under the name of West, Webb & Co, and there will be no change in policy.

We trust that the confidence you have shown in our firm in the past will continue and that we may rely on your continued custom. We shall certainly do everything possible to ensure that our present standards of service are maintained.

Yours sincerely

13.7 Appointment of a new partner

Dear

A large increase in the volume of our business has made necessary an increase in the membership of this company. It is with pleasure, therefore, that we announce the appointment of Mrs Briony Kisby as partner.

Mrs Kisby has been our Head Buyer for the past 10 years and is well-acquainted with every aspect of our policy. Her expertise and experience will continue to be of great value to the company.

There will be no change to our firm's name of Taylor, Hyde & Co.

We look forward to continuing with you our mutually beneficial business relationship.

Yours sincerely

13.8 Conversion of partnership to private company

Dear

The need for additional capital to finance the considerable growth in the volume of our trade has made it necessary to reorganise our business as a private company. The new company has been registered, with limited liability, with the name <u>Barlow & Hoole Limited</u>.

We wish to stress that this change is in name only, and the nature of our business will remain exactly as before. There will be no change in business policy.

The personal relationship which has been built up with all customers in the past will be maintained, and we shall continue to do our utmost to ensure that you are completely satisfied with the way in which we handle your future orders.

Yours sincerely

Glossary

1 **sound** reliable
2 **acquiring** obtaining
3 **scope** opportunity
4 **relocated** moved to a different place

Assignments on material included in this chapter can be found on pp 358–9.

Chapter 14

Sales letters and voluntary offers

Sales letters

A sales letter is the most selective of all forms of advertising. Unlike press and poster advertising, it aims to sell particular kinds of goods or services to selected types of customers. The purpose of the sales letter is to persuade the reader that they need what you are trying to sell, and therefore persuade the reader to buy it. You take something attractive and make it seem necessary, or you take something necessary and make it seem attractive.

The same rules discussed for circular letters in Chapter 13 also apply to sales letters, so when composing sales letters be careful to follow the rules listed on page 167.

Elements of the sales letter

A good sales letter must:

- arouse interest
- create desire
- carry conviction
- induce action

Each of these elements will now be considered in detail.

1 Arouse interest

Your opening paragraph must arouse interest and encourage the reader to take notice of what you have to say. Without care in this opening paragraph, your letter could end up in the waste-paper bin without being read. It may begin with a question, and instruction or a quotation. Here are some examples:

(a) An appeal to self-esteem

Are you nervous when asked to propose a vote of thanks, to take the Chair at a meeting, or to make a speech? If so, this letter has been written specially for you!

(b) An appeal to economy

Would you like to cut your domestic fuel costs by 20 per cent? If your answer is 'yes', read on . . .

(c) An appeal to health

'The common cold', says Dr James Carter, 'probably causes more lost time at work in a year than all other illnesses put together.'

(d) An appeal to fear

'More than 50 per cent of people have eye trouble and in the past year no fewer than 16 000 people in Britain have lost their sight. Are your eyes in danger?'

---

2 Create desire

Having aroused interest, you must now create a desire for the product or service you are selling. To do this, it must point out the benefits to the readers and how it will affect them.

If the letter is sent to a person who knows nothing about the product, you must describe it and give a clear picture of what it is and what it can do. Study the product and then select those features which make it superior to others of its kind. Stress the features from the reader's point of view.

To claim that a particular hi-fi system is 'the best on the market' or 'the latest in electronic technology' is of little use. Instead, stress such points as quality of the materials used and the special features that make the equipment more convenient or efficient than its rivals. The following description stresses such points:

This hi-fi system is carefully designed and incorporates the latest technological developments to give high quality sound including full stereo recording and playback on the twin-cassette deck. Its clearly arranged controls make for very simple operation. It is supplied with two detachable loudspeakers separately mounted in solid, polished teak cabinets, as finely finished as a Rolls-Royce.

In this description, note the final statement 'as finely finished as a Rolls-Royce' equates the product with one which is well known and recognised as a high level product. This creates a picture of a reasonably priced yet superb product.

3 Carry conviction

You must somehow convince your reader that the product is what you claim it to be. You must support your claims by evidence – facts, opinions. You can do this in a number of ways: invite the reader to your factory or showroom, offer to send goods 'on approval', provide a guarantee, quote your 100 years of experience in the field. In the following example of a letter from a cotton-shirt manufacturer, note how convincing it sounds. No manufacturer would dare to make such an offer without the firm belief in what is claimed. All the proof is supplied to give the reader complete confidence and to persuade them to buy.

Remember, we have manufactured cotton shirts for 50 years and are quite confident that you will be more than satisfied with their quality. This offer is made on the clear understanding that if they are not completely to your liking, you can return them to us without any obligation whatever and at our own expense. We will refund to you the full amount you paid.

As a caution, however, remember that it is against the law to make false or exaggerated claims. Remember also that the good name and standing of your business, as well as its success, depends upon honest dealing.

4 Induce action

Your closing paragraph must persuade the reader to take the action that you want – to visit your showrooms, to receive your representative, to send for a sample or to place an order. You must also provide the reader with a sound reason why they should reply. For example:

If you will <u>return the enclosed request card</u> we will show you how <u>you can have all the advantages of cold storage and at the same time save money</u>.

Sometimes the closing paragraph will give special reasons why the reader should act immediately:

The special discount now offered can be allowed only on orders placed by 30 June. So hurry now to take advantage of this limited offer.

You must make it easy for the reader to do these things, such as by providing a tear-off slip to complete and return, or by enclosing a prepaid card.

Before we look at some sample letters, remember: your readers will not be anywhere near as interested in the product, service or idea you have to sell as they are in how it will benefit them. You have to persuade your readers of the benefits of what you are selling, and tell them what it can do for them.

Specimen sales letters

Here are some examples of effective sales letters which follow the four-point plan of *interest*, *desire*, *conviction* and *action*.

14.1 Sales appeal to economy

Dear Ms Reading

Have you ever thought how much time your typist wastes in taking down your dictation? It can be as much as a third of the time spent on correspondence. Why not record your dictation – on our <u>Stenogram</u> – and she can be doing other jobs while you dictate?

[Interest]

You will be surprised at how little it costs. For 52 weeks in the year your <u>Stenogram</u> works hard for you, and you can never give it too much to do – all for less than an average month's salary for a secretary! It will take dictation anywhere at any time – during lunch-hour, in the evening, at home – you can even dictate while you are travelling or away on business, and simply post the recorded messages back to your secretary for typing.

[Desire]

The <u>Stenogram</u> is efficient, reliable, time-saving and economical. Backed as it is by our international reputation for reliability, it is in regular use in thousands of offices all over the country. It gives superb reproduction quality, with every syllable as clear as a bell. It is unbelievably simple to use – just slip in a preloaded cassette, press a button, and it is ready to record your dictation, interviews, telephone conversations, reports, instructions, whatever. Nothing could be simpler! And with our unique after-sales service contract, you are assured lasting operation at the peak of efficiency.

[Conviction]

Some of your business friends are sure to be using our <u>Stenogram</u>. Ask them about it before you place an order and we are sure they will back up our claims. If you prefer, return the enclosed prepaid card and we will arrange for our representative to call and arrange a demonstration for you. Just state the day and time which will be most convenient for you.

[Action]

Yours sincerely

14.2 Sales appeal to efficiency

Dear Mr Wood

Reports from all over the world confirm what we have
always known – that the RELIANCE solid tyre is the   [Interest]
fulfilment of every car owner's dream.

You will naturally be well aware of the weaknesses of the
ordinary air-filled tyre – punctures, split outer covers
under sudden stress, and a tendency to skid on wet road
surfaces, to mention only a few of motorists' main   [Desire]
complaints. Our RELIANCE tyre enables you to offer your
customers a tyre which is beyond criticism in those vital[1]
qualities of road-holding and reliability.

We could tell you a lot more about RELIANCE tyres, but
would prefer you to read the enclosed copies of reports
from racing car drivers, test drivers and motor dealers and   [Conviction]
manufacturers. These reports really speak for themselves.

You are already aware of our terms of dealing, but to
encourage you to hold a stock of the new solid RELIANCE,
we are pleased to offer you a special discount of 3% on any   [Action]
order received by 31 July.

Yours sincerely

14.3 Sales appeal to security

Dear Mr Goodwin

A client of mine is happier today than he has been for a
long time – and with good reason. For the first time since
he married 10 years ago, he says he feels really
comfortable about the future. Should he die within the
next 20 years, his wife and family will now be provided   [Interest]
for. For less that £2 a week now, his wife would receive
£50 per month for a full 20 years, and then a lump sum of
£10,000.

Such protection would have been beyond his reach a short
time ago, but now a new and novel scheme has enabled
him to ensure this security for his family. The scheme
need not be for 20 years. It can be for 15 or 10 or any   [Desire]
other number of years. And it need not be for £10,000. It
could be for much more or much less so that you give the
protection you want.

For just a few pounds each month you can buy peace of
mind for your wife and children – and for yourself. You   [Conviction]
cannot – you dare not – leave them unprotected.

Let me call on you to tell you more about this scheme
which so many families are finding so attractive. I shall
not press you to join; I shall just give you all the details
and leave the rest to you. Please return the enclosed   [Action]
prepaid reply card and I will call at any time convenient to
you.

Yours sincerely

14.4 Sales appeal to comfort

Dear Mrs Walker

What would you say to a gift that gave you a warmer and
more comfortable home, free from draughts, and a saving   [Interest]
of over 20% in fuel costs?

You can enjoy these advantages, not just this year but
every year, simply by installing our SEALTITE panel
system of double glazing². Can you think of a better gift
for your entire family? The enclosed folder will give you
some of the benefits which make SEALTITE the most   [Desire]
completely satisfactory double-glazing system on the
market, thanks to a number of features not provided in
any other system.

Remember that the panels are precision-made³ to fit your
own particular windows by experienced craftsmen.
Remember too that you will be dealing with a well-   [Conviction]
established company which owes its success to the
satisfaction given to scores of thousands of customers.

There is no need for you to make up your mind right now.
First why not let us give you a free demonstration in your
own home without any obligation whatsoever? However, if
you are looking for an investment with an annual average   [Action]
return of over 20%, then here is your opportunity. If you
post the enclosed card to reach us by the end of August,
we can complete the installation for you in good time
before winter sets in.

Secure your home with SEALTITE!

Yours sincerely

14.5 Sales appeal to leisure

Dear Mrs Hudson

'Modern scientific invention is a curse to the human race
and will one day destroy it', said one of my customers
recently. Rather a <u>rash statement</u>[4], and quite untrue, for   [Interest]
there are modern inventions which, far from being a curse,
are real blessings.

Our new AQUAMASTER washer is just one of them. It
takes all the hard work out of the weekly wash and makes
washing a pleasure. All you have to do is put your soiled
clothes in, press a button and sit back while the machine   [Desire]
does the work. It does everything – washing, rinsing and
drying – and (no offence intended) it does it quicker and
better than you could.

Come along and see the AQUAMASTER at work in our
showroom. A demonstration will take up only a few
minutes of your time, but it may rid you of your dread of   [Conviction]
washing day and make life much more pleasant.

I hope you will accept this invitation and come along soon
to see what this latest of all domestic time-savers can do   [Action]
for you.

Yours sincerely

14.6 Sales appeal to sympathy

This letter was sent together with a leaflet containing a form for readers to
return with a donation.

Dear Reader

You can walk about the house, at work, in the streets, in the country.
Yet this ability, which you take for granted, is denied to thousands of
others – those who are born crippled, or crippled in childhood by
accident or illness.

It is estimated that in Britain a deformed child is born, or a child
crippled by accident or illness, every 5 minutes. This means that every
day there could be 288 more crippled children.

Does this not strike you as unfair? Most of what is unfair in life is
something we can do little about, but here is one <u>grave</u>[5] inequality

which everyone can help with. The enclosed leaflet explains how you can help. Please read it carefully, while remembering again just how lucky you are.

Yours faithfully

14.7 Sales appeal to comfort

Dear Sir

At half the actual cost you can now have SOLAR HEATING installed in your home.

As part of our research and development scheme introduced two years ago, we are about to make our selection of a number of properties throughout the country as 'Research Homes' – yours could be one of them.

The information received from selected 'Research Homes' in the past two years has proved that SOLAR HEATING is successful even in the most northern parts of the United Kingdom. This information has also enabled us to <u>modify</u>[6] and improve our designs, which we will continue to do.

If your home is selected as one of the properties to be included in our research scheme, we would bear half the actual cost of installation.

If you are interested in helping our research programme in return for a solar heating system at half-price, please complete the enclosed form and return it by the end of May. Within three weeks we will inform you whether or not your home is one of those selected for the scheme.

Yours faithfully

14.8 Sales appeal to health

Dear Madam

Thousands of people who normally suffer from the miseries of cold, damp, changeable weather wear THERMOTEX. Why? The answer is simple – tests conducted at the leading Textile Industries Department at Leeds University have shown that of all the traditional underwear fabrics, THERMOTEX has the highest warmth insulating properties.

THERMOTEX has been relieving aches and pains, particularly those caused by rheumatism, for many years. It not only brings extra warmth, but also soothes those aches caused by icy winds cutting into your bones and chilling you to the marrow. THERMOTEX absorbs far less moisture than conventional underwear fabrics, so perspiration passes straight through the material, leaving your skin dry, but very, very warm.

Don't just take our word for it – take a good look at some of the testimonials shown in the enclosed catalogue. The demand for THERMOTEX garments has grown so much in recent years that we now often have to deal with over 20 000 in a single day.

The enclosed catalogue is packed with lots of ways in which THERMOTEX can keep you warm and healthy this winter. Just browse through it, choose the garment you would like, and send us your completed order form – there is no need even for a postage stamp! Warmth and health will soon be on their way to you. If you are not completely satisfied with your purchase, return it to us within 14 days and we will refund your money without question and with the least possible delay.

Let THERMOTEX keep you warm this winter!

Yours faithfully

Voluntary offers

An offer which is not asked for which is something sent to an individual or a small number of individuals is a form of sales letter. It serves the same purpose and follows the same general principles.

Such offers take a variety of forms, including offers of free samples, goods on approval, special discounts on orders received within a stated period, or more frequently offers to send brochures, catalogues, price lists, patterns, etc., upon return of a form or card, usually prepaid.

14.9 Offer to a newly established trader

Dear Sir

We would like to send our best wishes for the success of your new shop specialising in the sale of toys. Naturally you will wish to offer your customers the latest toys – toys which are attractive, hard-wearing and reasonably priced – but your stock will not be complete without the mechanical toys for which we have a national reputation.

We are sole importers of VALIFACT toys, and our terms are very generous, as you will see from the enclosed price list. In addition to the trade discount stated, we would allow you a special first-order discount of 5%.

We hope that these terms will encourage you to place an order with us, and feel sure you would be well satisfied with your first transaction. If you would like one of our representatives to call on you to ensure that you are fully briefed on the wide assortment of toys we can offer, please complete and return the enclosed card to say when it would be convenient.

Yours faithfully

14.10 Offer to a regular customer

Dear Mr Welling

We have just bought a large quantity of high quality rugs and carpets from the bankrupt stock of one of our competitors.

As one of our oldest and most regular customers, we should like you to share in the excellent opportunities our purchase provides. We can offer you mohair rugs in a variety of colours at prices ranging from £55 to £753; also premier quality Wilton and Axminster carpeting in a wide range of patterns at 20% below current wholesale prices.

This is an exceptional opportunity for you to buy a stock of high quality products at prices we cannot repeat, and we hope you will take full advantage of it. If you are interested, you may call at our warehouse to see the stock for yourself not later than Friday next, 14 October. Or alternatively call our Sales Department on 453 2567 to place an immediate order.

Yours faithfully

14.11 Offer to new home owners

Dear Newcomers

Welcome to your new home! We have no wish to disturb you as you settle in, but we would like to tell you why people in this town and the surrounding areas are very familiar with the name BAXENDALE.

Our store is situated at the corner of Grafton Street and Dorset Road, and we invite you to visit us to see for yourself the exciting range of goods that have made us a household name.

Our well-known shopping guide is enclosed, which you may like to browse through at your leisure. You will see practically everything you need to add to the comfort and beauty of your home.

As a special attraction to newcomers into the area, we are offering a free gift worth £2 for every £10 spent in our store. Presentation of the enclosed card, which is valid for one calendar month, will entitle you to select goods of your own choice as your free gift.

We sincerely hope you enjoy your new home.

Yours faithfully

14.12 Offer of a demonstration

Dear Mrs Thornton

The Ideal Home Exhibition opens at Earls Court on Monday 21 June, and you are certain to find attractive new designs in furniture, as well as many new ideas.

The exhibition has much to offer which you will find useful, but we would specially like to invite you to see our own display on Stand 26 where we shall be revealing our new WINDSOR range of <u>unit furniture</u>[7].

WINDSOR represents an entirely new concept in luxury unit furniture at very modest prices, and we hope you will not miss the opportunity to see it for yourself. The inbuilt charm of this range springs from the use of solid elm and beech, combined with expert craftsmanship to give a perfect finish to each piece of furniture.

I have pleasure in enclosing two admission tickets to the Ideal Home Exhibition, and look forward to seeing you there. I am sure you will not want to miss this opportunity to see the variety of ways in which WINDSOR unit furniture can be arranged to suit any requirements.

Yours sincerely

Useful expressions

Openings

1 We are taking the liberty of sending you a copy of our latest catalogue and price list.
2 As you have placed many orders with us in the past, we would like to extend our special offer to you.
3 We are able to offer you very favourable prices on some goods we have recently been able to purchase.
4 We are pleased to introduce our new . . . and feel sure that you will find it very interesting.
5 I am sorry to note that we have not received an order from you for over. . . .

Closes

1 We hope you will take full advantage of this exceptional offer.
2 We feel sure you will find a ready sale for this excellent material, and that your customers will be well satisfied with it.
3 We should be pleased to provide a demonstration if you would let us know when this would be convenient.
4 We hope you will take the opportunity to try this product, which is not only of the highest quality but also very reasonably priced.

Glossary

1 **vital** essential
2 **double glazing** double-glass window panels
3 **precision-made** manufactured to a high degree of accuracy
4 **rash statement** a statement made recklessly, without thought
5 **grave** very important
6 **modify** alter, rearrange
7 **unit furniture** furniture made in standard sections

Assignments on material included in this chapter can be found on pp 359–61.

Chapter 15

Personnel

Letters of application

A letter of application for a job is essentially a sales letter. In such a letter you are trying to sell yourself. The general principles of sales-letter writing (Chapter 14) will therefore apply: you must arouse *interest* in your qualifications; then, by your past record and testimonials, *conviction*; and finally, bring about the *action* you want the *prospective employer*[1] to take – to grant an interview and eventually give you the job.

1 Style of application

Unless an advertisement specifies that you must apply in your own handwriting, or the post is purely clerical or bookkeeping, your application should be typed. It is then easier to read and, if well set out, attracts attention at once and creates a favourable first impression.

Some applicants prefer to write a long letter containing all the relevant information about education, qualifications and experience – this is not advisable as the information is not easy to locate and it can sound rather boastful.

It is preferable to write a short letter applying for the post and stating that your curriculum vitae (or résumé) is enclosed – your curriculum vitae should give full details of your personal background, education, qualifications and experience. Do not duplicate such information in your covering letter.

2 Points of guidance

(a) Remember the purpose of your application is not to get the job, but to get an interview.
(b) Ensure your application is well-typed and neatly presented; make your application stand out from the rest.
(c) Be brief; give all the relevant information in as few words as possible.
(d) Write sincerely, in a friendly tone, but without being familiar.
(e) Do not make exaggerated claims or sound boastful; simply show a proper appreciation of your abilities.

(f) Do not suggest you are applying for the job because you are bored with your present one.
(g) If your main interest is the salary, do not state the figure you expect. Instead, mention what you are earning now.
(h) Do not send originals of your testimonials; send copies with your application, but take your originals along to the interview.

3 Checklist

A busy employer has little time for long rambling correspondence. You should avoid the temptation to include details in which the recipient is unlikely to be interested, however important they may be to you. You should also avoid generalising, and instead be quite specific in the information provided. For example, instead of saying 'I have had several years' relevant experience in a well-known firm of engineers', state the number of years, state the experience and give the name of the firm.

When you have written your letter, read it carefully and ask yourself these questions:

(a) Does it read like a good business letter?
(b) Will the opening paragraph interest the employer enough to prompt the rest to be read?
(c) Does it suggest that I am genuinely interested in the kind of work to be done?

If your answer to these questions is 'Yes', then you may safely send your letter.

15.1 Application for an advertised post

(a) Application letter

When your application is in response to an advertisement in a newspaper or journal, this should always be mentioned in the opening paragraph or in the subject heading. In this application, note that the writer's address is placed at the top right-hand corner of the letter, with all other details at the left in fully blocked style. (It would be satisfactory to place the date at the right, if preferred.)

26 Gordon Road
CHINGFORD
E4 6PY

15 May 19--

Mrs W R Jenkinson
Personnel Manager
Leyland & Bailey Ltd
Nelson Works
CLAPTON
E5 8HA

Dear Mrs Jenkinson

PRIVATE SECRETARY TO MANAGING DIRECTOR

I was interested to see your advertisement in today's <u>Daily Telegraph</u>, and would like to be considered for this post.

In my present post of Private Secretary to the General Manager at a manufacturing company, I have a wide range of responsibilities. These include attending and taking minutes of meetings and interviews, dealing with callers and correspondence in my employer's absence, and supervising junior staff, as well as the usual secretarial duties.

The kind of work in which your company is engaged particularly interests me, and I would welcome the opportunity it would afford to use my language abilities, which are not utilised in my present post.

A copy of my curriculum vitae is enclosed giving further details, together with copies of previous testimonials.

I hope to hear from you soon, and to be given the opportunity to present myself at an interview.

Yours sincerely

JEAN CARSON (Miss)

Encs

(b) Curriculum vitae

Your curriculum vitae (sometimes called a résumé) should set out all your personal details, together with your education, qualifications and working experience. It should be displayed attractively so that all the information can be seen at a glance. It should not extend to more than 2 pages. Wherever possible, the information should be categorised under headings and columns, as shown in Fig. 15.1.

```
CURRICULUM VITAE

NAME                    Jean Carson
ADDRESS                 26 Gordon Road
                        Chingford
                        Essex E4 6PY
TELEPHONE               081 529 3456
DATE OF BIRTH           26 May 1965
NATIONALITY             British
MARITAL STATUS          Single

EDUCATION

19-- to 19--            Woodford High School
19-- to 19--            Bedford Secretarial College
                        (Secretarial Course

QUALIFICATIONS

GCE A Level             English Language           19--
                        Mathematics                19--
                        Spanish                    19--
                        French                     19--

GCE O Level             Biology                    19--
                        Philosophy                 19--
                        Commerce                   19--
                        History                    19--
LCCI                    Private Secretary's Diploma 19--
LCCI Level 3            Typewriting                19--
                        Audio Typing               19--
                        Shorthand Typing           19--
                        English for Business       19--
RSA                     140 wpm Shorthand          19--
PITMAN                  160wpm Shorthand           19--

SPECIAL AWARDS

RSA Silver medal for shorthand 140 wpm
Governors' prize for first place in college examinations

WORKING EXPERIENCE

Sept 19-- to     Shorthand Typist
March 19--                              Bains, Hoyle & Co
                                        Solicitors
                                        60 Kingsway
                                        LONDON WC2B 6AB
```

| April 19-- to present | Personal Secretary to General Manager | Reliance Cables Vicarage Road Leyton LONDON E10 5RG |

INTERESTS

Music; Languages; Hockey; Golf; Swimming

REFEREES

1 Dr R G Davies
   Principal
   Bedford Secretarial College
   Righton Road
   Bedford MH2 2BS

2 Ms W Harris
   Partner
   Bains, Hoyle & Co
   60 Kingsway
   London WC2B 6AB

3 Mr W J Godfrey OBE
   Managing Director
   Reliance Cables
   Vicarage Road
   Leyton
   London E10 5RG

June 19--

Fig. 15.1 Curriculum vitae

15.2 Application using an introduction

Sometimes your application will result from an introduction by a friend or colleague. In this case, such an introduction should be mentioned in the opening paragraph as a useful way of attracting attention.

Dear Mr Barker

Mrs Phyllis Naish, your Personnel Officer, has told me that you have a vacancy for a Marketing Assistant. I should like to be considered for this post.

As you will see from my Curriculum Vitae, which is attached, I have several A levels as well as secretarial qualifications gained during an intensive one-year course at Walthamstow College of Commerce. I have been Shorthand Typist within the marketing department of Enterprise Cables Ltd for 2 years and have been very happy there, gaining quite a lot of valuable experience. However, the office is quite small and I now wish to widen my experience and hopefully improve my prospects.

My former headmistress has written the enclosed testimonial and has kindly agreed to give further details should they be needed. If you are interested in my application you will, of course, be able to obtain more information from my present employer.

I shall be glad to attend an interview at any time, and hope to hear from you soon.

Yours sincerely

15.3 An unsolicited application

An *unsolicited*[2] application is the most difficult to write, since there is no advertisement or introduction to tell you anything about the work, or indeed whether there is a vacancy. In such a situation, you must try to find out something about the company's activities and then show how your qualifications and experience could be used.

Dear Sir

For the past 8 years I have been a Statistician in the Research Unit of Baron & Smallwood Ltd, Glasgow. I am now looking for a change of employment which would widen my experience and at the same time improve my prospects. It has occurred to me that a large and well-known organisation such as yours might be able to use my services.

I am 31 years of age and in excellent health. At the University of London I specialised in merchandising and advertising, and was awarded a PhD degree for my thesis on 'Statistical Investigation in Research'. I thoroughly enjoy working on investigations, particularly where it involves statistical work.

Although I have had no experience in consumer research, I am familiar with the methods employed and fully understand their importance in the recording of buying habits and trends. I should like to feel that there is an opportunity to use my services in this type of research and that you will invite me to attend an interview. I could then give you further information and bring testimonials.

I hope to hear from you soon.

Yours faithfully

15.4 Application for post of Sales Manager

In this letter, note the clarity with which the writer gives information about previous experience and present responsibilities, without being long-winded, in order to 'sell themselves' well.

Dear Sir

I was very interested to see your advertisement for a Sales Manager in yesterday's <u>Daily Telegraph</u> and should like to be considered for this post.

My full particulars are shown on my curriculum vitae which is enclosed, from which you will see that I have had 10 years' experience in the sales departments of two well-known companies. My special duties at Oral Plastics Ltd include the training of sales personnel, dealing with the company's foreign correspondence and organising market research and sales promotion programmes. I thoroughly enjoy my work and am very happy here, but feel that the time has come when my experience in marketing has prepared me for the responsibility of full sales management.

Mr James Watkinson, my Managing Director, and Ms Harriet Webb, Sales Manager of my former company, have both consented to provide references for me; their details can be found on my curriculum vitae.

I shall be pleased to provide any further information you may need, and hope I may be given the opportunity of an interview.

Yours faithfully

15.5 Application for a teaching post

This letter of application is sent by a teacher-trainee to the Chief Education Officer of her local authority, enquiring about suitable teaching posts.

Dear Sir

At the end of the present term I shall complete my one-year teacher-training course at Garnett College of Education. For domestic reasons, I would like to obtain a post at a school or college in the area administered by your authority.

From my curriculum vitae, which is attached, you will see that I have 6 O level and 2 A level passes, together with advanced qualifications in many secretarial subjects. I have held secretarial positions in the London area for a total of 8 years, during which time I studied for my

RSA Shorthand and Typewriting Teachers' Diplomas. Having enjoyed the opportunity to teach these subjects in evening classes at the Chingford Evening Institute for 2 years, I was prompted to take up full-time teacher-training at Garnett.

I like young people and get on well with them, and I am looking forward to helping them in the very practical way which teaching makes possible. If there is a suitable vacancy in your area, I hope you will consider me for it.

Yours faithfully

15.6 Application for post of Data Processing Trainee

In this letter the writer gives details of his education and qualifications in his letter instead of in a separate curriculum vitae. This style is useful when the applicant does not have a lot of previous working experience to warrant a CV.

Dear Sir

I would like to apply for the post of Management Trainee in your Data Processing Department advertised today in The Guardian.

I obtained A level passes in Mathematics, Physics and German at Marlborough College, Wiltshire. The College awarded me an open scholarship to Queens' College, Cambridge, where I obtained a 'first' in Mathematics and a 'second' in Physics. After leaving University last year, I accepted a temporary post with Firma Hollander & Schmidt in order to improve my German and to gain some practical experience in their laboratories at Bremen. This work comes to an end in 6 weeks' time.

My special interest for many years has been computer work, and I should like to make it my career. I believe my qualifications in Mathematics and Physics would enable me to do so successfully.

I am unmarried and would be quite willing to undertake the training courses away from home to which you refer in your advertisement.

My former Housemaster at Marlborough, Mr T Gartside, has consented to act as my referee (telephone 234576), as has Dr W White, Dean of Queens' College, Cambridge (telephone 453453). I hope that you will take up these references and grant me the opportunity of an interview.

Yours faithfully

References (favourable)

Even if testimonials are provided at the time of sending an application letter, it is usual to state (either on your CV or covering letter) the names of one or two people who have consented to act as referees. Prospective employers may contact such referees either by telephone or letter to obtain further information about an applicant's work performance and character.

15.7 Letter taking up a reference

Dear Mrs Lambert

Mr James Harvey, at present employed by you as Foreign Correspondent, has applied to us for a similar post and has given your name as a reference.

I should be grateful if you would state whether his services with you have been entirely satisfactory and whether you consider him qualified to accept full responsibility for the French and German correspondence in a large and busy department.

I am aware that Mr Harvey speaks French and German fluently, but am particularly interested in his ability to produce accurate translations into these languages of letters that may be dictated to him in English.

Any other information you can provide would be appreciated, and of course will be treated as strictly confidential.

Yours sincerely

15.8 Favourable reply

In this reply, the writer recommends the employee very highly and without hesitation, feeling confident that he can carry out the duties required in the post stated.

Dear Mr Brodie

I am pleased to be able to reply favourably to your enquiry of 6 April concerning Mr James Harvey.

Mr Harvey is an excellent linguist and for the past 5 years has been in sole charge of our foreign correspondence, most of which is with European companies, especially in France and Germany.

We have been extremely pleased with the services provided by Mr Harvey, and should you engage him you may rely upon him to produce well-written and accurate transcripts of letters into French and German. He is a very reliable and steady worker and bears an excellent character.

We wish him success, but at the same time shall be very sorry to lose him.

Yours sincerely

15.9 Alternative reply

In this reply the writer is very cautious, implying that the applicant lacks the experience needed for control of a department. However, the writer is very careful not to say this in so many words.

Dear Mr Brodie

Thank you for your letter of 6 April concerning Mr James Harvey.

Mr Harvey is a competent linguist, and for the past 5 years has been employed as senior assistant in our foreign correspondence section. He has, however, always been conscientious[3] and hard-working. Whether or not he would be capable of taking full responsibility for a large and busy department is difficult to say, since his work with us has always been carried out under supervision.

Should you require any further information, please do not hesitate to contact me.

Yours sincerely

15.10 Enquiry letter requesting a reference

In this letter, another prospective employer requests information about the work and character of an applicant.

Dear Mr Jones

Mr Lionel Picton has applied to us for an appointment of Manager of our factory in Nairobi. We are leading manufacturers of engineered components used in the petrochemical industry and our requirements are for a qualified engineer with works manager's experience in medium or large batch production

Mr Picton informs us that he is employed by you as Assistant Manager of your factory in Sheffield, and we should be grateful for any information you can give us about his competence, reliability and general character.

Any information provided will be treated in strictest confidence.

Yours sincerely

15.11 Favourable reply

Dear Mr Gandah

Mr Lionel Picton, about whom you enquire in your letter of 10 August, has been employed by this Company for the past 10 years.

He served his apprenticeship with Vickers Tools Ltd in Manchester, followed by a three-year course for the Engineering and Work Study Diploma of the Institution of Production Engineers. He is thus technically well-qualified, and for the past five years has been our Assistant Works Manager responsible for production and associated activities in our Sheffield factory. In all aspects of his work he has shown himself to be hard-working, very conscientious and in every way a very dependable employee.

I can recommend Mr Picton without the slightest hesitation, and am sure that if he was appointed to manage your factory in Nairobi he would bring to his work a genuine spirit of service, which would be found stimulating and helpful by all who worked with him.

Yours sincerely

15.12 Applicant's thank you letter

Those who have provided references will naturally be pleased to know how the applicant has fared, whether successful or not. Applicants should therefore always inform and thank those who supported them, as in this letter.

Dear Mr Buttle

I would like to thank you for supporting my application for the post as Manager of the Barker Petrochemical Company in Nairobi.

I know that the generous terms in which you wrote about me had much to do with my being offered the post, and I am deeply grateful to you for the reference you provided for me.

Your help and encouragement has always been much appreciated and this will always be remembered.

Yours sincerely

15.13 Enumerated enquiry for a reference

In the following enquiry, the writer is looking for certain qualities. To make sure that each one is covered in a reply, the enquiry is presented in enumerated form.

Dear Miss French

Miss Jean Parker has applied for a post as Sales Administrator in our Sales Department. She states that she is presently employed by you and has given your name as a referee.

We should be grateful if you would answer the following questions as to her abilities and character:

1 Is she conscientious, intelligent and trustworthy?
2 Are her keyboarding and administrative skills satisfactory?
3 Is she capable of dealing with difficult situations presented by external bodies such as customers?
4 Is she capable of dealing effectively with figure work?
5 Is her output satisfactory?
6 Does she get on well with her colleagues?
7 Is her health and time-keeping satisfactory?

Any information you are kind enough to provide will be treated in strict confidence.

Yours sincerely

15.14 Reply

Dear Mr Kingston

In reply to your letter of 15 April, I have nothing to say but good about Miss Jean Parker. She has been employed as Assistant Sales Administrator in our general office for the past 2 years and I feel sure that you will find her in every way satisfactory.

In reply to each of the questions in your letter, I can give an unqualified[4] 'Yes'.

We will be sorry to lose Miss Parker, but realise that her abilities demand wider scope than is possible at this Company.

Yours sincerely

15.15 Favourable reference – Former Student

Dear Mrs Thompson

MISS CAROLINE BRADLEY

In reply to your enquiry of 3 June, I welcome the opportunity to support Miss Bradley's application for the post of your Marketing Assistant.

Miss Bradley was a student at this College during the year 19-- to 19--. Admission to this intensive one-year course is restricted to students with good school-leaving qualifications, and the fact that Miss Bradley was admitted to the course is in itself evidence of sound academic ability. Upon completing her course, she was awarded the title 'Student of the Year', being the student gaining highest qualifications over the one-year course.

In all other respects Miss Bradley's work and attitude were entirely satisfactory, and I can recommend her to you with every confidence. I feel sure that if she was appointed, she would perform her duties diligently and reliably.

Yours sincerely

15.16 Favourable reference – Department Manager

Dear Mrs Leighton

In reply to your letter of yesterday, Mr Stephen Walters is both capable and reliable. He came to us 5 years ago to take charge of our Hardware Department.

He knows the trade thoroughly and does all the buying for his department with notable success. I know that for some time he has been looking for a similar post with a larger store. While we would be sorry to lose his services, we would not wish to stand in the way of the advancement which a store such as yours could offer.

Yours sincerely

References (unfavourable)

If an employer is asked for a testimonial by an employee whose services have not been entirely satisfactory, the safest course of action is to tell the employee that their name may be given as a referee. There is always a danger that unfavourable reports may be seen by unauthorised people, so it is safer to make such comments either over the telephone or in person, instead of in writing. If, however, an unfavourable reference is put in writing, it should be worded with caution and restraint and with as little detail as possible.

15.17 Unfavourable reference

A reference such as the following would almost certainly prevent this girl from getting a good post anywhere, but if the writer sincerely believes in what is said then they should not fear to send it. The letter should of course, be marked 'Private and Confidential' and it should be sealed in an envelope marked in the same way and addressed to the person who made the enquiry.

Dear Ms Samson

I am replying to your letter of 18 January in which you enquire about Mr Ian Bell.

Mr Bell was employed as Clerk in this Company from February to October last year. We released him because his work fell below the standards we normally require. His punctuality also left a lot to be desired, and he had a disturbing influence on other members of our staff.

Mr Bell is an intelligent young man and with the exercise of a little self-discipline he could do well. However, from my personal experience I am afraid that I cannot conscientiously recommend him.

Yours sincerely

15.18 Alternative unfavourable reference

The letter in 15.17 is quite specific about the applicant's unsuitability. Perhaps a safer and wiser course would be to write in more general terms and to be less specific in criticism, as in the following letter.

Dear Ms Samson

I am replying to your letter of 18 January in which you enquire about Mr Ian Bell.

This young man was a member of our clerical staff from February to October last year, but I am sorry to say that we did not find him suitable. It is quite possible that he may do better in another office.

Yours sincerely

Interview letters

If a large number of applications are received for a post, it is unlikely that all applicants can be interviewed. In such cases, a shortlist will be drawn up comprising those applicants thought to be most suitable for interview.

15.19 Invitation to attend for interview

A letter inviting an applicant for interview should first acknowledge receipt of the application, and then go on to give a day, date and time for the interview. The name of the person the applicant should ask for should also be stated. Confirmation is often required.

Dear Miss Wildman

ADMINISTRATOR – TRAINING SECTION

Thank you for your application for the above post.

You are invited to attend for an interview with Mrs Angela Howard, Training Manager, on Friday 29 May at 3.30 pm.

Will you please let me know either by letter or telephone whether this appointment will be convenient for you.

Yours sincerely

15.20 Confirmation of attendance

Dear Miss Dotrice

ADMINISTRATOR – TRAINING SECTION

Thank you for your letter of yesterday inviting me to attend for interview on Friday 29 May at 3.30 pm.

I shall be pleased to attend, and will look forward to meeting Mrs Howard.

Yours sincerely

Offers of appointment

Letters appointing staff should state clearly the salary and any other conditions of appointment. If the duties of the post are described in detail on a Job Description and enclosed with the letter, it will not be necessary to duplicate such details in the letter itself.

15.21 Letter confirming offer of employment

If an appointment is made verbally at the interview, it should be confirmed by letter immediately afterwards.

Dear Miss Wildman

I am pleased to confirm the offer we made to you yesterday of the post of Administrator of our Training Section, commencing on 1 August 19--.

Your duties will be as outlined at the interview, and as described on the attached Job Description. In particular, you will report directly to the Training Manager, with overall responsibility for the course organisation.

This appointment carries a commencing salary of £9 000 per annum, rising to £10 500 after one year's service, and thereafter by annual review. You will be entitled to 4 weeks' annual holiday.

The appointment may be terminated at any time by either side giving 2 months' notice in writing.

Please confirm that you accept this appointment on the terms stated, and that you will be able to commence you duties on 1 August.

Yours sincerely

15.22 Letter offering appointment

When the appointment is not made at the interview, the offer will be made by letter to the selected applicant as soon as possible.

Dear Miss Jennings

Thank you for attending the interview yesterday. I am pleased to offer you the post of Shorthand Typist in our Sales Department at a starting salary of S$900 (Nine hundred Singapore dollars) per month. Your commencement date would be Monday 1 October.

As discussed, office hours are 9.00 am to 5.30 pm with one hour for lunch. You will be entitled to 3 weeks' annual paid holiday.

Please confirm in writing by return that you accept this appointment on these terms, and that you can take up your duties on 1 October.

Yours sincerely

15.23 Acceptance of offer of employment

Any offer letter should be accepted in writing immediately.

Dear Mr Broomfield

Thank you for your letter of 24 August offering me the post of Shorthand Typist in your Sales Department.

I am pleased to accept this post on the terms stated in your letter, and confirm that I can commence work on 1 October.

I can assure you that I shall do everything I can to make a success of my work.

Yours sincerely

15.24 Declining an offer of employment

If you do not wish to take up the offer of employment you should put this in writing immediately, and it is courteous to give a reason for declining the offer. In this way, the employer may make a second choice as soon as possible.

Dear Mr Broomfield

SUPERINTENDENT OF TYPISTS' TRAINING SECTION

Thank you for your letter of 24 August and for the courtesy extended to me at my interview.

I am sorry that I will be unable to take up the position as outlined in your letter. My present company has discussed with me their plans for expansion, and I have been offered the new post of Office Manager. You will appreciate that this post will offer me a challenge which I feel I must take up.

I wish you every success in appointing a suitable candidate.

Yours sincerely

15.25 Letter to unsuitable applicants

Once an offer of employment has been accepted by the selected applicant, it is courteous to write letters to the remaining applicants who were interviewd telling them that their application was unsuccessful.

Dear Miss Jones

SUPERINTENDENT OF TYPISTS' TRAINING SECTION

Thank you for attending the interview on 24 August for the above post.

I am sorry to inform you that on this occasion your application was unsuccessful. However, I am sure that your experience and qualifications will enable you to obtain a successful appointment in the future.

With best wishes for future applications.

Yours sincerely

Termination of Employment

15.26 Employee's letter of resignation

A Contract of Employment made for a stated period comes to an end when the period is completed unless both parties agree to extend it. If the contract is for an unstated period, it may be ended at any time by either of the parties giving the agreed period of notice.

Dear Miss Ward

I regret to inform you that I wish to give 2 weeks' notice of my resignation from the Company. My last day of work will be 30 June 19--.

I have been very happy working here for the past 2 years, and found my work challenging and enjoyable. However, I have obtained a post where I will have wider responsibilities and greater career prospects.

Thank you for your help and guidance during my employment, and best wishes for the future.

Yours sincerely

15.27 Employer's letter terminating employment (services unsatisfactory)

By the Trade Union and Labour Relations Act 1974 employees who feel they have been unfairly dismissed have the right to appeal to an Industrial Tribunal. An employer must be able to show that the dismissal was justified by referring to the employee's conduct, or inability/failure to do the job satisfactorily.

Where it is decided to terminate the employment of a person whose services have been unsatisfactory, it is advisable to do so verbally in the first place. The confirmatory letter should be worded carefully and tactfully.

Dear Miss Anderson

Following our discussion earlier this week, I regret to inform you that your services with the Company will not be required with effect from 31 August 19--.

As you know, there have been a number of occasions recently when I have had to point out the unsatisfactory quality of your work. Together with your persistent unpunctuality in spite of several warnings, this has led me to believe that you will perhaps be more successful in a different kind of work.

I hope you will find suitable employment elsewhere, and if another employer should wish you to start work before the end of the month, arrangements can be made for you to be released immediately.

Yours sincerely

15.28 Employer's letter terminating employment (services redundant[5])

The Redundancy Payments Act 1975 states that employees are entitled to *compensation*[6] for loss of employment due to redundancy, as in the case of the employer ceasing to carry on business, or having no further need of the employee's services. The amount of compensation payable is calculated on the basis of the employee's age, length of service and weekly earnings.

Dear Mr White

As you are aware, the reorganisation of our office has been the subject of an investigation by a firm of management consultants. They have made a number of recommendations which will result in a decrease in staff.

I very much regret having to inform you that your position as Ledger Clerk is one which will become redundant on 30 June. I am giving you as much notice as possible to enable you to begin looking immediately for alternative employment.

You will, of course, be entitled to a redundancy payment. This will amount to 2 weeks' salary for each of your 5 years' service, at the rate prevailing when your services end. This is calculated as follows!

£100 × 2 × 5 = £1,000

I would like to take this opportunity to say that your work has always been entirely satisfactory, and I shall be pleased to provide any prospective employer with a reference if required.

I do hope you will soon find another suitable post, and wish you all the best for the future.

Yours sincerely

Testimonials

As well as sending a copy of your curriculum vitae with an application letter, it is useful to send copies of any testimonials you may have. The originals of such open testimonials are addressed TO WHOM IT MAY CONCERN. They are generally given by your previous employers if they are requested, and you should always retain the originals, sending prospective employers photocopies only.

There is no legal obligation for anyone to give a testimonial, but if one is written it must state only what is true, otherwise the writer may become legally liable, either to the applicant for *libel*[7], or to the employer if the testimonial is at all misleading.

Any testimonial should give the following details of the employee:

- duration of employment
- post(s) held
- the duties carried out
- work attitude
- personal qualities
- a recommendation

15.29 Formal testimonial for Secretary

This testimonial was requested by an employee who worked at a company over a period of 8 years until she took up teacher training.

TO WHOM IT MAY CONCERN

Miss Sharon Tan was employed as Shorthand Typist in this Company's Sales Department when she left secretarial college in July 19--. She was promoted to my Personal Secretary in 19--. [Duration of employment/ Positions]

Her responsibilities included the usual secretarial duties involved in such a post, as well as attending meetings, transcribing minutes, and supervising and advising junior secretaries. [Duties]

Sharon used her best endeavours at all times to perform her work conscientiously and expeditiously. She was an excellent secretary, an extremely quick and accurate shorthand typist, and meticulous in the layout, presentation and accuracy of her work. I cannot overstress her exceptional work rate, which did not in any way detract from the very high standards she set for herself. [Working attitude]

Sharon enjoyed good health and was a good time-
keeper. She was very personable, friendly, sociable and
quick to share in a joke, and it was a great loss to both
myself and the Company when Sharon took up
teacher-training.

[Personal
qualities]

In my opinion, Sharon has the necessary character,
dedication and approach to be suitable for the position
of personal secretary or to enter the teaching
profession. I can recommend her highly, and may be
contacted for further information.

[Recommendation]

IAN HENLEY
Deputy Chairman

15.30 Testimonial for Head of Department

Here is another very favourable testimonial which was issued to someone who
left a private college after completing a 2-year contract as Head of Department.

TO WHOM IT MAY CONCERN

Norman Tyler has been employed by this College as Head of Business
Studies from August 19-- to 9 March 19--.

As well as capably handling the responsibilities for the overall
administration of his department, Norman ably taught Economics,
Commerce and Management Appreciation to students of a wide range of
ability and age groups on courses leading to Advanced LCCI
examinations.

Norman is a highly competent and professional teacher whose class
preparation is always thorough and meticulous. His committed
approach to teaching is matched by his administrative abilities. He has
made a substantial contribution to course planning, student
counselling, curriculum development and program marketing.

As a person, Norman possesses an outgoing personality and is an easy
mixer, who makes his full contribution to a team and is popular with
his students and colleagues alike.

Given his dedication and ability, I am confident that Norman will prove
to be a valuable asset to any organisation fortunate enough to have him
in their employ. It is with pleasure that I recommend him highly and
without hesitation.

FAISAL SHAMLAN
Principal

Sundry personnel matters

15.31 Transfer of employee to other work

Where it is necessary to transfer an employee from their normal work which has been enjoyed, the reasons for the transfer must be clearly explained and any advantages it may have pointed out and stressed. Perhaps there will be the prospect of more interesting and responsible work, more experience, better pay, improved prospects. With tact, it will be possible to convey what will be unwelcome or disappointing news to an employee without causing hurt feelings or offence. In this way, what might otherwise be received as unwelcome news may almost be turned into good news.

In this case, a long-standing employee is happily settled into a routine with no wish to change, but this has been made necessary due to technological changes within the company.

Dear Mr Turner

As Mrs Williamson has already discussed with you, we have arranged to appoint you as Section Supervisor in the Stores Department with effect from Monday 1 July. Your salary will be £14 200 per annum.

In your new post you will report directly to Mr James Freeman, Storekeeper, and you will be responsible for the work of the clerical staff employed in the department.

Your 30 years of loyal service in the Invoice Department have been greatly appreciated by the management, and we are sorry that it is necessary to move you from a department in which you are so thoroughly at home. Our only reason for doing so is that invoicing will be completely changed by the introduction of computerised methods. We feel sure that you will understand that it is uneconomic for us to retrain our older employees who might, in any case, find difficulty in adjusting to new ways of working.

In your new post you will find ample scope for your experience. We know you will do a good job, and hope you will find it enjoyable.

Yours sincerely

15.32 Recruitment of staff through an agency

Employers in need of office staff frequently make their requirements known to employment agencies. These agencies will introduce either full-time, part-time or temporary staff in return for a commission related to the amount of wage or salary paid.

Dear Sir/Madam

I hope you will be able to help me to fill a vacancy which has just arisen in my department.

My Secretary needs secretarial help, but only on a part-time basis. This will be an interesting post and ideal for someone who wishes to work for only a few hours each week. Applicants should be able to undertake normal secretarial duties and have shorthand and typewriting speeds of about 100 and 45 wpm respectively. Applicants of any age would be considered, but I would stress that willingness and reliability are preferable to someone with high qualifications.

The successful applicant would be required to work for 5 mornings each week for 3 hours each morning. However, I would be willing to consider an alternative arrangement if this is not convenient.

I propose payment based on an hourly rate of £4.00 to £5.50 according to age and experience.

Will you please let me know whether you have anyone on your register who would be suitable.

Yours faithfully

15.33 Request for an increase in salary

Any letter requesting an increase in salary should be worded very carefully. You should explain tactfully the reason why you feel a salary increase is justified.

Dear Mr Browning

My present appointment carries an annual salary of £8 500, reviewed in March last year. During my 5 years with this Company I feel I have carried out my duties conscientiously and have recently acquired additional responsibilities.

I feel that my qualifications and the nature of my work justify a higher salary and have already been offered a similar position with another company at a salary of £9 000 per annum.

My present duties are interesting and I thoroughly enjoy my work. Although I have no wish to leave the Company, I cannot afford to turn down the present offer unless some improvement in my salary can be arranged.

I hope a salary increase will be possible, otherwise I feel my only course will be to accept the offer made to me.

Yours sincerely

Useful expressions

Application letters

Openings

1 I wish to apply for the post . . . advertised in the . . . on . . ..
2 I was interested to see your advertisement in . . . and wish to apply for this post.
3 I am writing to enquire whether you have a suitable vacancy in your organisation which I might usefully fill.
4 I understand from Mr . . . , one of your suppliers, that there is an opening in your company for . . . .
5 Mrs . . . informs me that she will be leaving your company on . . . and if her position has not been filled, I should like to be considered.

Closes

1 I look forward to hearing from you and to being granted the opportunity of an interview.
2 I trust you will consider my application favourably and grant me an interview.
3 I look forward to the opportunity of attending an interview, at which I can provide further details.

Favourable references

Openings

1 Mr . . . has applied to us for the above post/position of . . . . We should be grateful if you would give us your opinion of his character and abilities.
2 We have received an application from Miss . . . who has given your name as a reference.
3 I am very glad of this opportunity to speak in support of Miss . . .'s application for a position in your company.
4 In reply to your recent enquiry, Ms . . . has been employed as . . . for the past 2 years.

Closes

1 Any information you can provide will be much appreciated.

2 We shall, of course, treat any information you are kind enough to provide in strictest confidence.
3 I am sure you will be more than satisfied with the work of Mr . . . .
4 I shall be sorry to lose . . . but realise that her abilities demand wider scope than are possible at this company.

Unfavourable references

1 I find it difficult to answer your enquiry about Mr . . . . He is a very likeable person, but I cannot conscientiously recommend him for the vacancy you mention.
2 The work produced by . . . was below the standards expected, and we found it necessary to release him.
3 Her poor time-keeping was very disturbing, causing some disruption to the work of the department.
4 We found her attitude quite a bad influence on other staff within the department.
5 Although . . . possesses the qualifications to perform such work, I have seen no evidence that she has the necessary self-discipline or reliability.

Offers of employment

Openings

1 Following your interview last . . ., I am pleased to offer you the position of . . . .
2 I am pleased to confirm the offer we made to you when you came for interview on . . . .
3 With reference to your interview with . . ., our Personnel Manager, I am pleased to offer you the position of . . . commencing on . . . .

Closes

1 Written confirmation of your acceptance of this post would be appreciated as soon as possible.
2 Please confirm in writing that you accept this appointment on the terms stated, and that you can commence your duties on . . . .
3 We look forward to welcoming you to the staff of . . . and hope you will be very happy in your work here.

Termination of employment

Openings

1 I very much regret that I wish to terminate my services with this Company with effect from . . . .
2 I am writing to confirm that I wish to tender my resignation. My last date of employment will be . . . .
3 As my family have decided to emigrate, I am sorry to have to tender my resignation.
4 It is with regret that I have to inform you that your position with this Company will become redundant on . . . .
5 There has been no improvement in your work performance and attitude despite our letters dated . . . and . . . . As a result we have no option but to withdraw your services with effect from . . . .

Closes

1 I have been very happy working here and thank you for your guidance during my employment.
2 I am sorry that these circumstances make it necessary for me to leave the Company.
3 We have been extremely satisfied with your services and hope that you will soon find another suitable post.
4 I hope you will soon find alternative employment, and extend my best wishes for your future.

Testimonials

Openings

1 Mr . . . has been employed by this Company from . . . to . . . .
2 Miss . . . worked for this company from leaving college in 19-- until she emigrated to Canada in March 19--.

Central section

1 Miss . . . enjoys good health and is a good time-keeper.
2 She uses her best endeavours at all times to perform her work expeditiously, and has always been a hard-working and conscientious employee.
3 Miss . . . made a substantial contribution to the work of the . . . department, and always performed her work in a business-like and reliable manner.
4 Mr . . . gave considerable help to his colleagues in improvements of teaching methods and materials, and also produced many booklets of guidance which are proving valuable to other teachers.

Closes

1 I have pleasure in recommending . . . highly and without hesitation.
2 We hope that . . . meets with the success we feel he deserves.
3 I shall be sorry to lose his services, but realise that his abilities demand wider scope than are possible at this company.
4 I can recommend Miss . . . to you with every confidence.

Glossary

1 **prospective employer** possible future employer
2 **unsolicited** not asked for
3 **conscientious** careful to do what is right
4 **unqualified** clear, complete, without question
5 **redundant** surplus to requirements
6 **compensation** payment for loss
7 **libel** a statement damaging a person's reputation

Assignments on material included in this chapter can be found on pp 361–3.

Chapter 16

Travel and hotels

In dealing with business travel it may be necessary to arrange for passports to be supplied or renewed, obtain visas when necessary, book travel by air or sea, and make accommodation reservations. Enquiries about such matters are usually made in the first instance by telephone to a travel agent, who will deal with most travel requirements on your behalf. Such arrangements need then only be confirmed in writing. This chapter looks at a variety of letters in connection with travel arrangements, including such confirmatory letters.

Passports

A passport is a document of identification issued by the government of a country to ensure protection of its subjects who travel overseas. British subjects of the United Kingdom should obtain a passport application form from any main post office or large travel agent. The completed application form, together with relevant documentary evidence and fee, should be sent to any of the regional offices of the Passport Division of the Foreign Office: London, Liverpool, Peterborough, Glasgow, Newport or Belfast. Postal applications are normally processed within 3–5 weeks of receipt. If a passport is required urgently, a personal visit to a passport office can ensure processing within about 5 days. Standard passports are *valid*[1] for 10 years, although one year passports are also available at a reduced fee. New regulations mean that husband and wife passports are no longer issued; any children should be included on the passports of both parties. Full particulars regarding passports are issued together with application forms.

16.1 Request for passport application form

Dear Sir

Early next year I intend to visit a number of countries in the Far East and Australasia. Please send me a passport application form and a list of the addresses to which applications for visas for the various countries should be sent.

I have not previously held or applied for a passport of any description.

Yours faithfully

16.2 Formal application for passport

Dear Sir

I have completed and enclose my application form for issue of a United Kingdom passport. Also enclosed are two passport photographs (one certified at the back), and a signed personal description slip, my birth certificate and a cheque for the passport fee.

I propose to leave England on 15 January and should be grateful if you would ensure that my passport is prepared and sent to me in good time to enable me to obtain the necessary visas.

Yours faithfully

Visas

Visas are required for travel to many countries. When travel arrangements are made through a travel agent, they will usually obtain any visa which is necessary. Alternatively, they may be obtained direct upon application to the visa department of the high commissioners (for British Commonwealth countries) or consuls (in foreign countries) of the countries concerned. A list of their addresses may be obtained from any passport office.

Applications for visas must be returned with the appropriate fee and any documents requested. These may include the applicant's passport, photograph, vaccination or other health certificate, travel ticket and perhaps a statement from an employer or other sponsor guaranteeing the applicant's financial security during overseas visits.

16.3 Request for visa application form

Dear Sir

Our Sales Director, Mr R Dickson, proposes to visit Australia in 2 months' time on the Company's business.

I understand a visa is necessary, and would be grateful if you could send me the appropriate application form, together with details of your visa requirements.

Yours faithfully

16.4 Formal application for visa

Dear Sir/Madam

I enclose the completed application form for an entry visa to enable Mr R Dickson, Sales Director of this Company, to visit Australia.

Mr Dickson will be leaving London on 5 August for a business tour of Singapore and Hong Kong. Subject to issue of the necessary visa, he proposes to fly to Perth, Western Australia, on 7 August. Thereafter he will be visiting Melbourne, Sydney and Cairns.

The purpose of Mr Dickson's visit to Australia is to gain information about recent developments in education there, with special reference to the use of our publications. He intends to visit departments of education, universities, commercial and technical colleges and other educational organisations, as well as leading booksellers. My Company would guarantee Mr Dickson's financial security during his stay, as well as payment of all expenses incurred.

The following supporting documents are enclosed:

1 Mr Dickson's passport.

2 A cheque for the visa fee.

3 A registered stamped addressed envelope for return of the passport.

4 A copy of the Company's catalogue of publications for your reference.

Should you require any further information, please do not hesitate to let me know.

Yours faithfully

Travel by air/sea

There are two main types of airline customer – the business traveller and the holidaymaker. Business travellers usually make their arrangements at very short notice, and as a rule make their *reservations*[2] direct with the airline, often by telephone. Holidaymakers, on the other hand, employ travel agents to make their arrangements well in advance.

16.5 Enquiry concerning flights

(a) Request

In this letter, the writer enquires with the Reservations Officer of British Airways regarding flights between London and New York.

Dear Sir/Madam

My Company will be arranging quite a number of business trips to New York in the near future.

Please send me information concerning flights (outward and return) including departure times and cost of single and return fares.

We are particularly interested in information relating to reduced fares.

Yours faithfully

(b) Reply

This reply is both courteous and helpful, giving confidence.

Dear Mrs Harben

Many thanks for your enquiry of 5 September.

I enclose a timetable giving details of outward and return flights between London and New York, together with a price list in which you will find details of both ordinary and discounted fares. As you will see from this list, discounted fares can be as little as one-third of the normal fare.

For all visitors to the United States, a visa will be necessary.

If I can be of any further assistance, please do not hesitate to contact me.

Yours sincerely

16.6 Enquiry concerning car ferry

In this letter, the writer requests details of car ferries, which are an alternative to flying to Europe, from a well-known operator.

(a) Enquiry

Dear Sir/Madam

Later this year I propose to tour Western Europe with friends, and I wish to take a car with me.

Please send me details of your car ferry service, including your terms and conditions for transporting a Mercedes-Benz and three passengers from Dover to Calais.

As this would be my first use of the service, I am not familiar with Customs and other formalities involved, and should be grateful for any information you can provide.

Yours faithfully

(b) Reply

Dear Mr Hanley

Thank you for your letter of 4 August requesting details of our car ferry service.

A brochure is enclosed giving all the information you require, together with prices and a timetable.

Formalities for touring Europe by car are now simpler than ever before. All that is necessary is for you to check in at our Dover office one hour before departure time, and to produce the following documents:

1 Your travel ticket.
2 Your passport.
3 Your car registration papers.
4 A valid British driving licence.
4 An international insurance 'green card'.

Your car must also carry a GB nationality plate.

If you require further details, please contact me. Meanwhile, I hope you will enjoy travelling with British Car Ferries Ltd.

Yours sincerely

16.7 Enquiry concerning sea journey

In this letter, the writer makes enquiries about travel on ocean liners.

(a) Enquiry

Dear Sir/Madam

I am interested in your sailings to New York during August or September this year, and should be pleased to receive any available literature giving information about the ships scheduled to sail during this period.

Please also let me have details of fares (single and return) for both first and second-class travel.

I look forward to hearing from you soon.

Yours faithfully

(b) Reply

Dear Mrs Morrison

Thank you for your letter of 11 June enquiring about sailings to New York.

In the enclosed copy of our Queen Elizabeth 2 sailing list you will find details of sailings and of first-class and tourist fares, including excursion fares in both classes.

A valid passport is, of course, necessary for all passengers, but an international certificate of vaccination is now no longer necessary. All passengers other than United States citizens and holders of re-entry permits, will also require a visa issued by a United States consul.

As the Company's liability for baggage is limited under the terms of the passenger ticket, we strongly urge passengers to insure against all risks for the full period of their journey. I shall be glad to supply details on request.

Please let me know if I can be of further assistance.

Yours sincerely

(c) Reservation of berths

Dear Sir

Thank you for recently forwarding information about sailings of Queen Elizabeth 2.

Will you please make a reservation for a first-class single cabin, in my name, on 3 August sailing to New York. Full payment is enclosed.

I look forward to receiving confirmation of my reservation, together with travel ticket.

Yours faithfully

16.8 Enquiry concerning holiday cruises

In this letter, the writer enquires about holiday cruises.

(a) Enquiry

Dear Sir

I am interested in learning more about 10–14 day holiday cruises offered by your organisation for this summer.

Please let me have the relevant brochure, as well as costs for tourist-class travel.

Yours faithfully

(b) Reply

Dear Mrs Tonks

Thank you for your enquiry of 10 February.

I have pleasure in enclosing our illustrated brochure, containing full details of the cruises about which you enquire, as well as tourist-class fares. Also enclosed is a leaflet showing the accommodation available for the coming summer, but as the booking position is constantly changing this leaflet can serve only as a broad guide of what we can offer.

Please let me know if you require further information or assistance.

Yours sincerely

Hotel accommodation

Most large hotels are organised as companies and enquiries should be addressed to 'The Manager'. Private hotels are much smaller and enquiries should be addressed to 'The Proprietor', by whom they are usually owned and managed.

When requesting information about a prospective booking, be sure to observe the following rules:

- Keep your letter short and to the point.
- State your requirements clearly and concisely. To avoid misunderstanding mention days as well as dates for which accommodation is required, as well as the exact period of your stay if it is known (e.g. 'from Monday 6 to Friday 10 July, inclusive').
- State times of arrival and departure if known.
- Request confirmation of the booking if there is time.

16.9 Booking company accommodation at a hotel

In this enquiry, a company writes to the Manager of a London hotel, requesting information about accommodation. Note the salutation 'Dear Sir/Madam'.

(a) Enquiry

Dear Sir/Madam

My company will be displaying products at the forthcoming British Industrial Fair at Earls Court and we shall require hotel accommodation for several members of staff.

Please send me a copy of your current brochure and details of terms for half board[3]. Please also indicate if you have one double and three single rooms available from Monday 13 to Friday 17 May inclusive.

I hope to hear from you soon.

Yours faithfully

(b) Reply

In replying, note that the Manager repeats details of rooms and dates to avoid misunderstanding. The opportunity is also taken to refer to the advantages offered by the hotel. This will build up a cordial relationship, and hopefully lead to further business.

Dear Miss Johnson

Thank you for your letter of 15 March.

As requested, I enclose a copy of our brochure in which you will find all the necessary details required.

We presently have one double and three single rooms available from Monday 13 to Friday 17 May inclusive. However, as we are now entering the busy season and bookings for this period are likely to be heavy, we recommend you to make your reservation without delay.

You will see from our brochure that this is a modern hotel, and I am sure your staff would be very comfortable here. We are well served by public transport to Earls Court, which can normally be reached from here in less that 15 minutes.

I hope to receive confirmation of your reservation soon.

Yours sincerely

(c) Confirmation of reservation

In the first instance you would normally telephone the hotel to make your reservation, and this would be confirmed in writing immediately.

Dear Mr Nelson

I refer to your letter of 17 March and our telephone conversation today.

I confirm reservation of one double and three single en suite[4] rooms from 13–17 May inclusive, with half-board. Guests' names are:

Mr & Mrs Philip Andersen
Mr Geoffrey Richardson
Miss Linda Clark
Mr Jonathan Denby

The account will be settled by Mr Philip Andersen, our Company's General Manager.

Yours sincerely

16.10 Booking private accommodation

(a) Enquiry

Dear Sir/Madam

I shall be passing through London next week and would like to reserve a single room for Wednesday and Thursday 18 and 19 October.

My previous stays at the Norfolk have always been very enjoyable, and I particularly like the rooms overlooking the gardens. If one of these rooms is avilable, I hope you will reserve it for me.

I expect to arrive at the hotel in time for lunch on the 18th and shall be leaving immediately after breakfast on the 20th.

Yours faithfully

(b) Reply

Dear Mr Robinson

Thank you for your letter of 10 October.

I was glad to learn that you have enjoyed your previous visits to the Norfolk. Unfortunately, a room overlooking the garden is not available for the dates you requested. However, I have several pleasant rooms on the south side of the hotel, away from traffic noise and with an open view of the surrounding countryside.

The charge for these rooms is the same as that for the room you occupied when you were here last July, namely £28 per night, though it has been necessary to increase meal charges slightly. You will find all details in the enclosed brochure.

I have provisionally booked for you one of the rooms referred to, for the two nights of Wednesday and Thursday, 18 and 19 October, and look forward to receiving your confirmation.

Yours sincerely

16.11 Booking private accommodation overseas

The writer here writes to a hotel overseas, mentioning that the hotel has been recommended by a friend.

(a) Enquiry

Dear Sir/Madam

Your hotel has been highly recommended by a friend who stayed there last year.

I will be arriving in Singapore at 1730 hours on Monday 15 April on flight SQ24, accompanied by three friends. We wish to stay in Singapore for 4 nights, i.e. 15–18 April inclusive, before arranging independent travel by land in Malaysia.

Could you please let me know if 2 twin-bedded rooms are available for this period, and what the charges would be. I also undertand that your hotel arranges local tours, and details would be appreciated.

I hope to hear from you soon.

Yours faithfully

(b) Reply

In this reply, the Reservations Officer takes the trouble to point out the benefits in the hotel's position and additions since the enquirer's friend visited.

Dear Mr Hill

I am pleased to learn from your letter of 2 February that The Lion Hotel was recommended to you.

A copy of our illustrated brochure is enclosed showing the hotel's many facilities, from which you will see the recent improvements made to our pool area, with adjoining gym and leisure facilities.

Our hotel's tour operator is Century Tours, and a brochure is attached giving details of their half and full-day tours. There would be no problem in reserving places on any of these tours when you actually arrive in Singapore.

I have taken the liberty of making a provisional reservation of 2 twin-bedded rooms from 15–18 April at a cost of S$95 per night. This reservation will be held until 1 March, and your confirmation would be appreciated before this date.

Arrangements can be made for our courtesy pick-up service to meet your flight SQ24 at 1730 on 15 April if you indicate this at the time of confirming your reservation.

You will find The Lion Hotel very convenient for transport both by

MRT (Mass Rapid Transport) and bus, as well as within 5 minutes' walking distance of Orchard Road.

I look forward to extending the hospitality of The Lion Hotel to your party, and hope to receive confirmation of your reservation before 1 March.

Yours sincerely

Holiday accommodation

Information about hotels, guest houses and holiday flats may be obtained from the annual holiday guides prepared by the publicity departments of the holiday resorts. These guides contain details also of the resort's attractions – places of interest, entertainments, sport, museums, art galleries and cultural activities. Copies are sent on request, usually free of charge, or for a small sum to cover postage.

16.12 Request for holiday guide

Requests for guides need only be very short and formal and, except where a payment is required, may be made on a postcard. Copies of the guide are usually sent out with a compliment slip instead of a formal letter.

Dear Sirs

Please send me a copy of your official holiday guide and a list of hotels and guest houses.

I enclose stamps to the value of 24p to cover postage.

Yours faithfully

16.13 Enquiry for hotel accommodation

(a) Enquiry

Dear Sir/Madam

I have obtained the name of your private hotel from the holiday guide received from your Information Centre.

Could you please let me know if you have accommodation for a family

of 5 for 2 weeks commencing Saturday 10 August. We shall require
2 twin-bedded rooms and 1 single room – the single room should be
near to the lift for my elderly mother.

If you can provide this accommodation, please send me a copy of your
brochure and also your terms for full board[5].

Yours faithfully

___

(b) Reply

Dear Mr Leeson

Thank you for your enquiry dated 15 April.

I am pleased to say that the accommodation you require is available for
the 2 weeks commencing Saturday 10 August. We can offer you two
adjacent[6] twin-bedded rooms on the first floor, with a single room on
the same floor conveniently located about 10 metres from the lift.
Should this distance present a problem, we could place a wheelchair at
your disposal.

Early confirmation of the accommodation offered is necessary, as
bookings for August are always heavy and I should not wish you to be
disappointed.

I enclose a brochure containing details of our charges, and hope you
will give us the opportunity to welcome your family to the Northcliffe.

Yours sincerely

___

16.14 Enquiry to a small private hotel

(a) Enquiry

Dear Sir/Madam

Your hotel has been recommended to me by Mr & Mrs John Windsor
who tell me they spent a very happy fortnight with you last summer.

I am planning to bring my family to St Annes for 2 weeks between
mid-July and the end of August, and hope you will be able to
accommodate us. We require one double and one twin-bedded room for
my wife and myself and our two young children.

Our holiday arrangements are fairly flexible and any 2

consecutive[7] weeks within the period mentioned would be suitable.

An early reply would be appreciated, so that our holiday arrangements can be completed as soon as possible.

Yours faithfully

(b) Reply

Dear Mr Wilkinson

Thank you for your letter of 10 April. I remember Mr & Mrs Windsor very well and should be pleased if you would pass on my thanks for their recommendation.

We are already fully booked for the month of August, but the flexibility of your arrangements enables us to offer you one double and one twin-bedded room for 2 full weeks from Saturday 18 July.

We are provisionally[8] reserving this accommodation for you, but would appreciate your written confirmation within one week.

Our brochure is enclosed for your information.

We look forward to welcoming you to St Annes and assure you that everything possible will be done to make your fortnight's stay a very happy one.

Yours sincerely

16.15 Enquiry to the proprietor of holiday flats

(a) Enquiry

Dear Sir/Madam

We wish to arrange a family holiday for 2 weeks from Saturday 14 August, and would be pleased to know if you have accommodation available which would be suitable for my husband and myself, as well as our two teenage children. We also wish to bring our dog, a clean and well-trained Irish Setter.

If you are able to accommodate us during this period, please let me know the facilities available in your holiday flats, together with your charges.

Yours faithfully

(b) Reply

Dear Mrs Turner

Thank you for your recent enquiry regarding holiday accommodation for your family for 2 weeks from Saturday 14 August.

I am pleased to say that we have a holiday flat available which would be suitable for your family. This flat is on the first floor, and comprises one double and two bunk beds, as well as cooker, fridge, sink, wardrobes and bedside drawers.

We do allow dogs in our holiday flats, and would refer you to the rules contained in our enclosed brochure. Schedules of prices are also shown on the separate leaflet.

We look forward to welcoming you to Thornton Holiday Flats, and would advise you to make an early reservation.

Yours sincerely

Useful expressions

Openings

1 I wish to visit . . . and would be pleased to know if you have a single room available on . . . .
2 I should be grateful if you would forward a copy of your current brochure.
3 Please let me know if you have available a first-class single cabin on the . . . leaving for . . . on . . . .
4 I was pleased to hear our hotel was recommended by . . . after his visit in . . . .

Closes

1 When replying, please include a copy of your current brochure.
2 I hope to receive an early reply.
3 I look forward to hearing that you can provide this accommodation.
4 As we wish to make arrangements in good time, I should appreciate an early reply.

Glossary

1 **valid** legally in order
2 **reservation** booking
3 **half board** breakfast and evening meal only
4 **en suite** with attached bathroom
5 **full board** including all meals
6 **adjacent** adjoining
7 **consecutive** running together
8 **provisionally** subject to confirmation

Assignments on material included in this chapter can be found on pp 363–4.

Chapter 17

Miscellaneous letters

There are many other occasions on which business letters are written. This chapter takes a look at a variety of business letters which cannot really be placed in any particular category, but all of which are still important in day-to-day business life.

17.1 Letter requesting appointment

(a) Request 1

Dear Mr Harrison

Our Mr Chapman has informed me that you have now returned from your visit to the Middle East. There are a number of points which have arisen on the book I am writing on <u>Modern Business Organisation</u>, and I should like the opportunity to discuss these with you.

I shall be in London from 15 to 19 September, and will telephone you on Monday 15 September to arrange a day and time which would be convenient for us to meet.

I look forward to the opportunity of meeting you again.

Yours sincerely

(b) Reply

Dear Mr Alexander

Thank you for your letter regarding <u>Modern Business Organisation</u>.

It will be a pleasure to meet you again and to renew the contact we had when we first discussed the matter of your book.

I note you will be telephoning me on Monday morning, and hope it will be possible to arrange to meet on either Tuesday or Wednesday afternoon.

I look forward to meeting you again.

Yours sincerely

(c) Request 2

Dear Mr Jones

I am very concerned about the difficulties you are having with the goods we supplied earlier this year.

I should very much like the opportunity to discuss this matter with you personally and wonder if it would be convenient to see you while I am in your area next week. My secretary will telephone you during the next few days to make a convenient appointment.

Yours sincerely

(d) Request 3

Dear Mrs Sirley

I should very much like to see you to discuss various matters of mutual interest. As I shall be in Bradford next week, I wonder if it will be convenient to call on you at 11 am on Thursday 12 September.

My secretary will call you within the next few days to confirm this appointment or, if necessary, arrange an alternative appointment.

I will look forward to seeing you.

Yours sincerely

17.2 Letter regarding unpaid subscription

(a) Request for payment

Dear Mrs Henderson

According to our records, your subscription for membership of this Society, due on 1 January, has not yet been received despite 2 reminders sent in February and March.

I am sorry to have to say that unless we receive your cheque within the next 10 days, we shall have to assume that you do not wish to continue your membership.

Yours sincerely

(b) Reply

Dear Mrs Betts

I am sorry not to have replied to your reminders sent earlier this year regarding my subscription to your Society. I have been overseas for the past 3 months, escaping the British winter by staying with my family in Australia.

I am now enclosing my cheque for £17.50 for this year's subscription, and apologise for any inconvenience.

Yours sincerely

17.3 Letter inviting speaker to conference

(a) Invitation

Dear Miss Forrest

Our Society will be holding a conference at the Moat House Hotel, Swansea, from 4 to 6 October, the theme of which will be 'Changes in the Role of the Secretary'. Approximately 100 delegates are expected, comprising mostly practising secretaries as well as some lecturer members.

We would be delighted if, once again, you would accept our invitation to speak on the subject of 'Effective Communication' on 5 October from 10.30 to 11.30 am. We would, of course, be prepared to pay you the usual fee of £50.

For your information, a copy of the detailed draft programme is enclosed. You will, of course, be welcome to attend other sessions of the conference on that day, and overnight accommodation will be provided for you on 4 October.

We look forward to hearing that you can accept our invitation. At the same time, please let us know if any visual aids will be required.

Yours sincerely

(b) Reply

Dear Ms Bolan

Thank you for your letter inviting me to speak at your conference on 5 October on the subject of 'Effective Communication'.

I am delighted to accept your invitation, and confirm that I will require overnight accommodation.

For my presentation, I will require use of an overhead projector and hope this can be made available.

I look forward to renewing my acquaintance with members of your Society at your conference, and wish you every success.

Yours sincerely

17.4 Letter declining invitation

Dear Mr Woodhead

I was very pleased to receive your letter of 2 May.

Much as I should like to present the prizes at your Speech Day on 15 June, I am sorry to say that I will be unable to do so, as I shall be abroad at the time. I must therefore regretfully decline your kind invitation.

I do hope that the day will be a great success.

Yours sincerely

17.5 Letter regarding conference accommodation

Dear Sir

Our Company will be holding a one-day conference on Saturday 18 May from 10.00 am to 5.30 pm, and we are looking for suitable accommodation for it.

About 200 delegates are expected to attend, and our requirements are as follows:

1 A suitable conference room with theatre-style seating.

2 A small adjacent room for the display of equipment and accessories.

3 A reception area for welcoming delegates.

4 Morning coffee at 11.30 am and afternoon tea at 3.30 pm.

5 A buffet luncheon to be served from 1.00 to 2.00 pm.

If you have suitable facilities available, please let us know the costs involved. At the same time, please send specimen menus for a buffet-style luncheon.

We hope to hear from you soon.

Yours faithfully

17.6 Dismissal of firm's representative

Dear Sir/Madam

We wish to inform you that Miss Rona Smart, who has been our representative in North-West England for the past 7 years, has now left our service. Therefore, she no longer has authority to take orders or to collect accounts on our behalf.

In her place we have appointed Mrs Tracie Coole. Mrs Coole has for many years had control of our sales section and is thoroughly familiar with the needs of customers in your area. She intends to call on you some time this month to introduce herself and to bring samples of our new spring fabrics.

We look forward to continuing our business relationship with you.

Yours faithfully.

NB If the representative left of their own free will and was a valued member of staff, the first paragraph of the above letter would be more suitably expressed as follows:

It is with regret that we inform you that Miss Rona Smart, who has been our representative for the past 7 years, has now decided to leave us to take up another appointment.

17.7 Appointment of new representative

Dear Sir/Madam

Mr Samuel Goodier, who has been calling on you regularly for the past 6 years, has now joined our firm as junior partner. His many friends will doubtless be sorry that they will see him much less frequently, and we can assure you that he shares their regret.

Mr Goodier hopes, however, to keep in touch with you and other customers by occasional visits to his former territory.

We have now appointed Mr Lionel Tufnell to represent us in the South West and Mr Goodier will introduce him to you when he makes his last regular call on you next week. Mr Tufnell has worked closely with Mr Goodier in the past, and he will still do so in the future. Mr Goodier will continue to offer help and advice in matters affecting you and other customers in the South West, and his intimate knowledge of your requirements will be of great benefit to Mr Tufnell in his new responsibilities.

Our business relations with you have always been very good, and we believe we have succeeded in serving you well. It is therefore with confidence that we ask you to extend to our new representative the courtesy and friendliness you have always shown to Mr Goodier.

Yours faithfully

Assignments on material included in this chapter can be found on pp 364–5.

Unit 4
Classified business letters

Chapter 18
Agencies

Many businesses with a large volume of foreign trade do their own buying and selling. A large manufacturing business, for instance, will often have its own export department and, if the volume of trade is sufficient, may establish branches abroad. However, there are many smaller firms who find it more economical to buy and sell through commission agents or commission houses, factors, brokers and other types of agent.

Any company considering appointing an agent should make a thorough investigation into such prospective agent's qualifications, experience and personal qualities beforehand, for example:

- Their reliability and financial soundness.
- Their technical ability to handle the goods to be marketed.
- Their market connections and the effectiveness of their sales organisation.
- The nature and extent of other agencies they hold, and in particular whether these are connected with the sale of competing products.

These matters are especially important when foreign agents are appointed, since they will be working without local supervision or control. It is advisable to make a formal appointment of an agent in writing, setting out in detail the terms of the agency.

Finding an agent

There are useful sources of information for those who want help in finding suitable agents. A British supplier, for instance, wishing to develop trade in an overseas country could make use of one or more of the following:

- The Export Services Division or the appropriate Regional Office of the Department of Trade.
- The Consular Section of the appropriate Embassy.
- HM Trade Commissioner in the country concerned.
- The Chamber of Commerce.
- Banks.
- An advertisement in selected journals in the country concerned.

Applications for agencies

When seeking an agency, the applicant will stress two things:

- The opportunities in the market waiting to be developed.
- The particular advantages that may be offered.

The applicant will mention such selling points as knowledge of the market, numerous connections, long-established position and wide experience, the efficiency of their sales organisation, the facilities for display offered by their showrooms and so on. The agent may also give the names of persons or firms who may be referred to and mention the rate of commission expected.

18.1 Application for home agency

(a) Application

Dear Sir/Madam

We understand from Knowles Hardware Ltd of Glasgow that you are looking for a reliable firm with good connections in the textile trade to represent you in Scotland.

For some years we have acted as Scottish agents for one of your competitors, Jarvis & Sons of Preston, but they have recently registered as a limited company and in the reorganisation decided to establish their own branch in Edinburgh. As they no longer need our services we are now free to offer them to you.

As we have had experience in marketing products similar to your own, we are familiar with customers' needs and are confident that we could develop a good market for you in Scotland. We have spacious and well-eqipped showrooms, not only at our Glasgow headquarters, but also in Edinburgh and Perth, and an experienced staff of sales representatives who would energetically promote your business.

We should be glad to learn that you are interested in our proposal and on what terms you would be willing to conclude an agreement. I will be visiting your town in 2 weeks' time and hope it will be possible to discuss details with you then.

Should you need them, we can provide first-class references, but for general information concerning our standing in the trade we suggest you refer to Knowles Hardware Ltd.

We hope to hear from you soon.

Yours faithfully

(b) Reply

Dear Mrs Matthews

Having carefully considered your letter of 10 September, we should like to discuss further your proposal for an agency in Scotland.

Your work with Jarvis & Co is well-known to us, and in view of your connections throughout the trade in Scotland we feel there is much you could do to extend our business there.

Our final decision would depend upon the terms and conditions. As you will be visiting our town in 2 weeks' time, we think it would be better to discuss these with you rather than to enter upon what may develop into lengthy correspondence.

Please let me know when we may expect you to call.

Yours sincerely

(c) Agency appointed

Dear Mrs Matthews

It was a pleasure to meet you yesterday, subsequent to my letter of 17 September.

We are now pleased to offer you an appointment as our sole agents for Scotland on the terms and conditions agreed verbally with you.

This appointment will be for a trial period of 12 months in the first instance. We will pay you a commission of 7% on the net value of all sales against orders received through you, to which would be added a del credere commission of 2½%.

As we are able to facilitate quick delivery there will be no need for you to maintain stocks of our goods, but we will send you full ranges of samples for display in your showrooms.

Please confirm these terms in writing as soon as possible, after which we will arrange for a formal agreement to be drawn up. When this is signed, a circular will be prepared for distribution to our customers in Scotland announcing your appointment as our agents.

We look forward to a successful business relationship.

Yours sincerely

18.2 Application for overseas agency

(a) Electrical engineering

Dear Sir/Madam

I was interested to see your advertisement in *The Daily Telegraph*, and wish to offer my services as representative of your company in Morocco.

I am 35 years of age, a chartered electrical engineer, and have a good working knowledge of Spanish and German. For the past 5 years I have acted in Egypt as agent for Moxon & Parkinson, electrical engineers in Warrington, Lancashire. This company has recently been taken over by Digital Equipment Ltd and is now being represented in Egypt by its own representative.

I have been concerned with work in the electronic field[1] since I graduated in physics at Manchester University at the age of 22. During my agency with Moxons I also had first-hand experience of marketing electronic and microprocessing equipment[2]. I feel I am well able, therefore, to promote the sale of your products in the expanding economies of the African countries.

For references I suggest you contact Moxon & Parkinson, as well as the two companies named below, with both of which I have had close business connections for several years:

Fylde Electronic Laboratories Ltd, 47 Blackpool Road, Preston, Lancs

Sexton Electronic Laboratories Ltd, 25 Deansgate, Manchester

I look forward to being able to give you more information at a personal interview.

Yours faithfully

(b) Textiles (from an agent abroad)

Dear Sir/Madam

We would like to offer our services as agents for the sale of your products in New Zealand.

Our company was established in 1906 and we are known throughout the trade as agents of the highest standing. We are already represented in several West European countries, including France, Germany and Italy.

There is a growing demand in New Zealand for British textiles, especially for fancy worsted suitings and printed cotton and nylon fabrics. The prospects for good quality fabrics at competitive prices are very good, and according to a recent Chamber of Commerce survey the demand for British textiles is likely to grow considerably during the next 2 or 3 years.

If you would send us details of your ranges, with samples and prices, we could inform you of their suitability for the New Zealand market, and also indicate the patterns and qualities for which sales are likely to be good. We would then arrange to call on our customers with your collection.

You will naturally wish to have references and may write to Barclays Bank Ltd, 99 Piccadilly, Manchester, or to any of our customers, whose names we will be glad to send you.

We feel sure we should have no difficulty in arranging terms to suit us both, and look forward to hearing from you soon.

Yours faithfully

18.3 Application for sole agency

(a) Importer's application

Dear Sir/Madam

We recently attended the International Photographic Exhibition in Cairo and were impressed by the high quality, attractive design and reasonable prices of your cameras. Having since seen your full catalogue, we are convinced that there is a promising market for your products here in Jordan.

If you are not already represented here, we should be interested in acting as your sole agents.

As leading importers and distributors of more than 20 years' standing in the photographic trade, we have a good knowledge of the Jordanian market. Through our sales organisation, we have good contacts with the leading retailers.

We handle several other agencies in non-competing lines and, if our proposal interests you, can supply first-class references from manufacturers in Britain.

We firmly believe that an agency for marketing your products in Jordan would be of considerable benefit to both of us, and we look forward to learning that you are interested in our proposal.

Mr Semir Haddad, our Purchasing Director, will be in England during May and will be pleased to call on you if we hear from you positively.

Yours faithfully

(b) Manufacturer's reply

Dear Mr Jamal

Thank you for your letter of 18 March and for your comments on our cameras.

We are still a young company, but expanding rapidly. At present our overseas representation is confined to countries in Western Europe, where our cameras are selling well. However, we are interested in the chance of developing our trade further afield.

When your Mr Semir Haddad is in England, we should certainly like to meet him with a view to discussing your proposal further. If Mr Haddad will get in touch with me to arrange a meeting, I can also arrange for him to look around our factory and see for himself the quality of the materials and workmanship put into our cameras.

Yours sincerely

18.4 Offer to act as *del credere* agent

Sometimes, in addition to the normal duties, an agent will be held personally liable for goods sold for the principal should the buyer fail to pay. Such agents are known as *del credere agents*[3], and are entitled to an extra commission for undertaking this additional risk.

(a) Offer

Dear Sir/Madam

The demand for toiletries in the United Arab Emirates has shown a marked increase in recent years. We are convinced that there is a considerable market here for your products.

There is every sign that an advertising campaign, even on a modest scale, would produce very good results if it were backed by an efficient system of distribution.

We are well-known distributors of over 15 years' standing, with branches in most of the principal towns. With knowledge of the local conditions, we feel we have the experience and the resources necessary to bring about a market development of your trade in this country. Reference to the Embassy of the United Arab Emirates and to Middle East Services and Sales Limited would enable you to verify our statements.

If you were to appoint us as your agents, we should be prepared to discuss the rate of commission. However, as the early work on development would be heavy, we feel that 10 per cent on orders placed during the first 12 months would be a reasonable figure. As the market would be new to you and customers largely unknown, we would be quite willing to act on a del credere basis in return for an extra commission of 2½ per cent to cover the additional risk.

We hope you will see a worthwhile opportunity in our proposal, and that we may look forward to your early decision.

Yours faithfully

(b) Reply

We are interested in your proposals of 8 July but, though favourably impressed by your views, are concerned that even a modest advertising campaign may not be worthwhile. We therefore suggest that we first test the market by sending you a representative selection of our products for sale on our account.

In the absence of advertising we realise that you would not have an easy task, but the experience gained would provide a valuable guide to future prospects. If the arrangement was successful, we would consider your suggestion for a continuing agency.

Meanwhile, if you are willing to receive a trial consignment, we will allow commission at 12½ per cent, with an additional 2½ per cent del credere commission, commission and expenses to be set against your monthly payments.

Please let us know as soon as possible if this arrangement is satisfactory to you.

Yours sincerely

18.5 Offer to act as buying agents for importer

Dear Sir/Madam

We understand from our neighbours, Firma Karl Brandt, that you have conducted your past buying of hardware in the German market through Firma Neymeyer and Schmidt of Bremen, and that in view of the collapse of their business you now require a reliable agent to take their place.

We are well known to manufacturers of hardware in this country and believe we have the experience and connections necessary to meet your needs. We therefore would like to offer our services as your buying agents in Germany.

Before transferring our business to Germany we had many years in the English trade and, knowing the particular needs of the English market, can promise you unrivalled service[4] in matters of prices, discounts and freights.

As Firma Brandt have promised to write recommending us to you, we would like to summarise the terms we should be willing to accept if we acted for you:

1 We are to have complete freedom in placing your orders.

2 All purchases to be made on your behalf and in your name.

3 All accounts to be passed to you for settlement direct with suppliers.

4 Commission, at 5 per cent payable quarterly, to be allowed us on cif values[5] of all shipments.

5 You will have full benefit of the very favourable terms we have arranged with the shipping companies, and of any special rates we may obtain for insurance.

We hope you will accept our offer and look forward to receiving your decision very soon.

Yours faithfully

18.6 Manufacturer's confirmation of agency terms

Drafting a formal agreement is a matter which calls for great care. It can be very time-consuming especially if any terms are disputed when drafting is completed. The terms and conditions to be included must, therefore, be clearly agreed by the parties before the agreement is drafted. A precaution similar to that illustrated in the following letter is one to be recommended. The legal touches can be added at the time of drafting.

Dear Sirs

We were pleased to learn from your letter of 14 November that you are willing to accept an agency for marketing our goods in Saudi Arabia. Set out below are the terms discussed and agreed with your Mr Williams when he called here earlier this month, but before drafting the formal agreement we should like you to confirm them.

1 The agency to operate as from 1 January 19– – for a period of 3 years, subject to renewal.

2 The agency to be a sole agency for marketing our goods in Saudi Arabia.

3 No sales of competing products to be made in Saudi Arabia either on your own account or on account of any other firm or company.

4 All customers' orders to be transmitted to us immediately for supply direct.

5 Credit terms not to be given or promised to any customer without our <u>express consent</u>[6].

6 All goods supplied to be invoiced by us direct to customers, with copies to you.

7 A commission of 5%, based on <u>fob values</u>[7] of all goods shipped to Saudi Arabia, whether on orders placed through you or not, payable at the end of each quarter.

8 A special <u>del credere</u> commission of 2½% to be added.

9 Customers to settle their accounts with us direct, and a statement to be sent to you at the end of each month of all payments received by us.

10 All questions of difference arising under our agreement to be referred to arbitration.

I shall be glad if you will kindly confirm these terms. A formal agreement will then be drafted and copies sent for your signature.

Yours faithfully

Offers of agencies

Sometimes a person seeking an agent will take the first step and make an offer to some person already known or recommended. Like the applicant seeking an agency, reference will be made to the market waiting to be developed, but concentration will rest on the special merits of the product in the efforts to persuade a correspondent to handle it. It is important to convince the prospective agent that the product is bound to sell well because of its exceptional quality, its particular uses, its novelty, its moderate price, etc., and because of the publicity with which it will be supported.

When offering an agency, it is not possible to include all the details, but enough information must be given to enable the correspondent to assess the worth of the offer. Failure to include essential basic information gives rise to unnecessary correspondence.

18.7 Offer of a provincial agency

(a) Offer

Dear Sirs

We have recently received a number of enquiries from dealers in the North of England for information about our range of haberdashery[8]. This leads us to believe there is a promising market waiting to be developed in that part of the country. Sales of our goods in other parts of the United Kingdom have greatly exceeded our expectations, but the absence of an agency in the North has meant poor sales in that region to date.

From our experience elsewhere, we believe that a really active agent would have little difficulty in rapidly expanding sales of our goods in the North of England. As we understand you are well experienced and have good connections in this area, we would like to know if you are interested in accepting a sole agency. We are prepared to offer you a 2-year agreement, with a commission of 7½% on net invoice values.

As we wish to reach a quick decision, perhaps you will be good enough to let us know if our offer interests you. If it does, then I would suggest an early meeting at which details of an arrangement agreeable to both of us could be discussed.

Yours faithfully

(b) Reply

Dear Ms Thompson

Thank you for your letter of 5 April offering us the sole agency for your haberdashery products in the North of England.

Your offer interests us and we are confident that we should be able to develop a good demand for your goods.

Your basic terms are agreeable to us, so perhaps you would let me know when it will be convenient for me to call on you. It would be helpful if you could offer a choice of dates.

I look forward to meeting you.

Yours sincerely

18.8 Offer of an overseas agency

(a) Offer

Dear Sir/Madam

We understand that you deal in stationery and related products, and would like to know if you are interested in marketing our products in your country on a commission basis.

We are a large and old-established firm specialising in the manufacture of stationery of all kinds, and our products sell well in many parts of the world. The enclosed catalogue will show you the wide range of our products, for which enquiries suggest a promising market for many of them waiting for development in your country.

If you are interested in our proposal please let us know which of our products are most likely to appeal to your customers, and also terms for commission and other charges on which you would be willing to represent us. We should be grateful if you could give us some idea of the market prospects for our products and suggest ways in which we could help you to develop the market.

We hope to hear favourably from you soon.

Yours faithfully

(b) Acceptance

Dear

I read with interest your letter of 15 May enclosing a copy of your catalogue and inviting me to undertake the marketing of your products in Zambia.

Provided we can agree on terms and conditions, I shall be pleased to accept your offer.

I already represent Batson & Sons of Manchester in office equipment. As my customers include many of the principal dealers in Zambia, I am sure they would provide a promising outlet for stationery and related products of the kind described in your catalogue.

I expect to be in London during July and would like to take the opportunity to discuss arrangements with you in detail. In the meantime, I suggest the following terms and conditions as the basis for a formal agreement:

1 All goods supplied to be invoiced direct to buyers, with copies sent to me.

2 Accounts to be made up and statements sent to me monthly, in duplicate, for distribution to buyers.

3 An agency commission of 5% to be payable on net amounts invoiced.

4 A del credere commission of 2½% in return for my guarantee of payments due on all accounts.

As initial expenses of introducing your products are likely to be heavy, I feel it reasonable to suggest an agreement extending over at least 3 years, though this is a matter we can discuss when we meet.

I shall be glad to learn that you are in general agreement with these suggestions.

Yours sincerely

18.9 Offer of a *del credere* agency

Where the agent acts on a *del credere* basis, the principal must be satisfied as to the agent's financial standing. Sometimes references from, for example, the agent's banker may be sufficient. In other cases, the agent may have to either provide a guarantor or deposit security, as in the following letter:

Dear

We thank you for your further letter of 20 June and are pleased to hear that you think a good market can be found for our goods in your country. We must confess, however, that credit on the scale you mention opens up a far from attractive prospect.

Nevertheless, we are willing to offer you an appointment on a <u>del credere</u> basis of 12% commission on the net value of all orders received through you, provided you are willing to lodge adequate security with our bankers here.

If security is deposited, we shall be willing to protect your interests by entering into a formal agreement giving you the sole agency for a period of 5 years.

We shall be glad to learn that you are willing to accept the agency on these terms.

Yours sincerely

Formal agency agreements

The terms of agency are sometimes set out in correspondence between the parties, but where dealings are on a large scale a formal agreement may be desirable. This should be drafted by a solicitor, or alternatively by one of the parties in consultation with the other. Matters to be covered in such an agreement may include all, or some, of the following:

- The nature and duration of the agency (i.e. sole agency, *del credere* agency for merely transmitting orders).
- The territory to be covered.
- The duties of agent and principal.
- The method of purchase and sale (e.g. whether the agent is to buy for their own account or 'on consignment [9]').
- Details of commission and expenses to be allowed.
- The law of the country by which the agreement is governed.
- The sending of reports, accounts and payments.
- The arrangements of *arbitration*[10] in the event of disputes.

The following illustrates the construction of a typical agency agreement, and is reproduced from *Specimen Agency Agreements for Exporters* by kind permission of the Institute of Export.

18.10 Specimen Agency Agreement suitable for exclusive and sole agents representing manufacturers overseas

SPECIMEN AGREEMENT 1

Suitable for exclusive and sole agents representing manufacturers overseas

AN AGREEMENT made this   day of
19   BETWEEN
whose Registered office is situate at

(hereinafter

called "the Principal") of the one part and

(hereinafter

called "the Agent") of the other part

WHEREBY IT IS AGREED as follows:

1.   The Principal appoints the Agent as and from the
to be its sole Agent in
(hereinafter called
"the area") for the sale of
manufactured by the Principal and such other goods and merchandise (all of which are hereinafter referred to as "the goods") as may hereafter be mutually agreed between them.

2.   The Agent will during the term of   years (and thereafter until determined by either party giving three months' previous notice in writing) diligently and faithfully serve the Principal as its Agent and will endeavour to extend the sale of the goods of the Principal within the area and will not do anything that may prevent such sale or interfere with the development of the Principal's trade in the area.

3.   The Principal will from time to time furnish the Agent with a statement of the minimum prices at which the goods are respectively to be sold and the Agent shall not sell below such minimum price but shall endeavour in each case to obtain the best price obtainable.

4.   The Agent shall not sell any of the goods to any person, company, or firm residing outside the area, nor shall he knowingly sell any of the goods to any person, company, or firm residing within the area with a view to their exportation to any other country or area without the consent in writing of the Principal.

5.   The Agent shall not during the continuance of the Agency hereby constituted sell goods of a similar class or such as would or might compete or interfere with the sale of the Principal's goods either on his

own account or on behalf of any other person, company, or firm whomsoever.

6.   Upon receipt by the Agent of any order for the goods the Agent will immediately transmit such order to the Principal who (if such order is accepted by the Principal) will execute the same by supplying the goods direct to the customer.

7.   Upon the execution of any such order the Principal shall forward to the Agent a duplicate copy of the invoice sent with the goods to the customer and in like manner shall from time to time inform the Agent when payment is made by the customer to the Principal.

8.   The Agent shall duly keep an account of all orders obtained by him and shall every three months send in a copy of such account to the Principal.

9.   The Principal shall allow the Agent the following commissions (based on fob United Kingdom values) in respect of all orders obtained direct by the Agent in the area which have been accepted and executed by the Principal. The said commission shall be payable every three months on the amounts actually received by the Principal from the customers.

10.   The Agent shall be entitled to commission on the terms and conditions mentioned in the last preceding clause on all export orders for the goods received by the Principal through Export Merchants Indent Houses, Branch Buying offices of customers, and Head Offices of customers situate in the United Kingdom of Great Britain, Northern Ireland and Eire for export into the area. Export orders in this clause mentioned shall not include orders for the goods received by the Principals from and sold delivered to customers' principal place of business outside the area although such goods may subsequently be exported by such customers into the area, excepting where there is conclusive evidence that such orders which may actually be transmitted via the Head Office in England are resultant from work done by the Agent with the customers.

11.   Should any dispute arise as to the amount of commission payable by the Principal to the Agent the same shall be settled by the Auditors for the time being of the Principal whose certificate shall be final and binding on both the Principal and the Agent.

12.   The Agent shall not in any way pledge the credit of the Principal.

13.   The Agent shall not give any warranty in respect of the goods without the authority in writing of the Principal.

14.   The Agent shall not without the authority of the Principal collect any moneys from customers.

15.   The Agent shall not give credit to or deal with any person, company or firm which the Principal shall from time to time direct him not to give credit to or deal with.

16.   The Principal shall have the right to refuse to execute or accept any order obtained by the Agent or any part thereof and the Agent shall not be entitled to any commission in respect of any such refused order or part thereof so refused.

17.   All questions of difference whatsoever which may at any time hereafter arise between the parties hereto or their respective

representatives touching these presents or the subject matter thereof or arising out of or in relation thereto respectively and whether as to construction or otherwise shall be referred to arbitration in England in accordance with the provision of the Arbitration Act 1950 or any re-enactment or statutory modification thereof for the time being in force.
18. This Agreement shall in all respects be interpreted in accordance with the Laws of England.
AS WITNESS the hands of the parties hereto the day and year first hereinbefore written..

(Signatures)

Appointing an agent – typical procedure

In this section we will look at a series of correspondence which evolves through a publishing company's desire to find a suitable agent to market its publications in Lebanon.

The publishing company decides to approach its bank in order to obtain the relevant information. The various letters shown can be adapted in order to apply to enquiries through other sources.

18.11 Publisher's letter to bank (addressed to the Manager)

Dear Sir

At a meeting of our Directors yesterday it was decided to try to develop our trade with the Lebanon. We propose to appoint an agent with an efficient sales organisation in that country to help us to market our publications.

We wonder if your correspondents in Beirut would be able to put us in touch with a suitable and reliable firm, and would be grateful for any help you can provide.

We hope to hear from you soon.

Yours faithfully

18.12 Bank's reply to publishers

Dear Miss Southern

Thank you for your letter of 24 August regarding the possibility of appointing a local agent in the Lebanon.

Our correspondents in Beirut are the Banque Nationale, whose postal address is:

Banque Nationale
PO Box 25643
Beirut

I have today written to their Manager explaining that you intend to appoint an agent in the Lebanon and asking him to provide you with any assistance possible.

No doubt you will now write to them direct, and I have told them to expect to hear from you.

Yours sincerely

18.13 Publisher's thanks to the bank

Dear Mr Johnson

Thank you for your letter of 26 August and for introducing our name to your correspondents in Beirut.

I have today written to the address provided, and would like to thank you very much for your help.

Yours sincerely

18.14 Publisher's letter to Beirut bank (addressed to the Manager)

Dear Sir

The Manager of Midminster Bank Ltd, London, has kindly given us your name. We are interested in appointing an agent to represent our interests in the Lebanon, and wonder if you can recommend a reliable person or firm.

We specialise in publishing educational books, including students'
books. If you could put us in touch with a distributor who has good
connections with booksellers, libraries and educational institutions, we
would be very grateful.

Please accept our thanks in advance for any help you can give us.

Yours faithfully

18.15 Reply from Beirut bank

Dear Miss Southern

The Manager of Midminster Bank, London, has already written
explaining your proposal to appoint a representative to further your
trading interests in the Lebanon. We were expecting to hear from you,
and your letter of 28 August reached us today.

We are pleased to introduce you to Messrs Habib Suleiman Ghanem of
Beirut. Messrs Ghanem have been our customers for many years. They
are a well-known, old-established and highly reputable firm with some
20 years' experience of the book trade in this part of the world. We can
recommend them to you with the certain knowledge that they would
serve you well.

We have taken the opportunity to contact Messrs Ghanem, who have
expressed interest in your proposal. I understand they will be writing
to you soon.

May I wish you success in your venture, and if we can be of further
assistance please do not hesitate to contact us.

Yours sincerely

18.16 Publisher's acknowledgement to Beirut bank

Dear Mr Jenkins

Thank you for your letter of 5 September giving us the name of Messrs
Habib Suleiman Ghanem. I wish to express my company's sincere
thanks for your recommendation and the trouble you have so kindly
taken to help us.

Messrs Ghanem appear to be well experienced to provide the kind of

service we need in the Lebanon, and we shall now look forward to
hearing from them.

Yours sincerely

18.17 Letter from prospective agents

Dear Miss Southern

Our bankers, the Banque Nationale, inform us that you require an
agent to assist in marketing your publications in the Lebanon. Subject
to satisfactory arrangements as to terms and conditions, we should be
pleased to represent you.

As publishers and distributors in Syria and the Lebanon for over 20
years, we have a thorough knowledge of the market. We are proud to
boast an extensive sales organisation and well-established connections
with booksellers, libraries and educational institutions in these two
countries.

We must mention that we are already acting as sole representatives[11] of
several other publishers, including two American companies. However,
as the preference in the educational field here is for books by British
publishers, so the prospects for your own publications are excellent,
especially those intended for the student market. Adequate publicity
would, of course, be necessary.

Before making any commitment, we shall require details of your
proposals for commission and terms of payment, and also some idea of
the amount you are prepared to invest in initial publicity[12].

We look forward to receiving this information from you very soon.

Yours sincerely

18.18 Publisher's reply to prospective agents

Dear Mr Ghanem

We were pleased to learn from your letter of 8 September that you will
consider an appointment as our agent.

Although we transact a moderate amount of business in the Middle
East, we have so far not had much success in the Lebanon and are now
hoping to develop our interests there.

We are enclosing a copy of our complete catalogue of publications. The published prices quoted are subject to the usual trade discounts.

We would reply to your various points as follows:

1 COMMISSION
   The commission at present allowed to our other agents is 10% on the invoice value of all orders, payable quarterly, and we offer you the same terms. We presume your customers would be able to settle their accounts direct with us on the basis of <u>cash against documents</u>[13], except of course for supplies from your own stocks.

2 PUBLICITY
   We feel that perhaps an initial expenditure of approximately £4,000 to cover the first 3 months' publicity would be reasonable. However, as we are not familiar with conditions in your country, this is a matter on which we would welcome your views.

In anticipation of your accepting our proposals, we enclose 2 copies of our standard agency contract, which includes terms relating to the stocks which you may decide to carry on our account. If you agree with our conditions, please add your signature to mine on both copies and return one copy to me.

We look forward to the prospect of welcoming you as our agents.

Yours sincerely

18.19 Letter accepting agency

Thank you for your letter of 19 September enclosing copies of your standard form of agency agreement, and for the copy of your catalogue. The catalogue covers an extensive range of interesting titles, which appear to be very reasonably priced.

With the proposed initial expenditure of £2,500 on advertising, backed by active support from our own sales staff, we feel that the prospects for many of your titles are very good, particularly where they are suitable for use in schools and colleges. We take it that you are prepared to leave the choice of <u>advertising media</u>[14] to us.

We are grateful for this opportunity to take up your agency here and, as your proposed terms are satisfactory, have pleasure in returning one copy of the contract, signed as requested.

Yours sincerely

18.20 Publisher acknowledges acceptance

Dear Mr Ghanem

Thank you for returning a signed copy of the agency contract with your letter of 26 September.

It is important that you carry stocks of those titles for which there is likely to be a steady demand. Perhaps when you have had an opportunity to assess the market, you will let us know the titles and quantities you feel will be needed to enable you to meet small orders quickly.

We will follow the development of our trade with keen interest and look forward to a happy and lasting working relationship with you.

Yours sincerely

Correspondence with agents

18.21 Agent requests increased commission

To ask for more money is never easy and to get it is often less so, especially when the amount payable has been fixed and included in an agreement freely entered into. Any request for increased commission must, therefore, be well founded and tactfully presented.

In the letter which follows the agent presents the case convincingly and with restraint. This ensures that it will have a fair hearing. No one receiving such a letter would wish to lose the goodwill clearly shown.

(a) Agent's request

Dear Sir/Madam

We would like to request your consideration of some revision in our present rate of commission. The request may strike you as unusual since the increase in sales last year resulted in a corresponding increase in our total commission.

Marketing your goods has proved to be more difficult than could have been expected when we undertook to represent you. Since then,

German and American competitors have entered the market and firmly established themselves. Consequently, we have been able to maintain our position in the market only by enlarging our force of sales staff and increasing our expenditure on advertising.

We are quite willing to incur[15] the additional expense and even to increase it still further because we firmly believe that the required effort will result in increased business. However, we do not feel we should be expected to bear the whole of the additional cost without some form of compensation. After carefully calculating the increase in our selling costs, we suggest an increase in the rate of commission by, say, 2%.

You have always been considerate in your dealings with us and we know we can rely on you to consider our present request with understanding.

Yours faithfully

(b) Principal's reply

Dear

Thank you for your letter of 28 August.

We note the unexpected problems presented by your competitors and appreciate the extra efforts you have made with such satisfactory results.

We feel sure that, in the long run[16], the high quality of our goods and the very competitive prices at which they are offered will ensure steadily increasing sales despite the competition from other manufacturers. At the same time we realise that, in the short term, this competition must be met by more active advertising and agree that it would not be reasonable to expect you to bear the full cost.

To increase commission would be difficult as our prices leave us with only a very small profit. Instead, we propose to allow you an advertising credit of £400 in the current year towards your additional costs, this amount to be reviewed in 6 months' time and adjusted according to circumstances.

We hope you will be happy with this arrangement and look forward to your confirmation.

Yours sincerely

18.22 Principal proposes reduced rate of commission

Any proposal by a principal to reduce an agent's commission must be well-founded and carefully presented, otherwise it would create ill-feeling and strain business relations. If the rate of commission is included in a legally-binding agreement, it cannot be varied without the agent's consent, and even that consent is not binding unless the principal gives the agent some concession in return.

Dear

It is with regret that I must ask you to accept a temporary reduction in the agreed rate of commission. I make this request because of an increase in manufacturing costs due to additional duties on our imported raw materials, and to our inability either to absorb these higher costs[17] or, in the present state of the market, to pass them on to consumers. In the event, our profits have been reduced to a level which no longer justifies continued production.

This situation is disturbing, but we feel sure it will be purely temporary. In the circumstances, we hope you will accept a small reduction of, say, 1½% in the agreed rate of commission. You have our promise that as soon as trade improves sufficiently, we shall return to the rate originally agreed.

Yours sincerely

18.23 Agent complains of slow delivery

When a buyer is thinking of placing an order, the three things which are of interest are quality, price and delivery. Often more importance is attached to the certainty of prompt delivery than to low price, though both are important. Therefore, in an increasingly competitive world, a manufacturer who regularly falls down on delivery dates is placed at a grave disadvantage and runs the risk of being forced out of business.

Dear

We enclose our statement of sales made on your account during March and of commission and expenses payable. If you will confirm our figures, we will credit you with the amount due.

These sales are most disappointing, but this is due entirely to late arrival of goods we ordered from you last January. Not having received the goods by mid-February, we cabled you on the 18th, but found on enquiry that the goods were not shipped until 3 March and consequently did not reach us until 20 March.

This delay in delivery is most unfortunate as the local agents of several of our competitors have been particularly active during the past few weeks and have taken a good deal of the trade that would normally have come our way had the goods been here. What is more disturbing is that these rival firms have now gained a good hold on the market which, until now, has been largely our own.

We have reminded you on a previous occasion of the competition from Japanese manufacturers, whose low prices and quick deliveries are having a striking effect on local buyers. If you wish to keep your hold on this market, therefore, prompt delivery of orders we place with you is essential.

Yours sincerely

18.24 Agent recommends lower price policy

An important reason for appointing a foreign agent is the gain in knowledge of local conditions and of the market for operation. Your agent will know what goods are best suited to the area and what prices the market will bear. Only an unwise exporter would ignore the advice of an agent on these and other matters of which they have special knowledge.

Dear

We are enclosing our customer's order number 252 for card-index and filing equipment.

To secure this order has not been easy because your quoted prices were higher than those which our customer·had been prepared for. The quotation was eventually accepted on the grounds of your reputation for quality, but I think we should warn you of the growing competition in the office-equipment market here.

Agents of German and Japanese manufacturers are now active in the market, and as their products are of good quality and in some cases cheaper than yours, we shall find it very difficult to maintain our past volume of sales unless you can reduce your prices. For your guidance we are sending you copies of the price lists of competing firms.

Concerning the present shipment, please send a draft bill of exchange for acceptance at 2 months for the net value of your invoice after allowing for commission and expenses.

Yours

18.25 Agent recommends credit dealings

(a) Agent's recommendation

Dear

After studying the catalogue and price list received with your letter of 31 March, we have no doubt we could obtain good orders for many of the items. However, we feel you are placing both yourselves and us at a disadvantage by adopting a cash settlement basis.

Nearly all business here is done on credit, the period varying from 3 to 6 months. Your prices, on the other hand, are reasonable, and your products sound in both design and quality. We therefore suggest that you could afford to raise your prices sufficiently to cover the cost and fall into line with your competitors in the matter of credit.

In our experience, to do so would be sound policy and greatly strengthen your hold on the market. With the best will in the world to serve you, we are afraid it would be neither worth your while, nor ours, to continue business on a cash basis.

If it would help you at all we should be quite willing to assume full responsibility for unsettled accounts and to act as <u>del credere</u> agents for an additional commission of 2½%.

We hope to hear from you soon.

Yours

(b) Manufacturer's reply

Dear

Thank you for your letter of 10 April. We are glad that you think a satisfactory market could be found for our goods, but are not altogether happy at the prospect of transacting all our business on a credit basis.

To some extent your offer to act in a <u>del credere</u> capacity meets our objections, and for a trial period we are prepared to accept on the terms stated, namely, an extra commission of 2½%. We make the condition, however, that you are willing either to provide a guarantor acceptable to us, or to lodge adequate security with our bankers.

Please let us know your decision on this matter.

Yours sincerely

18.26 Principal complains to agent

It is always unpleasant to have to make complaints, but if a criticism is necessary it must be written with care and restraint. Never assume that the agent, or whoever the other party may be, is at fault. A letter written with courtesy and understanding will usually bring a considerate reply and obtain the co-operation needed to put matters right.

(a) Poor sales

Dear Sirs

We are very concerned that your sales in recent months have fallen considerably. At first, we thought this might be due to the disturbed political situation in your country, but on looking into the matter more closely we find that the general trend of trade during this period has been upwards.

Of course, it is possible that you are facing difficulties of which we are not aware. If so, we should like to know of them since it is always possible for us to take measures to help. We therefore look forward to receiving from you a detailed report on the situation, and also any suggestions of ways in which you feel we may be of some help in restoring our sales to at least their former level.

Yours faithfully

(b) High expenses

Dear Sirs

We have received your October statement of sales and write to express our concern at the high figure included for expenses. This figure seems to be much too high for the volume of business done.

It is of course possible that there are special reasons for these high charges. If so, we feel it is reasonable to ask you to explain them. We are particularly concerned because, under pressure of competition, the prices at which we offered the goods had been cut to a level which left us with only a very small profit.

We shall be glad to receive your explanation and your assurance that expenses on future sales can be reduced. If for any reason this is not possible, then we should be left with no choice but to discontinue our business with you, for which we sincerely hope there will be no need.

Yours faithfully

Useful expressions

Agency applications

Openings

1 We should be glad if you would consider our application to act as agents for the sale of your . . . .
2 We thank you for your letter of . . . enquiring whether we are represented in . . . .
3 We have received your letter of . . . and should be glad to offer you a sole agency for the sale of our products in . . . .

Closes

1 We hope to hear favourably from you and feel sure we should have no difficulty in arranging terms.
2 If you give us this agency we should spare no effort to further your interests.
3 If you are interested, we can provide first-class references.

Agency appointments

Openings

1 Thank you for your letter of . . . offering us the sole agency in . . . for your products.
2 We thank you for your letter of . . . and are favourably impressed by your proposal for a sole agency.
3 We thank you for offering us the agency in . . . and appreciate the confidence you have placed in us.

Closes

1 We hope to receive a favourable response, and can assure you of our very best service.
2 We look forward to a happy and successful working relationship with you.

Glossary

1 **electronic field** the area of electronics
2 **microprocessing equipment** electronic equipment such as computers which have been greatly reduced in size
3 ***del credere* agent** an agent who guarantees payment
4 **unrivalled service** service which cannot be equalled
5 **cif values** values covering cost, insurance and freight
6 **express consent** permission clearly stated

7 **fob values** values cover cost of placing goods on board ship
8 **haberdashery** ribbons, lace and other small articles of dress
9 **on consignment** for sale on exporter's behalf
10 **arbitration** settlement of disputes by an independent person or body
11 **sole representatives** the only representatives
12 **initial publicity** advertising in the early stages
13 **cash against documents** payment made upon delivery of shipping documents
14 **advertising media** forms of publicity
15 **incur** be responsible for
16 **in the long run** eventually
17 **absorb these higher costs** accept without raising prices

Assignments on material included in this chapter can be found on p 365.

Chapter 19

International trade

Some exporters will deal direct with overseas buyers, but it is more usual for transactions to take place in any of the following ways:

1 The overseas buyer employs a commission agent in the exporter's country.
2 The exporter employs an agent living in the buyer's country.
3 The exporter sends the goods to a *factor*[1] in the importing country for sale 'on consignment'.

The exporter is known as the consignor, and the importer is known as the consignee.

Correspondence concerned with buying and selling overseas is generally carried out through fax or telex messages these days, for obvious reasons of speed. In fact new technology has now given us EDI (Electronic Data Interchange) which substantially reduces the amount of paperwork which needs to be sent between the parties concerned. If both exporter and importer have compatible systems, EDI results in huge savings in time, documentation and paperwork.

Import/export flow chart

The flow chart in Fig. 19.1 shows the traditional documentation and procedures involved in purchasing goods from abroad.

Commission agents

A commission agent may be either an individual or a firm employed to buy or to sell for a principal. In foreign trade, agents buy and sell in their own names, but for accounts of the principals. Their tasks include obtaining quotations, placing orders, supervising their fulfilment and arranging for the despatch of the goods. Agents also collect payments for the principal and sometimes hold themselves personally liable for payment should teh buyer fail to pay.

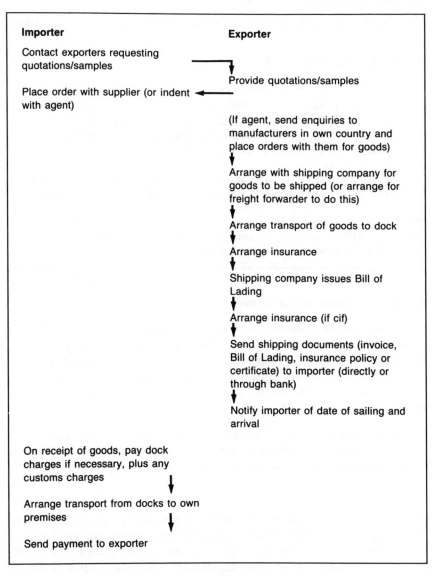

Fig. 19.1 Flow chart showing a typical transaction relating to purchase of goods from abroad.

19.1 Bahraini buyer deals with commission agent in London

(a) Agent acknowledges order

Your order number C75 of 10 February for 1500 fibreglass wash basins in assorted colours will be placed without delay. We have already written to a manufacturer in North London and will do everything we can to ensure early shipment.

We note your request for the basins to be arranged in tens and packed in cartons rather than wooden containers, in order to save freight.

We shall arrange insurance on the usual terms and the certificate of insurance will be sent to you through our bankers, along with our draft bill and other shipping documents.

(b) Agent requests quotation from manufacturers

We have received an order for 1500 (fifteen hundred) 40 cm circular fibreglass wash basins in assorted colours for shipment to Bahrain. Please quote your lowest price fob London, and state the earliest possible date by which you can have the consignment ready for collection at your factory.

Your price should include arrangement of the basins in tens and packing in cartons of a size convenient for manual handling.

(c) Agent sends advice of shipment

Assuming the manufacturer's quotation is accepted and that the date of delivery is known, the agent will telephone a freight forwarder to find out details of ships sailing to Bahrain and the closing date for accepting cargo. The freight forwarder will need to know the measurements concerned as well as weight and price of the consignment. Having received the required information, the agent will write to the client giving particulars of shipment.

YOUR ORDER NUMBER C75

The 1500 fibreglass wash basins which you ordered on 10 February will be shipped to you by the SS Tigris sailing from London on 25 March and due to arrive in Bahrain on 15 April.

The bill of lading, commercial invoice, consular invoice[2] and certificate of insurance, together with our draft[3] drawn at sixty (60) days' sight,[4] have been passed to the Barminster Bank Ltd, London, and should reach you within a few days. The enclosed copy of the invoice will give you advance information of the consignment.

We hope the goods will prove to be satisfactory.

(d) Agent passes documents to banker

Payment for the transaction is to be made by bill of exchange drawn at 60 days and sent through the agent's bank to the foreign buyer. The banker's correspondent in Bahrain will not hand over the shipping documents until the buyer accepts the bill as a sign of willingness to meet it when it is presented for payment in 60 days' time.

On receipt of the letter in 19.1, the client's bank in Bahrain would present the documents to the client and obtain a signature on the back of the bill of exchange saying that the payment terms are accepted. The documents will then be released and the goods may be collected.

Enclosed is a bill of lading, consular invoice, certificate of insurance and our invoice relating to a consignment of fibreglass wash basins for shipment by SS Tigris to Mr Faisal Ashkar of Bahrain.

Please forward these documents to your correspondent in Bahrain with instructions to hand them to the consignee against acceptance of our 60 days' draft, also enclosed.

Goods on consignment

Goods on consignment are goods which an exporter sends to an importer, but an invoice will not immediately be issued. The importer will hold the goods in stock until they are sold, at which point the exporter will draw up an invoice for whatever stock has been sold.

19.2 Company in Nairobi requests goods on consignment

(a) Buyer's request

We are the largest department store in Nairobi and have recently received a number of enquiries for your stainless steel cutlery. There are very good prospects for the sale of this cutlery, but as it is presently unknown here, we do not feel able to make purchases on our own account.

We would like to suggest that you send us a trial delivery for sale on consignment terms. When the market is established we would hope to place firm orders.

If you agree, we would render monthly accounts of sales and send you the payments due after deducting expenses, and commission at a rate to be agreed. Our bankers are the Nairobi branch of Midminster Bank Ltd, with whom you may check our standing[5].

We believe our proposal offers good prospects and hope you will be willing to agree to a trial.

(b) Seller's acceptance

Thank you for your letter proposing to receive a trial delivery of our cutlery on consignment, which we have carefully considered.

We are sending you a representative selection[6] of our most popular lines and hope you will find a ready sale for them. Your suggestion to submit accounts and to make payments monthly is quite satisfactory, and we will allow you commission at 10% calculated on gross profits.

The consignment is being shipped by SS Eastern Prince, leaving Southampton for Mombasa on 25 January. We will send the bill of lading and other shipping documents as soon as we receive them. Meanwhile a pro forma invoice is enclosed, showing prices at which the goods should be offered for sale.

We are confident that this cutlery will prove popular in your country, and look forward to trading with you.

(c) Agent submits account sales

When the agent has sold the goods, an account sales (Fig. 19.2) will be sent to the exporter showing the goods sold and the prices realised, together with the net amount due to the exporter after deducting commission and any charges or expenses incurred. The net amount may be placed to the credit of the exporter in the importing country, or it may be forwarded by means of a banker's draft (unless other means of payment, discussed in Chapter 11 are adopted).

We enclose our account sales for the month ending 31 March showing a balance of £379.20 due to you after deducting commission and charges. If you will draw on us for this amount at two months, we will add our acceptance and return the draft immediately.

ACCOUNT SALES
by U Patel & Co
15–17 Rhodes Avenue, Nairobi

25 October 19..

In the matter of stainless steel cutlery ex SS <u>Eastern Prince</u> sold

for account of E Hughes & Co Ltd, Victoria Works, Kingsway,

Sheffield.

Quantity	Description	@ per 100 £	£
100	Knives	170.00	170.00
100	Forks	170.00	170.00
50	Table Spoons	150.00	75.00
200	Tea Spoons	105.00	210.00
			625.00

Charges:

Ocean Freight	92.55	
Dock Dues and Cartage	37.40	
Marine Insurance	20.50	
Customs Dues	32.85	
Commission	62.50	245.80

Net proceeds, as per
banker's draft enclosed   379.20

Nairobi, 25 October 19..

E & OE   (signed) U Patel & Co

Fig. 19.2 Account sales. The account sales is a statement of goods sold by an agent for the consignor. It shows the amount due to the consignor after deduction of charges and agency commission.

(d) Principal sends payment

Thank you for sending your account sales for March. Our draft for the balance shown of £379.20 is enclosed.

Indents

When foreign buyers place orders through commission agents or *commission houses*[7] in the supplier's country, their orders are known as indents (see Fig. 19.3) and they give details of the goods required, their prices, packing and shipping instructions and method of payment. An indent, therefore, is not an order for goods, but an order to an agent to buy goods on behalf of the foreign buyer.

If the indent names the manufacturer who is to supply the goods, it is known as a 'closed' or 'specific' indent. If selection is left to the agent, the indent is said to be 'open' and the agent will then obtain quotations from a number of manufacturers before placing an order.

19.3 Foreign buyer deals with commission house

(a) Buyer (in Egypt) sends indent to commission house (in England)

We have received the manufacturer's price list and samples you sent us last month and now enclose our indent number 762 for goods to be shipped by the SS Merchant Prince due to leave Liverpool for Alexandria on 25 July. The indent contains full instructions as to packing, insurance and shipping documents.

It is important for the goods to be shipped either by the vessel named, or by an earlier vessel, and if there are any items which cannot be supplied in time for this shipment, they should be cancelled. When we receive the goods we shall pay you the agreed agency commission of 5%. The account for the goods will be settled direct with the manufacturers.

This is a trial order and if it is met satisfactorily we shall probably place further orders.

INDENT
No 64

N WHARFE & CO LTD
19–21 Victoria Street
CAIRO, EGYPT

10 February 19..

H Hopkinson & Co
Commission Agents and Shippers
41 King Street
MANCHESTER
M60 2HB

Dear Sirs

Please purchase and ship on our account for delivery not later than
31 March the following goods, or as many of them as possible. Arrange
insurance for amount of your invoice, plus 10% to cover estimated profit
and your charges.

Yours faithfully
for N WHARFE & CO LTD

J G Gartside
Director

Identification Marks etc	Quantity	Description of Goods	Remarks
NW 64 Nos 1–12	48	HMV Stereo Model 1636 Walnut finish	Pack 4 per case
NW 64 Nos 13–37	25 bales	Grey Shirting Medium weight About 1,000 metres per bale	Pack in oil bags
NW 64 Nos 38–39	500 pairs	Assorted House Slippers Men's (200) Women's (200) Children's (100)	Pack in plain wooden cases

Ship: By Manchester Liners Ltd
Delivery: cif Alexandria
Payment: Draw at 60 days from sight of documents
through Royal Bank, London

Fig. 19.3 Indent. An indent is an order sent to a commission agent to arrange
for the purchase of goods for the principal.

(b) Agent places order with a firm in Manchester

We have just received an order from Jean Riachi & Co of Mansura, Egypt. Particulars are shown in the enclosed official order form, together with details of packing and forwarding, case marks, etc.

The goods are to be ready for collection at your warehouse in time to be shipped to Alexandria by SS Merchant Prince due to sail from Liverpool on 25 July or by an earlier vessel if possible. Prompt delivery is essential, and if there are any items which cannot be included in the consignment they should be cancelled.

Invoices, priced ex warehouse, are to be in triplicate and sent to us for forwarding to our customers with the shipping documents. The account will be settled by our customers direct with you. As del credere agents, we undertake to be responsible should the buyer fail to pay.

This is a trial order and if it is completed satisfactorily it is likely to lead to further business. Your special care would therefore be appreciated.

Please confirm by return that you can accept this order, and arrange to inform us when the goods are ready for collection.

Bills of lading

The bill of lading, prepared by the shipping company, sets out the terms of the contract of carriage with the shipping company. It serves as the consignor's receipt for the goods taken on board ship. The bill of lading is also a document of title so that when it is transferred to the consignee it also gives the right to claim the goods to which it refers.

A bill of lading is usually prepared in a set of 3 originals and 3 copies. It will state the name of the vessel, the time of sailing, marks and identification on the cargo, the delivery address, and also the statement 'clean shipped on board', meaning the goods are not damaged and they are actually on board ship.

On issue of the bill of lading, the consignor must check that all details are correct and that it has been signed by the ship's captain. The bill of lading then goes, with other documents, to the bank to be forwarded to the consignee.

Import documentation and procedure

Whether goods are imported on consignment or against orders, import procedure is much the same. Before the ship arrives, the importer (who will be either a merchant dealing on their own account or an agent) will usually have received the shipping documents. The original documents would go through the bank, but it is normal practice for photocopies to be despatched by a courier service so that the importer can, in advance, go through the import procedures before the goods actually arrive. This makes things easier for the importer and saves a lot of time.

Shipping documents include:

1 An advice of shipment specifying the goods and stating the name of the carrying ship, its date of sailing and probable date of arrival.
2 A bill of lading.
3 An invoice (pro forma if the goods are imported on consignment).

When the ship arrives the importer must obtain release for the bill of lading and proceed as follows:

1 The importer must *endorse*[8] the bill of lading and present it to the shipping company, or their representative, at the port.
2 The freight must be paid (if not already prepaid by the exporter) and any other charges due to the shipping company.
3 The importer must prepare and submit the necessary import entries on official forms provided by the appropriate Customs authorities.

Import duties may either be specific (i.e. charged on quantity, as on wines and tobacco) or *ad valorem* (i.e. charged on invoice value, as on television sets and other manufactured goods). If the goods, or any of them, are required for immediate use, duty must be paid before they may be taken away.

Some goods imported into the United Kingdom are liable to VAT (value added tax) and this should generally be paid when the goods are cleared through customs.

19.4 An import transaction

(a) Importer (London) places order (Japan)

Our order for 20 Super Hitachi Hi-Fi Systems (SDT 400) is enclosed at the cif price of £550 each, as quoted in your letter of 10 June.

Through the Midminster Bank Ltd, 65 Aldwych, London WC2, we have arranged with the Bank of Japan, Tokyo, to open a credit in your favour for £6,000 (six thousand pounds) to be available until 30 September next.

Please notify us when the consignment is shipped.

(b) Importer opens credit

The importer writes to the Midminster Bank in London opening credit.

I have completed and enclose your form for an irrevocable credit of £6,000 to be opened with the Bank of Japan, Tokyo, in favour of Kikuki, Shiki & Co, Tokyo, for a consignment of music systems, the credit to be valid until 30 September next.

When the consignment is shipped the company will draw on the Bank of Japan at 30 days after sight, the draft to be accompanied by bills of lading (3/3), invoice and certificate or policy of insurance.

Please confirm that the credit will be arranged.

(c) Supplier in Japan presents documents to Bank of Japan, Tokyo

---

We enclose a 30 days' sight draft together with bill of lading (3/3), invoice, letter of credit and certificate of insurance relating to a consignment of music centres for shipment by SS Yamagata to Videohire Ltd, London.

Please send draft and documents to the Midminster Bank Ltd, 65 Aldwych, London WC2 4LS, with instructions to hand over the documents to Videohire Ltd only against their acceptance of the draft.

(d) Supplier sends advice of shipment

YOUR ORDER NO 825

We thank you for your order for 20 Super Hitachi Music Centres. I am glad to say we can supply these immediately from stock. We have arranged to ship them to your London warehouse at St Katharine Docks, London, by SS Yamagata, sailing from Tokyo on 3 August and due to arrive in London on or about the 25th.

The shipping documents will be delivered to you through the Aldwych Branch of the Midminster Bank Ltd against your acceptance of the 30 days' sight draft, as agreed in our earlier correspondence.

We hope you will find everything to your satisfaction.

(e) Importer acknowledges consignment

ORDER NO 825

Your consignment of Music Centres reached London on 27 August.

We take this opportunity to thank you for the care and promptness with which you have fulfilled our first order. We expect to place further orders in the near future.

Bonded warehouses

If imported goods on which duty is payable are not wanted immediately, they may be placed in a bonded warehouse, that is a warehouse whose owners have entered into a bond with the customs authorities as a guarantee that the goods will not be removed until duty on them has been paid.

This system enables payment of duty to be *deferred*[9] until the goods, which may be withdrawn by *instalments*[10], are needed. The main commodities dealt with in this way are tea, tobacco, beer, wines and spirits.

When goods are placed in a warehouse, bonded or free, the owner of the goods is given either a warehouse warrant or a warehousekeeper's receipt. A delivery order, signed by the owner of the goods, must be completed when goods are withdrawn.

19.5 Clearance of goods from warehouse

This letter is from a tea blender to their broker, who has bought a quantity of tea and holds the delivery order issued by the importer.

We refer to the 12 chests of Assam, ex City of Bombay, which you bought for us at the auctions yesterday and for which we understand you hold the delivery order.

Please clear all 12 chests at once and arrange with Williams Transport Ltd to deliver them to our Leman Street warehouse.

Useful expressions

Enquiries and orders

Openings

1 Thank you for your quotation of . . . and for the samples you sent me.
2 One of our best customers has asked us to arrange to purchase . . . .
3 Your letter of . . . enclosing indent for . . . arrived yesterday.

Closes

1 Please deal with this order as one of special urgency.
2 We look forward to receiving further indents from you.
3 We thank you for giving us this trial order and promise that we will give it our careful attention.

Consignments

Openings

1 We regret that we cannot handle your goods on our own account, but would be willing to take them on a consignment basis.
2 We have today sent a consignment of . . . by SS *Empress Victoria*, and enclose the shipping documents.
3 The consignment you sent us has been sold at very good prices.

Closes

1 You will of course credit our account with the amount due.
2 We look forward to hearing that you have been able to obtain satisfactory prices.
3 We will send you our account sales, with banker's draft, in a few days.
4 We enclose our account sales and shall be glad if you will draw on us at 2 months for the amount due.

Glossary

1 **factor** any agent who deals in their own name and has possession of the goods they are required to sell
2 **consular invoice** an invoice signed by the consul of the country to which goods are exported
3 **draft** a bill of exchange requiring acceptance
4 **sixty (60) days' sight** for payment within 60 days of acceptance
5 **check our standing** enquire as to our position in business
6 **representative selection** a selection covering all types of goods

7 **commission houses** a commission agency organised as a firm or company
8 **endorse** sign on the back
9 **deferred** delayed
10 **instalments** in separate lots

Assignments on material included in this chapter can be found on p 365.

Chapter 20

Banking (home business)

Commercial banks offer four main services:

1 They accept customers' deposits.
2 They pay cheques drawn on them by their customers.
3 They grant advances to customers.
4 They provide a payments mechanism for the transfer of funds between its own customers and those of other banks.

Kinds of bank account

Current accounts are the most usual type of bank account. Deposits in the account can be withdrawn on demand. This is the main method by which customers may utilise the full money transfer facilities of the bank, involving the use of cheques, credit transfers, *standing orders*[1] and *direct debits*[2]. Traditionally the current account holder did not receive interest on funds, but some banks now pay a small rate of credit interest. Besides their main services the bank offers customers a wide range of miscellaneous services including safe custody and night safe facilities, the provision of references, executor and trustee, and pension and insurance services, plus advice on how to start up a business.

Deposit accounts have been used in recent years by banks to attract customers. A range of deposit accounts are offered paying various rates of interest as well as the ordinary deposit account. On ordinary deposit accounts withdrawals are subject to 7 days' notice. Generally the amount of interest depends on the amount of money deposited, and, to some extent, on the length of notice of withdrawal required.

Opening accounts

Anyone wishing to open an account should legally provide satisfactory references or be introduced by an established customer of the bank. In practice, however, some banks do not necessarily take personal references in respect of customers but may rely on proof of identity and some form of credit referencing.

Statements

Periodic statements in loose-leaf form are provided to customers. These statements record all transactions affecting the customer's current account and the balance after each day's transactions.

Cheques

A cheque is a widely accepted form of payment today. Their acceptability has increased since the introduction of the cheque guarantee card in 1965, which guaranteed the payment of a cheque up to a stated amount (often £50).

A banker is entitled to refuse payment of a cheque in any of the following circumstances:

1 When the drawer has countermanded payment.
2 When the balance on the drawer's account is insufficient to meet the cheque.
3 When the cheque is post-dated, i.e. dated ahead of time.
4 When the cheque has become 'stale', i.e. over 6 months' old.
5 When the cheque contains some irregularity, e.g. a forgery or an unsigned alteration.
6 When the banker is aware that the drawer has died or committed an act of bankruptcy.

In any of these circumstances the cheque would be returned to the payee or other holder marked with the reason for its non-payment.

Bank charges

As long as personal customers keep their accounts in credit they are not liable to any bank charges.

Business customers will normally negotiate their charges with their bankers. Such charges are generally applied quarterly.

Correspondence with banks

Correspondence between the bank and its customers tends to be standardised and quite formal, as the range of correspondence in this chapter reflects.

Current accounts

20.1 Notification of signatures to bank

Only officers authorised by a company's board of directors may sign cheques for the company. The bank will want to see a copy of the board's resolution authorising the opening of an account and stating the manner in which (and the persons by whom) cheques are to be signed, with specimens of their signatures.

Dear Sir

At a meeting of the Board yesterday it was decided that cheques drawn on the Company's account must bear two signatures instead of one as formerly.

One of the signatures must be that of the Chairman or Secretary, and the other that of any member of the Board. This change takes place as of today's date.

There have been no changes in membership of the Board since specimen signatures were issued to you in July.

A certified copy of the Board's resolution is attached.

Yours faithfully

20.2 Account overdrawn – correspondence with bank

The following is the kind of letter a bank manager would send to a customer who has overdrawn on their account. While being polite, courteous and helpful the letter conveys to the customer the seriousness of an unauthorised overdraft.

(a) Letter from bank

Dear

On a number of occasions recently your account has been overdrawn. The amount overdrawn at close of business yesterday was £50.72 and I should be glad if you would arrange for the credits necessary to clear this balance to be paid in as soon as possible.

Overdrafts are allowed to customers only by previous arrangement and as I notice that your account has recently been running on a very

small balance, it occurs to me that you may wish to come to some
arrangement for overdraft facilities. If so, perhaps you will call to
discuss the matter. In the absence of such an arrangement I am afraid
it will not be possible to honour future cheques drawn against
insufficient balances.

Yours sincerely

(b) Customer's reply

Dear

Thank you for your letter of yesterday. I have today paid into my
account cheques totalling £80.42. I realise that this leaves only a small
balance to my credit and as I am likely to be faced with fairly heavy
payments in the coming months, I should like to discuss arrangements
for overdraft facilities.

I have recently entered into a number of very favourable contracts, but
they involve the early purchase of raw materials and as payments
under the contracts will not be made until the work is completed I am
really in need of overdraft facilities up to about £600 for 6 months or
so.

Perhaps you will suggest a day and time when it would be convenient
for me to call on you.

Yours sincerely

(c) Further letter from bank

Dear

In the circumstances you mention in your letter of yesterday I think
the bank may be able to help you and, if the arrangement is convenient
for you, will expect you next Thursday morning, the 10th, at
11.00 am.

Please bring with you details of the contracts you mention and also a
copy of your last audited balance sheet. We can then go more fully into
the question of overdraft facilities.

Yours sincerely

20.3 Drawer stops payment of cheque

When a payment of a cheque is stopped, as for example where the cheque has been lost in the post, payment is said to be *countermanded*[3]. Only the drawer of the cheque can countermand payment. This is done by notifying the bank in writing. An *oral notification*[4], even when made by the drawer in person, is not by itself enough and, as with a notification by telephone, it should be immediately confirmed in writing.

Dear Sir

I am writing to confirm our telegram of this morning to ask you to stop payment of cheque number 67582 for the sum of £96.25, drawn payable to the St Annes Electrical Co Ltd.

This cheque appears to have been lost in the post and a further cheque has now been drawn to replace it.

Please confirm receipt of this authority to stop the payment..

Yours faithfully

20.4 Complaint concerning dishonoured cheque

(a) Customer's letter to bank

Dear Sir

The Alexandria Radio & Television Co Ltd inform me that you have refused payment of my cheque number 527610 of 15 August for £285.75. The returned cheque is marked 'Effects not cleared'. I believe this refers to the cheques I paid in on 11 August, the amount of which was more than enough to cover the dishonoured cheque.

As there appears to have been ample time for you to collect and credit the sums due on the cheques paid in, I should be glad if you would explain why payment of cheque number 527610 was refused.

Yours faithfully

(b) Reply from bank

Dear

In reply to your letter of yesterday, I regret we were not able to allow payment against your cheque number 527610. It appears to have

escaped your notice that one of the cheques paid in on 11 August –
the cheque drawn in your favour by M Tippett & Co – was post-dated
to 25 August and that the amount cannot be credited to your account
before that date.

To honour your cheque would have created an overdraft of more than
£100 and in the absence of previous arrangement I am afraid we could
not grant credit for such a sum.

I trust this explanation will make matters clear.

Yours sincerely

20.5 Request for bank reference

It is contrary to banking custom to give information to private enquirers about
its customers. Therefore, when a buyer in seeking credit from a supplier gives
the bank as a reference, the suppliers must approach their own bank, not the
buyer's bank, and ask them to make the necessary enquiries. As a rule, the
information supplied in answer to such requests is brief and formal, and much
less personal than that obtainable through a trade reference.

(a) Supplier's request to bank

Dear Sir

We have received an order for £1,200 from Messrs Joynson and Hicks
of 18 Drake Street, Sheffield. They ask for credit and have given the
Commonwealth Bank, 10 Albert Street, Sheffield S14 5QP, as a
reference.

Would you be good enough to make enquiries and let us know whether
the reputation and financial standing of this firm justify a credit of the
above amount.

Yours faithfully

(b) Reply from bank

Dear Sir

As requested in your letter of 18 April we have made enquiries as to
the reputation and standing of the Sheffield firm mentioned.

The firm was established in 1942 and its commitments have been met regularly. The directors are reported to be efficient and reliable and a credit of £1,200 is considered sound.

This information is supplied free from all responsibility on our part.

Bank loans and overdrafts

When granting an advance to a personal customer, especially an overdraft, the bank may require some form of acceptable security. The security should be easy to value, easy for the bank to obtain a good legal title, and it should be readily marketable or realisable. The most common types of security accepted are life policies, shares, mortgages of land and guarantees.

Normally a bank will not require security from a customer to support a personal loan.

Interest on an overdraft is charged on a daily basis, while interest on a personal loan is calculated on the full amount borrowed.

20.6 Request for overdraft facilities

(a) Customer's request

Dear Sir

With the approach of Christmas I am expecting a big increase in turnover[5], but unfortunately my present stocks are not nearly enough for this. Because my business is fairly new wholesalers are unwilling to give me anything but short-term credit.

Therefore, I hope you will be able to help me by making me an advance on overdraft until the end of this year.

As security I am willing to offer a life policy, and of course will allow you to inspect my accounts, from which you will see that I have promptly met all my obligations.

Perhaps you will be good enough to let me know when it will be convenient to discuss this matter personally with you.

Yours faithfully

(b) Banker's reply

Dear Mr Wilson

Thank you for your recent letter requesting overdraft facilities.

We are prepared to consider an overdraft over the period you mention, and have made an appointment for you to see me next Friday 11 November at 2.30 pm. Please bring with you the life policy mentioned, together with your company's accounts.

Yours sincerely

20.7 Request for loan without security

Dear Sir

In April 19. ., you were good enough to grant me a credit of £5,000, which was repaid within the agreed period. I now require a further loan to enable me to proceed with work under a contract with the Waterfoot Borough Council for building an extension to their King's Road School.

I need the loan to purchase building materials at a cost of about £6,000. The contract price is £20,000, payable immediately upon satisfactory completion of the work on or before 30 September next.

I should be glad if you could grant me a loan of £5,000 for a period of 9 months.

I enclose a copy of my latest audited balance sheet and shall be glad to call at the bank at your convenience to discuss the matter.

Yours faithfully

20.8 Request for loan with security

Dear Sir

I am considering a large extension of business with several firms in Japan and as the terms of dealings will entail[6] additional working capital[7], I should be glad if you would arrange to grant me a loan of, say, £6,000 for a period of 6 months.

You already hold for safe keeping on my behalf £5,000 Australian 3% stock and £4,500 4% consols[8]. These I am willing to pledge as security.

At current market prices they would, I presume, provide sufficient cover for the loan.

You would be able to rely upon repayment of the loan at maturity[9] as, apart from other income, I have arranged to take into the business a partner who, under the terms of the partnership agreement, will introduce £5,000 capital at or before the end of the present year.

If you will arrange a day and time when I may call on you to discuss my request, I will bring with me evidence supporting the above statements.

Yours faithfully

20.9 Request for extension of loan

Dear Sir

On 1st August last you granted me a loan of £2,500 which is due for repayment at the end of this month.

I have already taken steps to prepare for this repayment, but unfortunately, due to a fire at my warehouse a fortnight ago, I have been faced with heavy unexpected payments. Damage from the fire is thought to be about £4,000 and is fully covered by insurance, but as my claim is unlikely to be settled before the end of next month, I should be glad if the period of the loan could be extended until then.

I am sure you will realise that the fire has presented me with serious problems and that repayment of the loan before settlement of my claim could be made only with the greatest difficulty.

Yours faithfully

20.10 Request to clear unauthorised overdraft

(a) Request by bank

Dear Mr Hendon

I notice that since the beginning of last September there have been a number of occasions on which your current account has been overdrawn[10]. As you know, it is not the custom of the bank to allow overdrafts except by special arrangement and usually against security[11].

Two cheques drawn by you have been presented for payment today, one by Insurance Brokers Ltd for £27.50 and one by John Musgrave & Sons for £87.10. As you are one of our oldest customers I gave instructions for the cheques to be paid although the balance on your current account, namely £56.40, was insufficient to meet them.

I am well aware that there is a substantial credit balance on your deposit account, and if overdraft facilities on your current account are likely to be needed in future, I suggest that you give the bank the necessary authority to hold the balance on deposit as overdraft security.

Yours sincerely

(b) Customer's reply

Dear Mr Standard

Thank you for your letter of 2 December.

I am sorry to have given you cause to write to me concerning recent overdrafts on my current account. Although the amounts involved are not large I agree that overdraft facilities should have been discussed with you in advance and regret that this was not done. I am afraid I had overlooked the fact that the balance carried on my current account in recent months had been smaller than usual.

Later this month I expect to receive payment for several large contracts now nearing completion. No question of overdraft facilities will then arise, but in the meantime I am pleased to authorise you to treat the balance on my deposit account as security for any overdraft incurred on my current account, and once again apologise for the inconvenience caused.

Yours sincerely

Credit cards

The use of credit cards has increased dramatically over the last few years. Many credit card companies are now in existence, and many major retail outlets now have credit card facilities for use in their own stores.

Credit card customers are given a credit limit on their account and they may buy goods and services up to this amount from any outlet displaying the credit card signs.

Each month the cardholder receives a statement from the credit card company detailing all purchases during the month together with the total amount outstanding and the minimum amount due for payment. Payment may be made by cheque through the post, by bank giro credit or by regular monthly direct debit. Where the full balance is not settled, interest is charged; this provides the credit card company with its main source of income. The credit card company also receives income from retailers who make use of its cards and who pay a percentage of each sale to the credit card company.

Advantages of credit cards

To personal customers

- No need to carry cash.
- Payments can be spread.
- Can be used to obtain cash.
- Can be used in most overseas countries.

To business customers

- Statements for company credit cards show all business expenses incurred by employees.
- No need to maintain large cash balances to reimburse employees' expenditure on business.

To the retailer

- Immediate payment when vouchers are paid in to the bank.
- Security is provided as the credit card company can be contacted to check the account when large sums are involved.

To banks operating the credit card company

- Cost effective way of granting credit (no need for continuous loan or overdraft).
- Credit can be provided to non-customers.
- Wider customer base.

Useful expressions

Openings

1 I have entered into partnership with Mr . . . and we wish to open a current account in the name of . . . .
2 I enclose a standing order for payment of £5 on the first day of each month to . . . .
3 I shall be removing to . . . at the end of this month and should be glad if you would transfer my account to your branch in that town.

4 According to the statement received
  from you yesterday . . .
5 The statement you sent me recently
  shows that . . .
6 On referring to the statement just
  received I notice that . . .

} my account was overdrawn
  during July

7 This is to confirm my telephone message this morning asking you to stop
  payment of cheque number . . . .
8 I am writing to ask you to consider a loan of £ . . . for a period of . . .
  months . . . .
9 Please arrange to buy for me the following securities within the price ranges
  shown:

Closes

1 Should you require further information please let me know.
2 I shall be glad to call on you should you need any further information.
3 I feel that the charges are excessive and should be glad of your explanation.
4 I should be most grateful if you could grant the credit asked for.
5 Should you require a guarantor, Mr . . . of . . . has kindly consented to act.

Glossary

1 **standing order** an order to make certain payments at stated times
2 **direct debit** similar to standing orders but instead of the customer stating the
  amounts and when to pay them the company tells the bank what to pay and when
3 **countermanded** cancelled
4 **oral notification** a verbal message
5 **turnover** total sales
6 **entail** make necessary
7 **working capital** the capital needed to keep a business running
8 **consols** short for 'consolidated annuities' – a form of British Government stock
9 **at maturity** when it becomes due
10 **overdrawn** withdrawn in excess of balance available
11 **security** bonds, certificates, or other property pledged to cover a debt

Assignments on material included in this chapter can be found on p 366.

Chapter 21

Banking (international business)

The cheque, which is the main means of settling business debts in the home trade, is not suitable for payments in international trade since it is payable only in the drawer's country. Settlement of overseas debts may be made in a number of ways: by banker's draft, banker's transfer (mail, telex and telegraphic), letters of credit, bill of exchange and promissory note.

The method of payment adopted by the importer will depend upon the arrangement made with the exporter when the order is placed and this in turn will depend on the exporter's knowledge of the importer and the extent of trust existing between them.

In recent years, SWIFT has come into operation (Society for Worldwide Inter-Bank Financial Telecommunication). All major banks throughout the world are members of SWIFT. This is an electronic mechanism which enables bankers all over the world to communicate with each other, thus speeding up the fund transfer mechanism and cutting down on paperwork. The traditional methods of payment, mentioned above, however, still exist and will be dealt with in this chapter.

Banker's drafts

Like cheques, banker's drafts are payable on demand, but unlike cheques they carry little or no risk since they are backed by the assets of the bank issuing them. An importer wishing to pay by draft would buy it at a local bank and send it to the exporter, who would simply pay it into their own bank account.

21.1 Payment by banker's draft

(a) Exporter's request for payment

We enclose your statement for the month of November showing an outstanding balance of £180.50.

We assume you will settle this outstanding amount by banker's draft in UK Pounds Sterling, and hope to receive payment soon.

(b) Importer's reply

We acknowledge receipt of your letter together with our November statement.

Our banker's draft for UK Pounds One hundred and eighty and 50 pence (UK£180.50) is enclosed.

Banker's transfers (mail, telex and telegraphic transfers)

The banker's transfer is a simple transfer of funds from the bank account of a debtor in their own country to the creditor's bank account in the creditor's country. This is one of the safest methods of sending money abroad. All the debtor has to do is to instruct their bank, either by letter or on a special form, to make the transfer. The debtor's bank then arranges for the creditor's bank to be credited with an amount in local currrency equal to the sum transferred. The calculation is made at the current rate of exchange.

As these transfers are arranged direct between the two banks, losses are impossible, but as delays may occur when the transfers are made by mail, it is now customary for the banks to communicate either by telegram or by telex, thus giving rise to what are commonly known as the *telegraphic transfer* and *telex transfer*. Exchange rates for these transfers are quoted in the daily press.

21.2 Payment by telegraphic transfer

Dear Sir

We have received your statement for the quarter ended 30 September and find that it agrees with our books. As requested, we have instructed our bankers, the Midland Bank Ltd, 2 Deansgate, Manchester, to telegraph the sum of £2,182.89 for the credit of your account at the Bank Nationalé, Sweden.

This payment clears your account up to 31 August. The unpaid balance of £623.42 for goods supplied during September will be telegraphed by our bankers on or before 15 November.

Yours faithfully

Bills of exchange

A bill of exchange is a written order by a creditor (the drawer) to the debtor (the drawee) requiring payment of the sum of money stated in the order to a named person or firm (the payee), usually on a stated future date. Dealings in bills of exchange are now almost entirely confined to international trade, though even here they have now been largely replaced by other forms of payment, especially by the system of bank credits.

A drawee who agrees to the terms of the bill, 'accepts' (i.e. undertakes to pay) and signs it; they then become liable to meet the bill when it falls due for payment.

In the example shown in Fig. 20.1:

the *drawer* is: Trevor Gartside,
the *drawee* is: C. Mazzawi,
the *payee* is: E. Hughes & Co.

Where goods are sent by sea and the exporter has complete confidence in the overseas buyer, the shipping documents may be sent directly, trusting that payment will be made for them according to the terms of the contract. Where these provide for the buyer's acceptance of the exporter's draft bill of exchange, the buyer is entitled to retain the documents when the goods have been accepted and returns the draft.

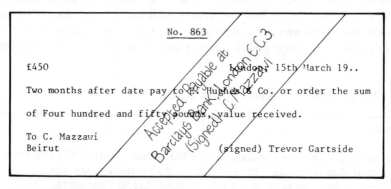

Fig. 20.1 Bill of Exchange. The bill of exchange is an order requiring the person to whom it is addressed to pay a stated sum of money to a named payee. It has almost disappeared from home trade and in international trade is now used much less frequently than in the past.

The exporter frequently requires the importer to arrange for the bill to be accepted by a bank or other financial house. This gives greater security to the person who holds the bill. Even when the importer accepts the bill, the exporter may require that it be marked payable at a named bank, as in Fig. 20.1. The holder must then present it to that bank for payment. This is called 'domiciling' a bill. Bills *domiciled in London*[1] are readily taken by the Bank of England for *rediscounting*[2].

21.3 Payment by bill of exchange

(a) Direct transaction with a trusted customer

Dear Sir

We thank you for your order of 25 June for 1,000 metres of poplin shirting at the quoted price of £0.86 per metre.

The shirting is now ready for despatch and will be shipped by the SS Tripoli sailing from Liverpool on 18 July.

We are pleased to enclose shipping documents. Also enclosed is our sight draft[3] drawn at 30 days as agreed. Please accept and return it immediately.

Yours faithfully

(b) Direct transaction with unknown customer

Dear Sirs

We are pleased to inform you that we can supply the fancy leather goods included in your order number 562 of 6 August and in accordance with our draft at 30 days for acceptance by your bankers.

Immediately we receive the accepted draft we will arrange to ship the goods and meanwhile are holding them for you.

Yours faithfully

21.4 Buyer requests extension of time

(a) Buyer's request

Dear Sirs

You informed me on 25 November that you intended to draw on me at 2 months for the amount due on your invoice number S 256, namely £461.54.

Until now I have had no difficulty in meeting my obligations and have always settled my accounts promptly. I could have done so now had it not been for the bankruptcy of one of my most important customers. I should therefore be most grateful if you could draw your bill at 3 months instead of the proposed 2. This would enable me to meet a temporarily difficult situation, forced upon me by circumstances that could not be foreseen.

Yours faithfully

(b) Seller's reply granting request

Dear Sir

I am replying to your letter of 30 November in which you ask for an extension of the tenor[4] of my draft from 2 to 3 months.

In the special circumstances you mention and because of the promptness with which you have settled your accounts in the past, we are willing to grant the request and enclose our draft, drawn at 3 months. Please add your acceptance and let me have it by return.

Yours faithfully

(c) Seller's reply refusing request

When refusing a request it is easy to give offence and lose a customer, but the example shown is a tactful and understanding letter and while it will give rise to disappointment it is unlikely to cause offence.

Dear Sir

I am sorry to learn from your letter of 30 November of the difficulty in which the bankruptcy of an important customer has placed you. I should like to say at once that I fully appreciate your wish for an extension of my draft and would very much like to help you. Unfortunately, I cannot do so because of commitments which I myself have to meet in 2 months' time.

In the circumstances you mention your request is not at all unreasonable and had I been able to grant it would gladly have done so, but as matters stand I am left with no choice but to ask you to accept the draft, as drawn at 2 months, and enclose it for your signature and return.

Yours faithfully

21.5 Bill dishonoured at maturity

When a buyer who has accepted a bill fails to meet it *at maturity*[5], the bill is said to be 'dishonoured' and the debt for which it was drawn is immediately revived. Dishonour entitles the drawer or other holder of the bill to take legal action against the acceptor either (a) on the bill, or (b) on the debt for which it was drawn.

(a) Drawer requests explanation

Dear Sirs

We were very surprised this morning when our bankers returned the bill we drew on you for £325 on 5 August, marked 'Refer to drawer'.

Since we are aware from personal knowledge that your firm is financially sound, we presume that failure to honour the bill was due to some mistake. We shall therefore be glad if you will explain the reason. At the same time we must ask you to send by return the sum due on the bill.

Yours faithfully

(b) Drawer threatens legal action

Dear Sir

I regret to say that our bill number 670 for £162.72 of 15 December was not met when we presented it to the bank today.

In view of your earlier promise to meet your obligations on the bill, we are both surprised and disappointed that payment has not been made. We should like to feel that there has been some misunderstanding and ask you to explain why the bill was not honoured[6].

At the same time, we are making a formal request for payment of the sum due and shall be glad to receive your remittance. Should payment not be made, then I am afraid we shall have no choice but to start proceedings for dishonour.

Yours faithfully

21.6 Dishonoured bill protested

When a foreign bill (but not an inland bill) is dishonoured, it must be 'protested' as a preliminary to legal action. A 'protest' is a formal declaration by a *notary public*[7] that the terms of the bill have not been fulfilled. Its purpose is to prevent the drawee (the acceptor) from denying that the bill was presented for payment (or for acceptance if it is dishonoured by non-acceptance).

In the following letter the supplier gives the buyer a further opportunity to pay, even after protest.

Dear Sir

Although you gave your <u>unqualified acceptance</u>[8] to our bill number 670 of 15 December for £162.72, we write to remind you that it was not met when presented for payment yesterday.

Non-payment has obliged us to make formal protest of the bill and we now offer you this further and final opportunity to meet your obligations by payment of the sum of £165.22 to cover the amount for which the bill was accepted and the expenses of protest as follows:

Nominal value of the bill	£162.72
Expenses of protest	2.50

We hope to receive payment within the next day or two so as to avoid our having to take further proceedings.

Yours faithfully

Documentary bills

The above examples refer to transactions conducted between importer and exporter direct, but it is more usual for the exporter to gain protection by using the services of the banks. There are three main methods, each requiring the exporter to prepare a documentary bill (i.e. a draft bill of exchange with shipping documents attached) and to leave it with the bank, which passes it to its foreign branch or correspondent, who then deals with the importer.

1 The importer is ordered to pay the draft either to the exporter, to their order, or to the bank.
2 The exporter again draws on the importer, but asks the bank to discount the draft against the security of the shipping documents, which are passed to the banker.
3 The exporter requires the importer to arrange for a letter of credit, the purpose of which is to enable the exporter to draw on a named bank when the shipping documents are presented. The letter of credit against which the bill is drawn must state the maximum amount and the duration of the credit, the usance (i.e. the term) of the bill and the shipping documents that are to be sent with the bill.

Where the draft on the importer is drawn for a term, say 60 days, the banker presenting it will hand over the shipping documents only against acceptance (*D/A terms*[9]), but where it is drawn payable on demand, this will be done only against payment (*D/P terms*[10]).

In practice, instructions to the banks are usually given on special forms provided by the banks themselves, thus making certain that all important points are covered. In the correspondence that follows, instructions to the banks are given in letters of the kind that would be sent where special forms are not provided.

21.7 Documentary bill presented through bank

(a) Exporter's letter to importer, D/P terms

Dear Sirs

We were pleased to receive your faxed order of 29 June and have arranged to ship the electric shavers by SS Tyrania, leaving London on 6 July and due to arrive at Sidon on the 24th.

As the urgency of your order left no time to make the usual enquiries, we are compelled to place this transaction on a cash basis and have drawn on you through Midminster Bank Ltd for the amount of the enclosed invoice. The bank will instruct their correspondent in Sidon to pass the bill of lading to you against payment of the draft.

Special care has been taken to select items suited to your local conditions. We hope you will find them entirely satisfactory and that your present order will be the first of many.

Yours faithfully

(b) Exporter's letter to importer, D/A terms

Dear Sirs

YOUR ORDER NO B 614

We are pleased to inform you that arrangements have now been made to ship the dress goods you orderd on 15 October. The consignment will leave London on 1 November by SS Manchester Trader, due to arrive at Quebec on the 22nd.

In keeping with our usual terms of payment we have drawn on you at 60 days and passed the draft and shipping documents to our bankers. The documents will be presented to you by the National Bank of Canada against your acceptance of the draft in the usual way.

Yours faithfully

21.8 Exporter's instructions to bank (D/P terms) (to be read with 21.7(a))

Dear Sirs

On 6 July we are shipping a consignment of 2,000 electric shavers to the Sidon Electrical Co of whom we have little knowledge and whose standing we have been unable to check. We therefore think it would be unwise to surrender the enclosed documents on a D/A basis and enclose a sight draft on the consignees, with bill of lading and insurance certificate attached.

Will you please arrange for your correspondent in Sidon to obtain payment of the amount due before handing over the documents, and notify us when payment has been made.

Yours faithfully

21.9 Documentary bill sent through exporter's bank

Exporters sometimes send the documentary bill direct to a bank in the importer's country, but more usually deal with their own bank, who arrange for the bill to be presented to the foreign buyer by their branch or correspondent abroad.

(a) Exporter's letter to bank

Dear Sirs

We have today shipped by SS Seafarer a consignment of haberdashery to the Nigerian Trading Co., Lagos. Since the standing of this company is unknown to us, we do not wish to hand over the shipping documents against their mere acceptance of a bill of exchange. Therefore we enclose a sight draft on them, together with bill of lading and the other shipping documents. In the circumstances, we shall require payment of the draft in full before the documents are handed over and shall be glad if you will instruct your correspondent in Lagos to arrange for this.

Yours faithfully

(b) Exporter's advice of shipment to Nigerian Trading Co.

When sending the above letter to their bankers, the exporters will send advice of shipment to the Nigerian Trading Co. and explain the arrangements made for payment.

Dear Sirs

The goods which you ordered on 2 October have been shipped to you today by SS Seafarer, due at Lagos on 2 December.

We have taken special care to include in the consignment only items suited to conditions in Nigeria. We hope you will be pleased with our selection and that your first order will lead to further business between us.

From the enclosed copy invoice you will see that the price of £865.75 is well within the maximum figure you stated. We have drawn on you for this amount at sight through the Barminster Bank, who have been instructed to hand over documents against payment of the draft. We hope you will understand when we explain that the urgency of your order left us with insufficient time to make the usual enquiries and that we therefore had no choice but to follow our standard practice with new customers of placing the transaction on a cash basis.

We look forward to your further orders, and subject to satisfactory references and regular dealings, would be prepared to consider open-account terms[11] with quarterly settlements.

Yours faithfully

21.10 Documentary bill sent direct to importer's bank

Dear Sir

We enclose shipping documents for 10,000 bags of rice shipped by SS Thailand, which left Bangkok for London on 15 October.

Please hand the documents to Messrs B Stephenson & Co of London EC2P 2AA, as soon as they are ready to take them up against payment of £4,260 (four thousand two hundred and sixty pounds), less interest at 2½% from date of payment to 31 December next and credit our account with the proceeds, after deducting your charges.

Yours faithfully

An exporter in need of immediate funds will sometimes ask their bank to advance money on a documentary bill. The bank will in return require their execution of a *letter of hypothecation*. This is a letter authorising the bank to sell the goods should the bill be dishonoured by the importer. An exporter who regularly obtains such advances often signs a *general letter of hypothecation*, which covers all future transactions.

Bankers' commercial credits

From the exporter's point of view the documentary bill suffers from the defect that the foreign buyer may fail to honour the bill. To avoid this risk a system of *banker's commercial credits* or *documentary credits* has been developed. The system is now widely used and works in the following manner.

1 Importers ask their own bank to open a credit in favour of the exporter, usually on a specially printed application form.
2 The importer's bank then sends a letter of credit to the exporter or, more usually, arranges for one of its branches or correspondents in the exporter's country to do so.
3 From this point the exporter deals with the correspondent bank and when the goods are shipped prepares the shipping documents and presents them (more often than not with a bill of exchange drawn on the correspondent bank) to the correspondent bank, which 'pays' for them within the limits of the authorised credit and sends them to the importer's bank.
4 The importer's bank in turn passes the documents to the importer either against payment or against an acceptance of a bill of exchange, if one accompanies the documents.

In effect, the importer's bank is temporarily providing the funds from which the exporter is paid, though it will usually require the importer to maintain a sufficient balance in their account to cover the credit.

The credit can be either *revocable*[12] or *irrevocable*[13]. Under a revocable letter of credit the importer is free to modify or even cancel the credit without so much as giving notice to the exporter, but an irrevocable credit can be neither amended nor withdrawn without the permission of the exporter to whom it is granted; the exporter can therefore rely on being paid.

Within the broad pattern illustrated above, there may sometimes be slight differences, but they do not affect the general principles on which the system works. Correspondence connected with these credits is very technical, as is evident from the complicated nature of the printed forms used by the banks, and should be handled by someone who is thoroughly familiar with the practice.

21.11 A documentary credit – stages in transactions

Perhaps the best way to study the system of bank commercial or documentary credits is to follow a transaction through. In this transaction, Messrs A H Brooks & Son are a firm of London fur dealers. They have agreed to take monthly deliveries of furs from the North American Trading Company over a period of 6 months and to open a credit on which the company can draw as shipments are made. Correspondence would take place on the following lines:

(a) Buyer approaches bank

Dear Sirs

We have just concluded an agreement to purchase monthly shipments of furs from Canada over the next 6 months and would like to make use of foreign-payment facilities by opening a series of monthly credits for £2,000 each in favour of the North American Trading Company. It has been agreed that we provide credits with a bank in Quebec against which our suppliers would draw for the value of shipments as they are made.

Will you please let us know on what terms your bank would be prepared to arrange necessary credits and to handle the shipping documents for us.

Yours faithfully

(b) Bank offers to provide credits

Dear

Thank you for your enquiry of 15 March. We shall be pleased to handle the shipments referred to and to arrange for the necessary documentary credits with our Quebec branch against deposit of bill of lading and other shipping documents. If you will complete and return the enclosed form we will make the arrangements.

Our commission charges for revocable documentary credits would be ⅛ to ¼% on each of the monthly credits, to which must be added ¼% for irrevocable credits and also our charges for such items as telegrams and postages. In return for these charges you have our assurance that your interests would be carefully protected.

Yours sincerely

(c) Buyer instructs bank

Dear

I have completed and enclose the form of application for a documentary credit received with your letter of 17 March and shall be glad if you will arrange to open for our account with your office in Quebec irrevocable credits for £2,000 a month in favour of the North American Trading Company, the credits to be valid until 30 September next.

To enable them to use the credits the company must present the following documents: bills of lading in triplicate, one copy of the invoice, the certificate or policy of insurance and certificate of origin, and draw on your Quebec office at 60 days after sight for each consignment. The documents relate to five cases of mixed furs in each consignment at the value of about £350 per case, cif London.

Yours sincerely

(d) Bank agrees to open credit

If the bank agrees to open a credit, they will usually notify the buyer on one of their own standard printed forms. If, instead, this is done by letter, they would write in some such terms as the following.

Dear

As instructed in your letter of 20 March we are arranging to open a documentary credit with our branch in Quebec in favour of the North American Trading Company, valid until 30 September. You will find enclosed a copy of our instruction opening the credit and we shall be glad if you will check it to ensure that it agrees with your instructions. As soon as the credits are used we shall debit your account with the amount notified to us as having been drawn against them.

We shall take all necessary steps to make sure that your instructions are carefully carried out, but wish to make it clear that we cannot assume any responsibility for the safety of the goods, or for delays in delivery since these are matters beyond our control.

Yours sincerely

(e) Buyer notifies exporter

The bank in London now sends to its Quebec office a copy of the form completed by Brooks & Son to authorise the opening of the credit.

Dear

This is to inform you that we have now opened irrevocable credits in your favour for £2,000 a month with the Royal Bank of Canada, Quebec, valid until 30 September next.

The terms of the credit authorise you to draw at 60 days on the bank in Quebec for the amount of your invoices after each shipment of five cases. Before accepting the draft, which should include all charges to London, the bank will require you to produce the following documents: bills of lading in triplicate, one copy of the invoice covering cif London, a certificate or policy of insurance and certificate of origin. We will expect your first consignment about the middle of next month.

Yours sincerely

(f) Bank issues letter of credit

The next step is for the Quebec office of the bank to notify the North American Trading Company that the credit is available. They may use a printed form for the purpose. But if they were to send the advice by letter and if the London office had requested them to 'confirm' the credit, the letter would be in something like the following form.

Dear

On instructions from Messrs A H Brooks & Son, received through our London office, we have opened monthly irrevocable credits for £2,000 in your favour, valid until 30 September next. You have authority to draw on us at 60 days against these credits for the amount of your invoices upon shipment of furs to Messrs A H Brooks & Son.

Your drafts must be accompanied by the following documents, which are to be delivered to us against our acceptance of the drafts: bills of lading in triplicate, commercial invoice, insurance certificate or policy and certificate of origin.

Provided you fulfil the terms of the credit we will accept and pay at maturity the drafts presented to us under these credits and, if required, provide discounting facilities at current rates.

Yours sincerely

In the foregoing letter the irrevocable credit is issued by the London Branch of the Royal Bank of Canada and is 'confirmed' by the Quebec branch of the same bank in the final paragraph of its letter to the exporter. But where the bank issuing the credit does not have a branch of its own in the exporter's country it will arrange for the credit to be notified to the exporter through a correspondent bank. Unless the issuing bank has authorised or requested its correspondent to 'confirm' the credit, and it does so, the correspondent is under no obligation to 'accept' the exporter's drafts. If it does confirm the credit, it enters into a definite undertaking with the exporter to accept drafts drawn under the credit, provided they conform to its terms. This undertaking is independent of, and in addition to, that of the bank issuing the irrevocable credit, thus providing the exporter with a twofold assurance of payment.

(g) Exporter presents documents

Dear

Referring to your advice of 30 March, we enclose shipping documents
for the first of the monthly consignments to Messrs A H Brooks & Son.

As required by them we have included all charges in our invoice, which
amounts to £1,725.71 and enclose our draft at 60 days for this sum.
We shall be glad if, after acceptance, you will discount it at the current
rate and remit the net amount to our account with the Banque de
France, Quebec.

We thank you for your help in this matter.

Yours sincerely

Note: The Quebec office now sends the shipping documents to its London
office with a statement of the amount of the draft charged against the credit.

(h) Bank debits buyers

As instructed by your letter of 20 March, our Quebec office has just
accepted for your account a bill for £1,725.71 drawn by the North
American Trading Company for a first consignment of furs to you by
SS <u>Columbia</u>. We have debited your account with this amount and our
charges amounting to £15.30.

The ship left Quebec on 22 April and is due to arrive in London on 2
May. The shipping documents for this consignment are now with us
and we shall be glad if you will arrange to collect them.

Yours sincerely

Useful expressions

Buyer to exporter

Openings

1 We have received your invoice number . . . and agree to accept your draft
   at 60 days after sight for the amount due.
2 As requested in your letter of . . . we have instructed the . . . Bank to open
   a credit for £. . . in your favour.
3 We are sorry to have to ask for the term of your bill dated . . . to be extended
   for one month.

4 I regret that at the moment I cannot meet in full my acceptance, which is due for payment on . . . .

Closes

1 Please let us know whether you are prepared to give us open-account terms.
2 Please draw on us for the amount due and attach the shipping documents to your draft.
3 We should like to pay by bill of exchange at 60 days after sight and should be glad if you would agree to this.
4 As requested, we will arrange to open an irrevocable credit in your favour.
5 Our acceptance will be honoured upon presentation of the bill at the . . . branch of the . . . Bank.

Exporter to buyer

Openings

1 We have considered your letter of . . . and are pleased to grant the open-account terms asked for.
2 As requested in your letter of . . . we have drawn on you for the amount of our April account at 3 months from . . . .
3 As agreed in our earlier correspondence we have drawn on you for the amount of the invoice enclosed.

Closes

1 Please accept the draft and return it as soon as you can.
2 We are quite willing to put your account on a documents-against-acceptance basis.
3 We have instructed our bank to hand over the shipping documents against acceptance (payment) of our draft.
4 Shipping documents, and our draft for acceptance, have been passed to the . . . Bank.
5 As arranged, we have instructed our bank to surrender (hand over) the documents against payment (acceptance) of our draft.
6 As soon as the credit is confirmed, we will ship the goods.

Buyer to bank

Openings

1 I enclose accepted bill, drawn on me by . . ., and should now be glad to receive the shipping documents.
2 Please accept and pay the following drafts for me and, at maturity, debit them to my account.

3 Please arrange with your correspondents in . . . to open a credit in favour of . . . .

Closes

1 Please accept the above draft for me and debit your charges to my account.
2 Will you please state the amount of your charges for arranging the necessary credits.

Exporter to bank

Openings

1 We enclose our sight draft on . . . of . . . and also the shipping documents.
2 Please surrender the enclosed documents to . . . of . . . when they accept our draft, also enclosed.
3 Kindly instruct your correspondent in . . . to release the documents only on payment of our sight draft for £. . . .

Closes

1 We ask you to obtain acceptance of this draft before surrendering the shipping documents.
2 Please present the bill for acceptance and then discount it for the credit of our account.
3 Please present this acceptance for payment at maturity and credit us with the proceeds.

Glossary

1 **domiciled in London** marked as payable in London
2 **rediscounting** to discount a bill is to obtain payment for it before the due date, at a figure below face value
3 **sight draft** a bill of exchange payable immediately upon acceptance
4 **tenor** the period for which a bill of exchange is drawn
5 **at maturity** when payment becomes due
6 **honoured** paid when due
7 **notary public** usually a solicitor specially authorised to witness deeds and other important documents
8 **unqualified acceptance** a full and complete acceptance
9 **D/A terms** documents against acceptance
10 **D/P terms** documents against payment
11 **open-account terms** credit terms with periodic settlement
12 **revocable** can be altered or cancelled
13 **irrevocable** cannot be altered or cancelled

Assignments on material included in this chapter can be found on p 366.

Chapter 22

Transport

Carriage by sea

Transporting goods by sea is still attractive in view of the increase in size and speed of ships, and the greatly increased use of the container. Ships are now built specifically to carry particular types of bulk cargoes such as oil, mineral ores, meat and fruit.

Liners and tramps

It is usual to classify ships into liners (ships which sail at regular times on set routes) and tramps (ships which have no set times or routes, but go wherever they can find suitable cargoes). Hardly any tramps are used these days for long-distance hauls, except within the United Kingdom. Tramps are essentially cargo boats, ready at any time to make any particular voyage.

Liners may be either passenger liners or cargo liners. Passenger liners usually take a certain amount of miscellaneous cargo, while cargo liners often provide a limited amount of accommodation for passengers.

The contracts entered into between shipowner and shipper (i.e. the consignor) may take the form of *either*

a charter party (where a complete ship is hired)

or

a bill of lading (where the ship carries cargoes belonging to various different shippers).

Chartering of ships

When goods are shipped in large consignments, and this applies especially to *bulk cargoes*[1], it may be an advantage to hire or charter a complete ship, either for a particular voyage (a voyage charter) or for an agreed period of time (a time charter). The documents setting out the terms and conditions of the contract between the shipowner who provides the ship and the merchant (the charterer) who hires it is called a charter party. Standard forms of charter party have been drawn up, but many shipowners prefer to draw up their own forms.

Ship chartering is usually arranged through shipbrokers, and in London there is a special centre where these brokers conduct business, namely, the Baltic Exchange.

The shipping conference system

A shipping conference is an association formed by shipping lines, British and foreign, serving a particular sea route. There are some 300 of these conferences, each serving its own particular route or area, e.g. North Atlantic, South African and Australian. The purpose of the conference is to fix and maintain *freight rates*[2] at a *remunerative*[3] level, and to ensure that a sufficient minimum of cargo is always forthcoming to feed the regular sailings they undertake to provide. They do this by establishing 'ties' between shippers and themselves. The 'tie' may take the form of a *deferred rebate*[4] to shippers who confine their shipment to vessels owned by members of the conference; but the rebate system has now been largely replaced by a *preferential rate system*[5].

The conference system has advantages for both shipper and shipowner. For the shipper it provides the certainty of regular sailings and reliable delivery dates; for the shipowner it ensures that, in return for undertaking to maintain regular sailings, shippers will place their cargoes with him rather than elsewhere. This helps the conference shipowner to keep ships employed.

The container service

The use of containers provides a highly efficient form of transport by road, rail and air. Its fullest benefits are felt in shipping, where costs may be considerably reduced. Containers are constructed in metal and are of standard lengths ranging from 10 to 40 feet (approximately 3–12 metres).

The container service has the following advantages:

1 Containers can be loaded and locked at factory premises at nearby container bases, making *pilferage*[6] more difficult.
2 There is reduced risk of goods getting lost or mislaid in transit.
3 Handling is greatly reduced, with lower costs and less risk of damage.
4 Mechanical handling enables cargoes to be loaded in a matter of hours rather than days, thus reducing the time ships spend in port and greatly increasing the number of sailings.
5 Temperature-controlled containers are provided for types of cargo which need them.

22.1 Enquiry for sailings and freight rates

Enquiries of this nature will normally be conducted by telephone or fax. The consigner (or agent) will need to know freight rates and dates of sailings.

We shall shortly have ready for shipment from Liverpool to Alexandria, four cases of crockery. The cases measure 1¼ × 1¼ × 1 m, each weighing 70 kg.

Please quote your rate for freight and send us details of your sailings and the time usually taken for the voyage.

22.2 Shipping company's reply to enquiry in 22.1

The SS Princess Victoria will be loading at number 2 dock from 8 to 13 July inclusive. Following her is the SS Merchant Prince, loading at number 5 dock from 20 to 24 July inclusive.

The voyage to Alexandria normally takes 14 days. The freight rate for crockery packed in wooden cases is £97.00 per tonne.

We shall be glad to book your four cases for either of these vessels and enclose our shipping form. Please complete it and return it as soon as possible.

22.3 Agent issues forwarding instructions

When notified by the supplier that the goods are ready, the agent either arranges to collect them and despatch them to the docks, or will ask the supplier to do so. The shipping form is then returned to the shipping company making arrangements for the goods to be received at the docks.

(a) Agent's advice to supplier

Thank you for informing us that the items ordered on 16 June are now ready for collection.

Please arrange to send the consignment by road to Liverpool to be shipped by SS Merchant Prince, due to sail for Alexandria on 25 July and to load at number 5 dock from 20 to 24 July inclusive. All cases should be clearly marked and numbered as shown in our official order. Invoices, in triplicate, and your account for transport charges, should be sent to us.

All the necessary arrangements have been made with the shipping company.

(b) Agent's instruction to shipping company

We have today arranged for H J Cooper & Co. Ltd, Manchester, to forward to you by road, the following cases to be shipped to Alexandria by SS Merchant Prince on 25 July.

4 cases of crockery, marked ⟨JR⟩ , numbers 1–4

The completed shipping form is enclosed, together with 4 copies of the bill of lading. Please sign and return 3 copies of the bill and charge the amount to our account.

Shipping and forwarding agents

A shipping and forwarding agent carries out all the duties connected with collecting and delivering the client's goods. These services are particularly valuable in foreign trade because of the complicated arrangements which have to be made. For exporters, the shipping company collects the goods, makes all the arrangements for shipping them, and notifies their despatch to the forwarding agent in the importing country. The latter takes delivery of the goods and either forwards them to the buyer or arranges for them to be warehoused if the buyer does not want them immediately.

Packing, shipping and forwarding agents are specialists and know the best methods of packing particular types of goods and the most suitable form of packing to use for the country to which the goods are being sent.

By assembling and repacking in larger lots, small consignments intended for the same destination, the forwarding agent can obtain lower freight rates. It is therefore often cheaper, and certainly much simpler, for suppliers to employ a forwarding agent than to deal directly with the shipping and road transport organisations. Many importers and exporters, however, prefer to reduce their costs by dealing direct with clearing or forwarding agents in the countries of their suppliers (if they are importers) or of their customers (if they are exporters).

22.4 Advice of shipment to forwarding agent in buyer's country (Alexandria)

Please note that we have shipped the following goods to you by SS Merchant Prince, which left Liverpool yesterday and is due to arrive at Alexandria on 9 August.

Mark and Numbers	Goods	Gross Weight	Value
JR 1–4	4 cases crockery	280 kg	£3,250

Insurance in the sum of £2,200 is provided as far as Alexandria only.

A copy of the bill of lading and the invoice are enclosed. Please arrange to handle the consignment and deliver it to Messrs Jean Riachi & Co, Mansura, who will be responsible for all charges.

The consignment is urgently required, so your prompt attention will be appreciated.

22.5 Advice of shipment to buyer

The consignment having been shipped and the buyer's forwarding agent notified, the agent will now write to inform the buyer of receipt of the consignment. The letter sent takes the form of an advice of despatch.

YOUR INDENT NO 762

We are pleased to inform you that all goods ordered on your above indent have now been shipped by SS Merchant Prince, which sailed from Liverpool yesterday and is due to arrive in Alexandria on 9 August.

The consignment will be handled on arrival by Messrs Behren & Co, who will make all the arrangements for its delivery to you.

The bill of lading and invoice, together with our account for commission and charges are enclosed. The suppliers have been informed that you will settle their account direct.

We hope to hear from you soon that the goods have arrived safely.

Forwarding agents

Where exporters arrange shipment through a forwarding agent in their own country, the agent handles the whole transaction. This includes arranging for the goods to be collected and transported to the docks and paying the charges, making the arrangements with the shipping company, paying the freight, insuring the goods, preparing the bill of lading and dealing with any other documents which may be necessary (e.g. consular invoice, *certificate of origin*[7], certificate of value and weight, export licence, etc.). Then, when the goods have been shipped, the exporter's agent advises the shipping and forwarding agent in the buyer's country, who deals with them when they arrive at the port. In short, a forwarding agent does everything and, as a specialist in the business, does it well.

22.6 Suppliers seeks forwarding agent's services

We have a consignment of tape recorders now waiting to be shipped to
Messrs Tan & Co of Kuala Lumpur. Will you please arrange for the
consignment to be collected from the above address and arrange
shipment to Klang by the first possible sailing. When it arrives at
Klang, the consignment will be handled for our customers by
Mr J Collins, with whom you should make the necessary
arrangements.

The recorders are packed in three cases and the enclosed copy of the
invoice shows quantities and a total value of £2,800. Insurance should
be taken out for £2,900 to include cover for expenses.

When the goods are shipped, please send the original bill of lading and
one copy to us, together with the certificate or policy of insurance and
any other necessary documents.

Carriage by air

Bills of lading, used for consignments by sea, are not used for consignments
by air because the goods usually reach their destination before a bill of lading
could be prepared. Instead, the consignor is required to prepare an airway bill
giving particulars of the consignment. This normally consists of a number of
copies, some of which are treated as originals, one for the issuing air carrier,
one for the consignee and one for the consignor. The remaining copies serve
for other possible carriers and for customs and record purposes.

It is common practice for the airline or its agent to prepare the airway bill
from details supplied by the consignor on a special form – an Instructions
for Despatch of Goods form – provided by the airline or by the forwarding
agents.

Like the bill of lading, the airway bill serves as a receipt for the goods taken
on board and is evidence of the contract of carriage, the terms of which are
set out in detail on the back. Unlike the bill of lading, however, the airway
bill is not a document of title.

With carriage by air, the consignor may also use the services of a forwarding
agent, or may deal with the airline direct through its cargo-booking section.
The more usual practice is to use an agent.

Air cargo is charged by weight except for bulky commodities, which are
charged by volume. To encourage movement of traffic by air, special rates are
charged for a wide range of enumerated articles. Valuables, however, are subject
to a surcharge to cover extra handling costs.

22.7 Enquiry for air freight rates (through agent)

We shall shortly have a consignment of electric shavers, weighing about 20 kg, for a customer in Damascus, which we wish to send by air from London.

Please send us details of the cost and any formalities to be observed. The invoice value of the consignment is £1,550 and we should require insurance cover for this amount plus the costs of sending the consignment.

22.8 Forwarding agent's reply

Thank you for your enquiry regarding your consignment to Damascus. All our charges, including freight, airway bill fee, insurance and our own commission, are shown on the attached schedule.

To enable us to prepare your airway bill we shall need the information requested in the enclosed form. Three copies of a certified commercial invoice and a certificate of origin will also be necessary.

Your consignment should be in our hands by 10 am on the morning of departure day. Please telephone me when you are ready to deliver the consignment to our officer at the airport; we can then prepare to receive it and deal with it promptly. Alternatively, we can make arrangements to collect the goods.

We hope to receive instructions from you soon.

Carriage by road

Road transport is generally cheaper than rail for both passengers and goods, although rail is cheaper for such bulk commodities as oil, sand and timber.
   The most important features of road transport are:

1 The ease with which it adapts itself to different situations and the fact that a direct delivery service is provided
2 Routes are easily varied according to traffic flow
3 It is safer for fragile goods and calls for simpler packing than for goods sent by rail
4 It is particularly suitable for short distance traffic, mainly because small truck loads can be dealt with easily and quickly.

Documents used

When goods are handed to a carrier the contract of carriage takes the form of a consignment note or waybill (if transport is by road, rail or air). The originals of these documents are handed to the *consignors*[8] and serve as their receipts. The carrier keeps a copy for himself and a further copy is passed on to the *consignee*[9] with the goods.

22.9 Enquiry for freight rates

Early next month we shall have a consignment of motor-car spares for delivery from our address to a company in Aberdeen.

These spares will be packed in two wooden cases, each measuring $1 \times 1 \times 0.75$ m and weighing about 80 kg.

Please let us know by return:

1 Your charge for collecting and delivering these cases.

2 If you can collect them on the 3rd of next month.

3 When delivery would be made to the consignee.

An early reply would be appreciated.

22.10 Supplier notifies despatch of goods

Your Order No 825

We have today despatched by Williams Transport Ltd two wooden cases containing the motor-car spares which you ordered recently.

Would you please unpack and examine them as soon as possible after delivery and in the event of any damage notify us and also the carriers at once.

We understand the goods will be delivered to you in 3 days' time.

22.11 Buyer notifies receipt of goods

Our Order No 825

The two cases of motor-car spares despatched by Williams Transport Ltd were delivered yesterday in good condition.

The case is being returned to you by Williams Transport. Please credit us with the amount charged for it on your invoice.

22.12 Removal of household furniture

(a) Request for quotation

Early next month we will be moving from the above address to 110 Normanshire Drive, Chingford. I would like a quotation on the cost of your removal services.

Our present house has six rooms, all of which are fully furnished. You will no doubt wish to inspect our furniture so perhaps you will arrange to send one of your representatives around.

I hope to hear from you soon.

(b) Quotation

We are writing to confirm the arrangement made with our representative for the removal of your furniture from St Annes to Chingford on 3 May.

Our charge for the removal, including insurance cover in the sum of £15,000, will be £350. We enclose a form of agreement setting out the terms and conditions and shall be glad if you will sign and return it.

Our van, with three workmen, will arrive at your house at 7.30 am on 3 May. The loading should be completed in about three hours. We should be able to deliver to your Chingford address and complete unloading by 4.30 pm on the following day.

Please let me know if you have any queries.

(c) Claim for damage to property during removal

When your workmen removed the furniture from my house in St Annes on 3 May, the staircase was badly damaged. The new owner of this house has obtained an estimate for the repair in the sum of £120 and he is now claiming this amount from me.

I realise the insurance policy you provided only covered damage to furniture. However, as the damage now reported is claimed to have been caused by your workmen, I have advised the new owner to contact you directly.

Carriage by rail

Over long distances and for bulk commodities such as oil, sand and timber, rail is cheaper than road. However, unlike road transport, it cannot collect and deliver without the help of some other form of transport. This sometimes causes delay, involves double handling, calls for more *elaborate*[10] packing, increases the risk of theft and damage, and *consequently*[11] increases costs. The railways are increasingly meeting these problems by using 'containers'.

Goods may be carried either at owner's risk or at company's risk, rates for the former being lower. Rates also vary with the class of goods.

Unless otherwise agreed between buyer and seller, responsibility for collecting and transporting the purchases lies with the buyer. If a carrier is engaged, then the carrier becomes the buyer's agent. Once the goods have been taken over by the agent, the seller's responsibility for them ceases and the buyer becomes liable for any loss or damage which may be suffered.

22.13 Claim for losses due to pilferage

(a) Buyer's complaint

OUR ORDER NO 326

The consignment of cotton shirts despatched on 21 June was delivered yesterday in a very unsatisfactory condition.

It was clear that two of the cases (numbers 4 and 7) had been <u>tampered with</u>[12]. Upon checking the contents we found that case number 4 contained only 372 shirts and case number 7 only 375 shirts instead of the 400 invoiced for each case.

Before reporting the matter to the railway, would you please confirm that each of these cases did, in fact, contain the invoiced quantity when they left your warehouse. At the same time please replace the 53 missing shirts with others of the same quality.

You will no doubt be claiming <u>compensation</u>[13] from the railway, in which case we shall be glad to assist you with any information we can provide. Meanwhile, the cases are being held for inspection, together with the contents.

(b) Supplier's reply

We were sorry to learn from your letter of 27 June that two of the cases sent to you on 21 June had been tampered with. We confirm that when they left our warehouse each of these cases contained the full quantity of 400 shirts. The cases were in good order when they left our premises, and in support of this we hold the carrier's clean receipt.

As we sent the goods by rail at your request, the railway company must be regarded as your agents. We cannot, therefore, accept any resonsibility for the losses and can only suggest that you make the claim for compensation directly with the railway company. We are, of course, quite willing to support your claim in whatever way we can.

The 53 missing shirts will be replaced, but we will have to charge them to your account. In the circumstances we will allow you an extra discount of 10%.

Please let us know in what way we can help in your claim for compensation.

(c) Buyer's claim on railway

We regret to report that two of the cases covered by your consignment receipt number S5621 were delivered to us in a condition that left no doubt of their having been broken into during transit. The cases in question are numbers 4 and 7.

This was noticed when the cases were delivered by your carrier and accordingly we added to our receipt 'Cases 4 and 7 damaged; contents not examined'. A later check of the contents revealed a shortage of 53 shirts.

The consignment was sent by our suppliers on carrier's risk terms. Therefore, we must hold you responsible for the loss. Our claim is enclosed for the invoiced value of the missing shirts (at £4.00 each) which is £212.00. In support of our claim we enclose a certified copy of our supplier's invoice.

The two cases and their contents have been put aside to await your inspection.

Useful expressions

Openings

Enquiries

1 We thank you for your enquiry of . . . and quote as follows for the shipment of . . . to . . . .

2 Thank you for your enquiry regarding sailings to Johannesburg in August.
3 We are due to ship a large quantity of . . . to . . . and need you to obtain a ship of about . . . tons capacity.
4 Please let us know the current rates of freight for the following:
5 Please quote an inclusive rate for collection and delivery of . . . from . . . to . . . .

Goods despatched

1 We have today sent to you a consignment of . . . by SS . . . .
2 We have given instructions to . . . to forward the following consignment to you by rail:

Closes

1 Please inform us of the date on which the ship closes for cargo.
2 Please complete and return the enclosed instructions form with a signed copy of the invoice.
3 We hope to receive your shipping instructions by return.

Glossary

1 **bulk cargoes** those not packed but loaded loose
2 **freight rates** transport charges
3 **remunerative** profitable
4 **deferred rebate** a discount to be allowed later
5 **preferential rate system** a system offering lower freight rates to Conference members
6 **pilferage** small thefts
7 **certificate of origin** a document entitling importer to preferenetial customs duties
8 **consignor** the one who sends the goods
9 **consignee** the one to whom the goods are sent
10 **elaborate** complicated
11 **consequently** as a result
12 **tampered with** improperly interfered with
13 **compensation** an amount of money that makes good the loss

Chapter 23

Insurance

Insurance was originally applied to losses at sea, where risks were always great, but it is now provided to cover almost any kind of occurrence that may result in loss. Its purpose is to provide compensation for those who suffer from loss or damage; in other words, it is a *contract of indemnity*, that is to say a contract to restore to their original position a person who suffers loss. They are not allowed to receive more than they lose, and gain nothing from insuring for a sum greater than the value of the good(s) insured. If a ship worth £20,000 is insured for £25,000, the owner would receive only £20,000 if the ship is lost.

A different kind of insurance is that which provides for payment of a fixed sum in advance to a person when they reach a given age, or to any dependents upon their death. In Britain, this type of insurance is termed *assurance*. It is concerned not with compensation for loss that *may or may not occur*, but with providing security for events that are *certain to occur*.

The insurance contract

A contract of insurance is one between a party who agrees to accept the risk (the insurer) and a party seeking protection from the risk (the insured). In return for payment of a *premium*[1] the insurer agrees to pay the insured a stated sum (or a proportion of it) should the event insured against occur. Premiums are quoted as a percentage of the sum insured – in Britain, at so many pence per £100 (e.g. 25p%).

A person wishing to take out life assurance or accident insurance must usually submit a *proposal form*[2] containing questions which must be answered truthfully. Any other information that is likely to influence the insurer's judgement concerning the risk must also be made known, otherwise the insurer may void the contract. It is not the practice to use proposal forms in marine insurance and only rarely are they used in fire insurance, but, as with other forms of insurance, all information affecting the risk must be disclosed.

If the proposal is accepted the insurer is required by law to issue a policy, which sets out the terms of the contract, including the risk to be covered, the sum insured and the premium to be paid. If at a later date it is desired to alter the terms of the insurance, this is usually done by *endorsing*[3] the existing policy and not by issuing a new one.

A person cannot legally insure a risk for which there is no legal interest.

Anyone may insure their own property, but not that of a neighbour; they may insure the life of a person who owes them money, but only up to the amount owing; shipowners may insure their ships, but not the cargo carried, except for the value of the *freight*[4] lost if the cargo were lost.

23.1 Enquiries for insurance rates

(a) Cash in transit

Dear Sirs

We normally pay into the bank each morning our takings for the preceding business day. The sums involved are sometimes considerable especially at the weekends: takings on a Saturday may amount to as much as £3,000.

We therefore wish to take out insurance cover for the following:

1 Against loss of cash on the premises, by fire, theft, or burglary.

2 Against loss of cash in transit between our premises and the bank.

3 Against accident or injury to staff while engaged in taking money to the bank, or bringing it from the bank.

We bank with the local branch of the Barminster Bank – about half a mile from our premises.

Please let us know on what terms you can provide cover for the risks mentioned.

Yours faithfully

(b) Goods sent by sea

Dear Sirs

We shall shortly have a consignment of tape recorders, valued at £20,000 cif Quebec, to be shipped from Manchester by a vessel of Manchester Liners Ltd.

We wish to cover the consignment against all risks from our warehouse at the above address to the port of Quebec. Will you please quote your rate for the cover.

Yours faithfully

(c) *Request for special rate*

Dear Sirs

We regularly ship consignments of bottled sherry to Australia by both passenger and cargo liners of the Enterprise Shipping Line. Will you please say whether you can issue an all-risks policy for these shipments and, if so, on what terms. In particular we wish to know whether you can issue a special rate in return for the promise of regular monthly shipments.

Yours faithfully

23.2 Applications for insurance cover

(a) *Continuation of 23.1(c)*

Dear Sirs

We thank you for your reply to our enquiry of 6 June. The terms you quote, namely 35p%, less 5% special discount for regular shipments, are acceptable. We understand that these terms will apply to all our shipments of bottled sherry by regular liners to Australian ports and cover all risks, including breakages and pilferage[5].

Our first shipment will be on 2 July for 20 cases of sherry, valued at £2,600, and we shall be glad if you will arrange open-account terms[6] with quarterly settlements.

We look forward to receiving the policy within the next few days.

Yours faithfully

(b) *Insurance of warehouse stock*

(i) *Application*

Dear Sirs

Thank you for your letter of 15 April quoting rates for insurance cover of stock already in our warehouse at the above address. The value of the stock held varies with the season, but does not normally exceed £50,000 at any time. Please arrange cover in this sum for all the risks mentioned in your letter and on the terms quoted, namely, 50% per annum, as from 1 May next.

Yours faithfully

(ii) Acknowledgement

Dear Sir

We acknowledge with thanks your letter of yesterday asking us to
cover you in the sum of £50,000 at 50p% per annum on stock in your
warehouse at 25 Topping Street, Lusaka, as from 1 May. The policy is
now being prepared and it should reach you in about a week's time.

Yours faithfully

(c) Cargo insurance

Dear Sirs

Please arrange full a.a.r.[7] cover in the sum of £5,000 for shipment of
20 Hi-fi music centres to Quebec by MV Merchant Shipper, scheduled to
sail from Manchester on 2 July. The goods are packed in 5 cases
marked AHB 1 - 5, now lying in our warehouse at 25 Manchester Road,
Salford.

Please let us have the policy, and one certified copy, not later than
30 June, and charge the cost to our account.

Yours faithfully

Insurance brokers

Insurance of business risks, and especially of *maritime*[8] risks, calls for special
knowledge, and the advice and help of a qualified insurance broker is often
of great advantage. A broker advises clients on the risks they should cover,
recommends the kinds of insurance best suited to their particular needs and
places the risks with the most suitable insurers.

23.3 Requests to brokers to arrange insurance

(a) Example 1

Dear Sir

Will you please arrange to take out an all-risks insurance for us on the
following consignment of cameras from our warehouse at the above
address to Valletta:

6 c/s Cameras, by SS <u>Endeavour</u>, due to leave Liverpool on 18 August.

The invoiced value of the consignment, including freight and insurance, is £11,460.

Yours faithfully

(b) Example 2

Dear Sirs

Referring to your Ms Taylor's call this morning, we have decided to accept the quotation of 60p% by the Britannia Insurance Co for insurance to cover the transit by road from our works in Birmingham to the Acme Engineering Co, Bristol of two 1¼ tonne boilers on 15 July.

Please arrange the necessary cover and send us the policy as soon as you can.

Yours faithfully

Insurance premiums

Statistics enable insurers to assess the extent of particular risks with considerable accuracy. This helps them to fix their premiums at levels that are fair both to themselves and to the insured. Since premiums vary with the degree of risk, lower rates are charged when protective measures such as fire alarms, *automatic sprinklers*[9], *fire extinguishers*[10] and fire-resistant materials are used.

23.4 Request for reduction in premium

Dear Sirs

POLICY NO F 623104

I am writing to ask you to review the rate of premium charged under the above fire policy for goods in our <u>transit shed</u>[11] at No 4 Dock. The shed, as you know, is also used as a <u>bonded store</u>[12] and storage warehouse.

I make this request because I feel that not enough weight could have been given to the following conditions when the present rate of premium was fixed:

1 The shed is not artificially heated.

2 No power of any kind is used.

3 All rooms are provided with automatic sprinklers, fireproof doors, and fire extinguishers of the latest type.

4 A water main runs round the entire dockside and can be tapped[13] at several points within easy distance of the shed.

When these conditions are taken into account the present rate of premium seems to be unreasonably high. We look forward to your being able to reduce it sufficiently to bring it more into line with the extent of the risk insured under the policy.

Yours faithfully

Householders' policies

Most fire insurance companies offer a wide range of cover on the buildings and contents of private dwellings under what are known as 'Householders' or 'All-risk' policies designed to give protection in one document from a variety of risks besides those usually covered by a fire policy, including storms, riots, burst pipes, burglary, theft, accidents to servants, liability to third parties, accidental breakage of mirrors, etc., but not losses due to war. It is a condition of such cover that both buildings and contents are insured for their full value.

23.5 Application for householder's insurance

(a) Application

Dear Sirs

I have recently bought the property at the above address with possession as from 1 July and wish to take out accidental damage cover on both building and contents in the sums of £80,000 and £15,000 respectively[14]. The former figure represents the estimated rebuilding cost of the property and the latter the full value of the contents.

Please send me particulars of your terms and conditions for the policy and, if one is required, a proposal form.

Yours faithfully

(b) Reply

Dear Sir

HOUSEHOLDERS' COMPREHENSIVE INSURANCE

We thank you for your enquiry of 19 June and enclose a copy of our prospectus containing particulars of our policies for householders.

You will see that we offer two types of cover for buildings. Cover 'B' (premium rate 21p%) is similar to cover 'A' (premium rate 24p%) but excludes cover for accidental damages. For contents we provide only one type of cover, the rate for this being 70p% per annum. As you will see from the prospectus, our comprehensive policies provide a very wide range of cover.

I enclose a proposal form, as requested, and shall be glad if you will complete and return it not later than 7 days before the date from which the policy is to run.

Yours faithfully

23.6 Request for increase in cover

Dear Sirs

HOUSE CONTENTS POLICY NO H 96154

On 2 June I sent you a cheque for £175.00 as the premium due for renewal of the above policy.

I now wish to increase the amount of cover from its current figure of £25,000 to £30,000 (thirty thousand pounds) with immediate effect. Please confirm that you have arranged for this and send me the customary insert indicating the change for inclusion in the policy schedule.

From the conditions that apply to your householders' policies I understand that no charge for the increase in the amount of cover referred to above will be made before my next renewal date.

Yours faithfully

23.7 Notice of increase in premiums

Some insurance companies encourage household policy-holders to increase the amount of cover for buildings and contents by deferring payment of the higher rate of premium until the next renewal of the policy, as in the above letter. Under this arrangement it is possible for the insured to obtain extra cover free of charge for a period of up to twelve months under a policy that is renewable annually.

The following is a letter from an insurance company to its household policy-holders, referring to underinsurance due to inflation.

Dear

Unfortunately, our efforts to encourage household policy-holders to revise the sums insured to take account of inflation[15] have been poorly supported. In the past 5 years the monetary value of property[16] and contents has more than doubled, but most householders have failed to provide for this and in consequence are grossly[17] underinsured. The problem of underinsurance has often been made worse because the initial cover[18] was inadequate[19] from the start. On some recent claims research shows the amount of underinsurance to have been well over 50%.

In this situation we have been reluctantly compelled[20] to introduce in all household insurance a provision[21] automatically increasing the amount of cover at each renewal of the policy. The increase, currently[22] 6%, will be reflected[23] in the amount of premium payable and allowance for this will be made in your next renewal notice.

Yours sincerely

23.8 Request for information concerning cover

Dear

POLICY NO MH 816/89068

Upon receiving your renewal notice on 21 July last I sent you a cheque for £25.50 to extend cover of my premises under the above policy. Unfortunately, I have no record of the amount of cover provided by the premium paid and should be obliged if you would please inform me.

Should the amount of the cover be less than £29,000 I should like to increase it to this amount with immediate effect. Please arrange for this if necessary and send me your account for the amount of additional premium payable. I will then send you a cheque in payment.

Yours sincerely

Holiday insurance

When a holiday is to be taken abroad it is a wise precaution to insure not only against loss of baggage and other personal property but also against personal accident and illness while away from home. If one is taken ill, the costs of medical and hospital care must be borne privately and can be very high. In return for a small premium many insurance companies now provide cover for this. The travel agencies are usually willing to make the necessary arrangements on request.

23.9 Holiday insurance – application and claim

(a) Application

Dear Sirs

I shall be touring Italy and Sicily in a Peugeot 405 GL, 19.. model, during the 4 weeks commencing 3 July.

Will you please inform me of the terms and conditions on which you could issue a policy to cover loss of and damage to baggage and other personal property. I should also like to consider cover against personal accident and illness and should be glad if you would send me particulars. The car is already separately insured.

Yours faithfully

(b) Insurer's reply

Dear

Thank you for your enquiry of 8 June concerning insurance to cover your tour of Italy and Sicily.

We are pleased to enclose a leaflet setting out the terms and conditions of the insurance for both personal property and injury and illness, and also a proposal form. The cover for injury and illness extends to the full cost of medical and hospital treatment and of any special arrangements that may be necessary for your return home.

Please complete and return the proposal form by 26 June at the latest, otherwise we may have difficulty in issuing the policy in time.

Yours sincerely

Fidelity insurance

An employer often seeks protection from the dishonesty of persons employed in positions of trust by taking out a 'Fidelity Guarantee' policy. Employees may be insured either individually or on a group basis under a collective policy guaranteeing a separate amount for each employee. Alternatively, a floating policy may be taken out in which the names of the various employees appear but with one amount of guarantee for the whole.

23.10 Enquiry for a Fidelity Guarantee policy

Dear Sirs

We have recently apointed Mrs Tessa Campbell as our chief accountant. She came to us with excellent references, but as a purely precautionary measure we wish to cover her by a fidelity bond for £100,000.

Please inform us on what terms you can provide this cover and, if one is necessary, send me a proposal form.

Yours faithfully

Temporary cover

No contract comes into being until the proposal made is accepted by the insurer, but where a person wants immediate cover while the proposal is being considered, the insurer is usually willing to grant temporary protection and to issue a *cover note*[24] upon request. The note is usually expressed to provide cover up to a stated date.

In the following correspondence the insurer does not issue a cover note, but nevertheless makes it clear that in fact the property is covered.

23.11 Request for cover pending issue of policy

(a) Householder's request

Dear Sirs

1 MARGATE ROAD, ST ANNES-ON-SEA, LANCS

I have recently bought the property at the above address. A covenant[25] in the deeds requires the property to be insured with your company against fire. In a letter to me dated 30 October the solicitors handling the transfer for me stated that you would be getting in touch with me about this.

Not having heard from you, I am writing as a matter of urgency, to ask you to insure the property under your usual full-cover householder's policy in the sum of £100,000 as from 7 December inclusive. This is the date fixed for the legal transfer of the property to me. The sum mentioned covers the purchase price of £80,000 and estimated rebuilding costs.

In view of the urgency is it too much to ask for your assurance that you will hold the property covered as from and including next Thursday 7 December? I ask this because I am in no position to accept the risks of non-insurance while the policy is being prepared.

Yours faithfully

(b) Insurer's reply

Dear

COMPREHENSIVE INSURANCE
1 MARGATE ROAD, ST ANNES-ON-SEA, LANCS

We thank you for your letter of yesterday and are pleased to inform you that we will hold this property covered for £100,000 as from 7 December on the terms and conditions of the company's comprehensive policy.

A proposal form is enclosed and we shall be glad if you will complete it and return it to us immediately.

Yours sincerely

Claims

Claims for loss or damage should always be made promptly by letter and supported by whatever information or evidence can be offered at the time. If a claim relates to goods delivered, it should be made immediately the loss or damage is discovered:

1 To the insurer, if the goods have been insured by the buyer.
2 To the seller where the insurance has been taken out by them.

23.12 Claim for damage to house property

When a claim is made it is usually necessary for a form of claim to be completed, as in this correspondence.

(a) Householder's claim

Dear Sirs

POLICY NO PK 850046

I am sorry to have to report a slight accident to the Formica[26] top of the sink-unit work-table, which was burnt and cracked when an electric soldering iron was accidentally knocked over upon it.

I have made enquiries and am informed that replacement cost of the damaged Formica will be about £30 (thirty pounds). There will also be an additional charge for fixing.

I should be glad to have your permission to arrange for the work to be carried out. Should you wish to inspect the damage I am at home on most days, but it would be helpful if I could be told when to expect your representative.

Yours faithfully

(b) Insurer's reply

Dear

POLICY NO PK 850046

We refer to your letter of 14 September and our representative's recent call on you, and enclose a claim form. Please complete and return this to us as soon as possible with the contractor's estimate for replacement of the damaged work-table top. We will then deal with the matter immediately.

Yours sincerely

23.13 Insurer requests further information

Sometimes a person suffering a loss gives incomplete, or even inaccurate, information, hoping that by doing so excessive compensation may be recovered. In such cases the insurer either will ask for further information, as in the following letter, or will *dispute*[27] the claim. Such cases are fairly numerous and varied, and the following is only one of the many kinds of letter the insurer may send. It relates to a claim by a contractor for loss of business suffered as a result of damage to a lorry in a road accident.

A person who suffers loss must do whatever possible to limit the loss, otherwise they may fail to get compensation in full.

Dear

We refer to your claim of 17 February for £500 as compensation for loss of business due to damage to your lorry.

Before we can deal with your claim we shall need the following further information from you:

1 What is the actual financial loss suffered as a result of the accident, and how is it calculated?

2 What steps, if any, were taken to hire a suitable lorry until the damaged lorry could be replaced?

3 If no steps to hire were taken, please give the reason.

Immediately we receive the information asked for we will deal with your claim.

Yours sincerely

23.14 Buyer requests seller to make claim

Where, on behalf of the buyer, the seller insures goods in transit, the buyer will report the loss or damage to the seller and ask him to make the claim, as in the following letter.

Dear Sirs

OUR ORDER NO C 541

When the SS Lancastria arrived at Famagusta on 10 November, it was noticed that one side of case number 12 containing the radio receivers was split. We therefore had the case opened and the contents examined by a local insurance surveyor in the presence of the shipping company's agents. The case was invoiced as containing 24 Hacker 'Mayflower' receivers, eight of which were badly damaged.

We enclose the surveyor's report and the shipping agents' statement.

As you hold the insurance policy we should be grateful if you would take the matter up for us with the insurers.

Eight replacement receivers will be required. Please arrange to supply these and charge to our account.

We hope no difficulty will arise in connection with the insurance claim and thank you in advance for your trouble on our behalf.

Yours faithfully

23.15 Claim for damage by fire

(a) Claim

Dear Sirs

POLICY NO AR 3854

I regret to report that a fire broke out in our factory stores last night. The cause is not yet known, but we estimate the damage to stock to be about £30,000. Fortunately, no records were destroyed so that there will be no difficulty in assessing the value of the loss.

Please arrange for your representative to call and let me have your instructions regarding salvage[28].

Yours faithfully

(b) Insurer's reply

Dear

FIRE POLICY NO AR 3854

Thank you for your letter of yesterday reporting the fire in your factory stores.

As a first step will you please make your claim on the enclosed form. Meanwhile, I am arranging for Mr J Watson, a loss adjustor, to call and assess the damage.

Should you need help in completing the claim form he will be able to give it to you.

Yours sincerely

23.16 Insurer declines to meet claim in full (continuation of 23.15)

Whenever it is necessary to convey disappointing or unwelcome news, as when a claim is rejected, or in any other circumstances likely to cause disappointment, the opening paragraph of the letter should be in terms that prepare the receiver for what is coming and soften the blow when it does come. This indirect approach to unwelcome news is used in the following letter.

Dear

POLICY NO AR 3854

When we received your letter of 5 June we sent Mr J Watson to inspect and report on the damage caused by the fire. He has now submitted his report, which confirms your claim that the damage is extensive. He reports, however, that much of the stock damaged or destroyed was either obsolete[29] or obsolescent[30]. We therefore regret that we cannot accept as a fair estimate of the loss the figure of £30,000 mentioned in your letter – a figure which we understand is based on the cost of the goods.

Our own estimate of the stock damaged or destroyed, based on present market values, does not exceed £20,000. We feel that this valuation is a very generous one, but are prepared to pay on it under the policy. We shall be glad to learn that you will accept it in full settlement of your claim for the value of the stock lost.

Yours sincerely

23.17 Claim for injury to worker

(a) Claim

Dear Sirs

POLICY NO 56241

Our foreman, Mr James MacDonald, met with an accident on 2 March. He crushed his thumb when operating a machine. At the time, we did not think the accident was serious enough to report, but Mr MacDonald has returned to his work after an absence of 3 weeks and is still unable to carry on his normal duties. We therefore wish to make a claim under the above policy and shall be glad if you will send us the necessary claim form.

Yours faithfully

(b) Insurer's reply

Dear

POLICY NO 56241

We have received your letter of 27 March and noted your claim for the accident to Mr J MacDonald.

Under the terms of the policy this claim should have been submitted within 3 days of the accident. More than 3 weeks have now passed. Consequently, your claim for compensation under the policy has been forfeited.

Nevertheless, as an exceptional measure, we have decided to overlook its late submission, though we are bound to say that it should have been clear from Mr MacDonald's prolonged absence from work that his accident was more serious than you had supposed and that there seems to be no good reason why the claim should not have been made earlier.

I am enclosing a claim form as requested, but must emphasise that future claims cannot be entertained where the terms of the policy are not complied with.

Yours sincerely

23.18 Request to support illness claim

Claims arising from accident, sickness or similar causes must be supported by medical evidence either from the attendant doctor or from the institution treating the patient.

A patient recovering from an operation is required by their insurance company to provide evidence of any stay in hospital. In the following letter a doctor is asked to complete the form received from the company. By providing the details and enclosing an addressed envelope the patient tries to help a busy doctor.

Dear Dr Edwards

The London Life Insurance Co Ltd, of which I am a member, have asked for completion of the enclosed form of claim for benefits for the period I was in your hospital, and later the Avala Nursing Home.

I have pencilled in the details requested on that side of the form which the company wish you to complete; this may assist you.

To the form I have attached 4 accounts covering both hospital and nursing home accommodation for 6 weeks as follows:

Hospital (23 April to 7 May 19. .)
Nursing Home (7 May to 2 June 19. .)

The company ask that you will return the completed claim to them. I shall be grateful if you will do so and enclose an addressed envelope for the purpose.

Yours sincerely

Marine insurance

Most of the world's business in marine insurance is centred in London though there are other important markets. At the heart of these activities is Lloyd's, a London corporation of insurers who issue most kinds of policy, but are especially active in marine insurance. Lloyd's membership comprises insurers (or underwriters as they are called) and brokers. The underwriters work in *syndicates*[31] specialising in different types of risk. All insurance business with underwriter members must be placed through Lloyd's brokers, but anyone who chooses to place business with insurance companies rather than with Lloyd's may employ any broker, or may deal with the matter directly.

Under the Marine Insurance Act of 1906 all marine insurance contracts must be in the form of a policy. Marine policies may be either *valued* or *unvalued*, both classes being further subdivided into *voyage policies*, *time policies*, *mixed policies* and *floating* or *open policies*. A *valued policy* is one based on values agreed in advance and stated in the policy. With an *unvalued policy* the value of any loss (within the limit of the sum insured) is left to be assessed at the time of the loss.

A *voyage policy*, like a voyage charter, covers a particular ship for a stated voyage (e.g. London to Melbourne). A *time policy*, like a time charter, covers a particular ship for an agreed period of time not exceeding twelve months (e.g. from noon 5 April 1991 to noon 5 April 1992). A *mixed policy* combines the features of both time and voyage policies.

Policies may be issued to cover 'All risks', or they may contain clauses relieving the underwriter of certain risks. The premium for an all-risks policy is naturally higher than that for a policy with exemptions.

23.19 Request for an all-risks policy

(a) Request

Dear Sir/Madam

We wish to insure the following consignment against all risks for the sum of £2,000.

4 c/s Fancy Leather Goods, marked ☐ AS

1–4

These goods are now lying at Number 2 Dock, Liverpool, waiting to be shipped by SS Rajputana, due to leave for Bombay on Friday 23 June.

We require immediate cover as far as Bombay and shall be grateful if you will let us have the policy as soon as it is ready. In the meantime please confirm that you hold the consignment covered.

Yours faithfully

(b) Reply

Dear

Thank you for your letter of 16 June asking us to cover the consignment of 4 cases of fancy leather goods from Liverpool to Bombay.

The premium for this cover is at the rate of £2.30% of the declared value of £2,000. The policy is being prepared and will be sent to you within a few days. Meanwhile, we confirm that we hold the consignment covered as from today.

Yours sincerely

23.20 Request to insure goods at docks

Dear Sir

Please arrange to insure for one calendar month from today the following consignment ex SS Ansdell from Hamburg:

2 cases Cameras, marked 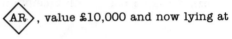 , value £10,000 and now lying at Royal Victoria Dock.

Please confirm that you hold the consignment covered and, when sending the policy, enclose your account for the premium.

Yours faithfully

Floating and open-cover policies

Floating policies are sometimes used by merchants engaged in regular overseas trade. A policy of this kind covers a number of shipments by any ship to any port or ports that may be agreed. The merchant takes out a policy for a round sum, say £50,000. As each consignment is shipped it is 'declared' on a special form provided by the underwriter, who records the value on a duplicate copy of the policy and issues a *certificate of insurance* stating that the consignment is covered. When the sum insured has been fully declared, that is, used up, a new policy is taken out.

Floating policies are sometimes referred to as 'Open' or 'Declaration' policies; but they are not greatly used today, being largely replaced by long-term policies issued on open cover. These open-cover policies extend the floating policy principle and cover all shipments for certain voyages or trades for an extended period, usually a year, *irrespective of their aggregate value*[32], which may not be known, but with a specified limit for each shipment. The arrangement avoids any risk that a shipment will be left uninsured through oversight.

23.21 Enquiry for open-policy terms

(a) Enquiry

Dear Sirs

Please quote your rate for an all-risks open policy for £100,000 to cover shipments of general merchandise[33] by Manchester Liners Ltd, from Manchester and Liverpool to Atlantic ports in Canada and the United States.

As shipments are due to begin on 30 June, please let us have your quotation by return.

Yours faithfully

(b) Reply

Dear

I am replying to your enquiry of yesterday. Our rate for a £100,000 A R open policy on general merchandise by Manchester Liners from Manchester and Liverpool to Atlantic ports in Canada and the United States is £2.10% of declared value.

This is an exceptionally low rate and we trust you will give us the opportunity to handle your insurance business.

Yours sincerely

(c) Acceptance

Dear

Thank you for your letter of 19 June quoting your rate for an open policy of £100,000 covering consignments on the routes named.

The rate of £2.10% is satisfactory and we shall be glad if you will now prepare and send us the policy and meanwhile let us have your cover note and statement of charges for the following, our first, shipment under the policy:

3 c/s General Merchandise (Textiles), marked Value £2,500.

Yours sincerely

23.22 Application for an open policy

Dear Sirs

We shall shortly be making regular shipments of fancy leather goods to South America by approved ships and shall be glad if you will issue an a/r open policy for, say, £50,000 to cover these shipments from our warehouse at the above address to port of destination.

All goods will be packed in wooden cases and despatched by road to Southampton and, less frequently, to Liverpool.

Yours faithfully

23.23 Declaration of shipment off open policy

When accepting application in 23.23 the underwriter will send the policy (original) to the merchant and also a supply of declaration forms, one of which the merchant will complete and send to the underwriter each time goods are shipped.

Dear Sirs

POLICY NO 18752

Please note that under the above open policy, dated 18 March 19.., we have today shipped a third consignment, valued at £1,620, by SS Durham Castle, due to sail from Southampton tomorrow. We enclose the necessary declaration form. This leaves an undeclared value on the policy of £48,380 and perhaps you will be good enough to confirm this figure.

Yours faithfully

23.24 Renewal of an open policy (continuation of 23.24)

Dear Sir

POLICY NO 18752

We enclose a completed form declaring a further consignment, valued £2,325.

This will be the last full declaration under the above policy as the undeclared balance now stands at only £825, which will not be sufficient to cover our next consignment in December. Will you therefore please issue a new policy on the same terms and for the same amount, namely £50,000, as the current policy. When we make the next shipment, we shall declare it against the present policy for £825 and against the new policy for the amount by which the value of the shipment exceeds this amount.

Yours faithfully

Average

Average is a term used in marine insurance to refer to partial losses. *Particular average* means partial loss or damage caused by accident to the ship or to some particular cargo. Such losses are borne by the owner of the particular property suffering the damage. *General average* on the other hand refers to loss or damage *deliberately incurred*[34] for the common good at a time when a ship and its cargo are in danger, as when cargo is thrown overboard to save the ship in a storm. Losses of this kind are shared by all who have a financial interest in the *venture*[35] in *proportion to*[36] the value of their interests.

As a rule, the manufacturer or merchant insures goods 'against all risks' and receives a WA policy containing a 'with average' clause. This means that the underwriters pay for partial losses. Under an FPA policy, which contains a 'free from particular average' clause the underwriters pay only for total losses. An FPA policy will therefore be issued for a lower premium than a WA policy.

Motor insurance

The owner of a motor vehicle must possess a current road licence and is also required by law to insure against accidents to third parties, against death and bodily injury, and up to £250,000 for damages to property (1988 Road Traffic Act). It is customary, but not compulsory, to insure against loss or damage to the vehicle. All these risks may be covered by what is termed a 'comprehensive' policy, i.e. a single policy providing all-inclusive cover.

23.25 Renewal of policy

Dear Mr Wrenshell

POLICY NO M 346871

Your policy and certificate of insurance as required by the Road Traffic Acts will expire at noon on 3 April next.

To maintain the insurance in force instructions should be given to your broker not later than, but preferably 5 days before, the date on which the policy expires so that you may receive the new certificate of insurance in time. You will realise that it is an offence under the Road Traffic Acts to use a vehicle on the road without a current certificate of insurance.

As a protection to you against any failure to observe the Acts I am enclosing a temporary cover note and certificate of insurance, but would remind you that this extension of cover applies only to that part of the policy, namely third party personal injury liability and damage to third party property, which is necessary to comply with[37] the requirements of the Road Traffic Acts. The temporary cover note should be kept carefully until the certificate of insurance reaches you.

Yours sincerely

Useful expressions

Requests for cover

Openings

1 Please quote your lowest All Risks rates for shipments of . . . to . . . .
2 Please hold us covered for the consignment referred to below (on the attached sheet).
3 We should be glad if you would provide cover of £. . . on . . ., in transit from . . . to . . . .
4 We wish to renew the above policy for the same amount and on the same terms as before to cover . . . .

Closes

1 Please inform us on what terms this insurance can be arranged.
2 Please send us the necessary proposal form.
3 We leave the details to you, but wish to have the consignment covered against All Risks.
4 The consignment is covered by our open policy Number . . . and we shall be glad to receive your certificate of insurance.

Replies to requests for cover

Openings

1 As requested in your letter of . . . we quote below our terms for arranging cover for . . . .
2 As requested in your letter of . . . we will arrange cover for the amount stated and on the terms required.
3 We note from your letter of . . . that you wish to renew open policy number . . . covering . . . .

Closes

1 The policy is being prepared and should reach you by . . . . In the meantime we are holding you covered.
2 We undertake all classes of insurance and would welcome the opportunity to transact further business with you.

Claims

Openings

1 I regret to report the loss of . . . insured with you under the above policy.
2 I regret to report a fire in one of the bedrooms at this address.
3 I have completed and enclose the form of claim for loss of . . . .
4 With reference to your letter of . . . in which you claim for . . . (To enable us to consider your claim dated . . . for . . .), please complete and return the enclosed claim form.

Closes

1 Please let us know what particulars (information) you need from us when we submit our claim.
2 If you will make out your claim on the enclosed form we will attend to it immediately.
3 Your claim will be carefully considered when we receive the information asked for.

Glossary

1 **premium** the payment made for insurance
2 **proposal form** a written request for insurance cover
3 **endorsing** writing on the back of a document
4 **freight** the charge for carriage of goods
5 **pilferage** small thefts
6 **open-account terms** credit terms with periodic statements
7 **a.a.r.** against all risks
8 **maritime** relating to the sea
9 **automatic sprinklers** a system which, when overheated, releases water
10 **extinguisher** an appliance for putting out fires
11 **transit shed** a shed through which goods pass
12 **bonded store** a warehouse for goods liable to customs duty
13 **tapped** used for drawing water
14 **respectively** relating to each in turn
15 **inflation** a rise in the general level of prices
16 **property** premises
17 **grossly** very much; considerably
18 **initial cover** the value insured at the beginning
19 **inadequate** insufficient
20 **reluctantly compelled** forced unwillingly
21 **provision** a term or condition in an agreement
22 **currently** at the present time
23 **reflected** included; covered by
24 **cover note** a document giving temporary insurance cover pending issue of policy
25 **covenant** a clause in a deed (a sealed contract)
26 **Formica** the trade name for a form of hard protective boarding

27 **dispute** to contest; oppose
28 **salvage** items that can be recovered
29 **obsolete** out of date
30 **obsolescent** becoming out of date
31 **syndicates** groups formed for a common purpose
32 **irrespective of their aggregate value** apart from their total worth
33 **merchandise** articles of commerce
34 **deliberately incurred** done intentionally
35 **venture** the voyage and its risks
36 **in proportion to** according to
37 **comply with** carry out; observe

Assignments on material included in this chapter can be found on pp 366–7.

Appendix

Assignments in practical letter writing

Letter writing tasks from most major examining bodies are shown here. They are categorised into the different types of letter, and within each section the assignments progress in difficulty.

The following abbreviations are used to indicate the examinations from which these questions are taken:

LCCI (The London Chamber of Commerce and Industry)
    EFB English for Business
    EFC English for Commerce
    SSC Secretarial Studies Certificate
    PSC Private Secretary's Certificate

PITMAN (Pitman Examinations Institute)
    EFS English for the Secretary
    EBC English for Business Communications

Chapter 1 Introducing the business letter

In the following organisations, identify which are partnerships and which are companies formed with limited liability. Where it is not a UK company, can you identify in which part of the world the company operates?

Sir Thomas Marsden & Co
H Hopkinson Sons plc
Messrs Johnson and Jones
Hopkinson Transport Pte Ltd
Brighter Windows Inc
Junior Clothing PLC
Clark's Manufacturing Co Ltd
Trainers Incorporated
Reef Traders Pty Ltd

2

Set out complimentary closes, signatures and designations for the following letters:
(a) A letter addressed 'For the attention of Mr Gary Hatton, Purchasing Manager', from Mr Derek Holmes, General Manager.
(b) A letter beginning 'Dear Caroline' to be signed by Ms Jacqueline Hatton, Training Manager.
(c) A letter beginning 'Dear Miss Clark', to be signed by Miss Angela Marshall in the absence of Mr Jeffrey Garrison, Managing Director.

3

Set out the reference/date/(attention line?) inside address/salutation and complimentary close/signature/name/designation/(enclosures?) for the following letters (you may assume all letters will be dated today and typed by you):
(a) A letter from Mrs Eileen England, Managing Director, to Mr Russell Conway, General Manager of Electronic Keyboards PLC, 21 High Street, Ashton, Sheffield S31 2RT, enclosing a cheque.
(b) A letter to Mrs Joy French, Purchasing Director, Phillips Tool Manufacturers Pte Ltd, Block 24, Jurong East Industrial Estate, Singapore 2933, from Michael Johnson, General Manager of Johnson Tools plc (UK).
(c) A letter for the attention of Mr John McInally, Sales Manager of Gordon Grills Ltd, 24 Jingle Hill, Leeds LS34 3JT, from Ms Linda Peters, Purchasing Manager.

4

Imagine the letters in Assignment 2 have to be continued onto a second page. Set out correct continuation sheet headings for the letters.

5

Set out correctly addressed envelopes for the letters in Assignment 2.

Chapter 2 Getting the message across

1

Rewrite these sentences in a more suitable tone:
(a) We no longer stock the goods you ordered.
(b) The goods were perfectly OK when we packed them, so the breakages must have been caused by rough handling by the railway authorities in transit. You should take this up with them.
(c) The curtains you bought were from a faulty batch and we are now replacing them.
(d) We cannot deliver the goods until you pay for the previous order we sent you.

2

Rewrite these sentences so that they sound more natural:
- (a) Please be good enough to inform us when you will be able to deliver to us the goods we have ordered.
- (b) I have pleasure in informing you that the goods you require are now available and will be delivered to you within the course of the next few days.
- (c) Please favour us with your early reply giving your comments on the matter to hand.

3

Rewrite these sentences in simple language:
- (a) We wish to apologise for the error we made pertaining to your order which was the fault of our despatch section.
- (b) I am writing to request you to forward to me an up-to-date catalogue and price list of all your goods.
- (c) I am sorry to have to inform you that we will not be in a position to despatch the goods as ordered by you until the beginning of next month, because of late despatch from our suppliers.
- (d) We express our regret that we are unable to repair your garage roof at the present moment in time due to pressures of other work in hand.

4

Rewrite the following sentences, replacing the commercial jargon with more suitable expressions:
- (a) Enclosed please find our current catalogue.
- (b) We hope to receive your comments on this matter at your earliest convenience.
- (c) We sincerely trust that the goods will sufficiently interest you to secure your valued order.
- (d) We are very glad to accept your kind offer with full appreciation of your kind consideration in this matter.
- (e) We sincerely hope that you will be able to give your consideration to this request in the very near future.

Chapter 3 Structuring the body of the letter

1

As the office manager of a large fruit-packing company you have been asked to investigate the costs of a day's summer outing for both the office and factory workers. Write a letter to a local coach company asking for a quotation for the hire of coaches for a day's excursion of your choice. Specify the number of people, the time of departure and return, and the destination. Make up any necessary details.

(LCCI EFB1 1991)

2

You have recently seen in your local paper an advertisement for a domestic appliance which you would like to purchase if you were satisfied with its performance. Write a letter of about 100 words to the distributor, mentioning the appliance advertised and requesting that a representative be sent to your home in order to give a demonstration of its operation. Offer a choice of days and times.

(LCCI EFB1 1991)

3

Your local authority proposes to demolish a building of historical (or architectural) interest in your own town in order to provide space for a supermarket (or an office block). Write a letter of about 100 words to the editor of a local newspaper, either supporting or opposing the proposal. Give sensible reasons to justify your attitude.

(LCCI EFC1 1991)

4

Study the structure of the following letter and note how it falls into the four-point plan as discussed. Then underline or highlight the points which require comment in the reply.

LONDON CHILDREN'S TELEVISION
Broadcasting Centre
Eastern Avenue
London SW1 2TV   Telephone 071-875 4322

Ref SY/EF

3 December 1990

Mrs J Hamley-Brown
Marketing Director
Comlon International plc
Comlon House
West Street
London SW1Y 2AR

Dear Mrs Hamley-Brown

APPEARANCE ON 'JOLLY ROGER'

It was a pleasure to meet you last week, and I am now able to confirm that we are pleased to accept your kind offer to help with our programme reviewing the 'Jolly Roger year'.

Your account of the sale of miniature toys just after last Christmas in aid of our Appeal for the Third World will make an enjoyable reminder of one of our most successful appeals.

I should be grateful if you would let me have a first draft of your script by 14 December.

We hope to hold a programme planning meeting to discuss the script with you on 18 December at 1000 hours. Please let me know if this will be convenient.

I look forward to seeing you at the meeting.

Yours sincerely

Susan Yim (Ms)
Producer
JOLLY ROGER Programme

(Adapted from LCCI SSC 1990)

Mrs Hamley-Brown wishes you to compose a letter for her signature in reply to 4. Plan your reply carefully and present a letter for her signature, incorporating the following notes:
- Have already written some of the script – need to know how long it should be. Also worried about what to include in it: should it outline Comlon's commercial operations? What about the level of language suitable for a children's programme?
- Confirm attendance at meeting.

(Adapted from LCCI SSC 1990)

Chapter 4 Enquiries and replies

Your employer Mr B Turnbridge of Turnbridge & Scott, Architects, Pinacle House, High Road, Watford WE6 9PL, wishes to have information about a new photocopier he has seen advertised in *Business World*. Write a letter to the Manager, Excell Copiers, Newbridge Office Block, Luton LU5 7RF, explaining where Mr Turnbridge saw the advertisement and asking for details of the XR66 machine. It is most important that the copier they buy is able to reduce and enlarge easily. A demonstration would be appreciated if this is possible.

(PITMAN EBC Elementary)

2

Write a correctly laid out reply, in 150–200 words, to the following letter of enquiry:

Gable Insurance Bureau
200 Ramsay Lane
Coventry
CV32 2VJ   Telephone 586828

SG/SAT

11 March 1991

Ideal Decorators
75 Fisher Street
Birmingham
BP57 8OP

Dear Sirs

EXTERNAL AND INTERNAL DECORATION OF OFFICES

Every 4 years we have our offices redecorated – including painting and new wallpaper – both externally and internally. James Coggan of Canterbury Street, Coventry, did this for us for many years but has now retired. Mr Coggan recommended your company to us.

We would like to have this job done when the offices are closed for our annual holidays during the first 3 weeks in August. Can you undertake this for us? If so, you must guarantee that the job will be finished on time so that we can open our office to the public on a prescribed date. If you are interested, would you please contact us to make an appointment for your representative to visit us to give an estimate for the job?

Mr Coggan said that he used to co-operate with you in jobs quite frequently some years ago but has lost touch with you recently. He has now moved to Devon and if you would like his address to resume contact with him, we can supply you with it.

We look forward to hearing from you.

Yours faithfully

Simon Gable

(LCCI EFC1 1991)

3

Clacton Business Properties has just received the following letter, which Richard Berry gives to you saying, 'Draft a reply to this letter under my name, please. Tell Mr Singh that at present there are no main-street premises available. There are, however, two empty shops in Dexter Avenue, just off the main street. Get details of them from Mary Smith to enclose with my reply, will you? If Mr Singh is interested in the properties in Dexter Avenue, ask him to contact us and we shall be happy to show him round them. If he *must* have a shop on the main street, say we will send him details immediately any come on the market.'

Write an appropriate reply to the letter.

35 Bingham Terrace
London LV2 2NO

Clacton Business Properties
112 Morse Avenue
Clacton
Essex
PO21 3MP

23 April 1991

Dear Sirs

A business colleague of mine has recommended you as a reputable business property agency and so I am writing to you as I wish to open a shop in your area.

I own four shoe shops in London and would like to dispose of one of them and open another one in Clacton. Have you any suitable premises for sale in the main street of Clacton? As I sell several brands of footwear it must be quite a large property.

Do you arrange mortgages? If not, could you advise me of where to apply for one?

If you find suitable premises for me, could you sell the shop I wish to close in London? If so, how do your rates of commission compare with those in London?

When I open the Clacton shop I shall have my son as its manager. He, naturally, would like to live in Clacton so could you please send me details of any houses – detached with four bedrooms – that you may have for sale?

I look forward to hearing from you.

Yours faithfully

M Singh

(LCCI EFB2 1991)

Chapter 5 Quotations, estimates and tenders

As Manager of the Dalmeny Hotel, Ramsgate, you are considering installation of a generator designed to provide an independent electricity supply. Write a letter to Lighting Installations Ltd asking for an estimate. Point out that the hotel has 60 bedrooms on 3 floors and the usual public rooms. Ask for suggestions and advice.

Compose a reply to Assignment 1 from the Manager of Lighting Installations Ltd recommending that the 'Starlight' system would meet their requirements. However, before submitting an estimate you would like to arrange for the premises to be inspected. Suggest a date and time in the following week, and ask for a phone call if the appointment will not be convenient.

Chapter 6 Orders and their fulfilment

You received an order (number MH345) from Mason Haberdashery Company requesting delivery within 3 days. Write a letter to the Purchasing Manager telling him that the goods have been despatched by parcel post today. Tactfully point out the inconvenience of fulfilling orders at such short notice, and ask for more notice in the future.

You belong to the Easy Listening Record Club, Globe House, Teddington, Middlesex, MB7 9UP. They operate a system whereby you gain bonus certificates if you pay promptly. Recently you purchased two records, paid within the required time and thus qualified for five bonus certificates. When you received the next newsletter and list of records on offer you should have also been sent these five bonuses, but they were not in the envelope. Write a letter to the club clearly explaining the situation. State the titles of the two records you bought and give the date on which you made the payment. Your club membership number is C975TP and should be used as your reference.

(PITMAN EBC Elementary)

Chapter 7 Invoicing and settlement of accounts

One of your customers has deducted 2½% from the amount owing on his last statement, but he settled his account 3 weeks after the period allowed for credit had expired. Write a tactful letter pointing this out and stating that the amount unpaid (£7.32) will be carried forward to the next statement.

Your company has bought goods on credit, but is now in financial difficulties because of a fire which destroyed much of your stock. You have naturally placed a claim with your insurance company but this will take some time to resolve. Write a letter to one of your major suppliers saying you are presently unable to make payment on their latest statement and asking them if you may defer payment for 3 months. Your letter must explain the situation fully and endeavour to create confidence.

Write a letter from Mr Tillbrook, Sales Manager of Ace Paper Ltd, 76 Longton Road, Great Clacton, Essex CM7 2TH, to Mr Parkhurst, Purchasing Manager of Good Read Books, West House, Middleton, Suffolk SJ7 5MQ, telling him that in view of the long connection between the two firms and the prompt way in which invoices have been paid they are going to allow them an extra 5% trade discount on all their orders from 1 January next. Inform him also that as from that date Mr Tillbrook is being promoted and that the new Sales Manager will be Mr Andrew Jackson who will be calling to visit Mr Parkhurst before the end of the year. Date the letter 1 November.

(PITMAN EBC Elementary)

Chapter 8 Letters requesting payment

Your Company is finding it difficult to meet accounts promptly owing to bad trade in your area during the winter months. You have received a statement from Garson Toys, a major supplier, requesting payment of a large sum which you are presently unable to meet. Compose a convincing letter explaining the situation and requesting an extension of credit for a few months.

A long-standing customer in Dubai, United Arab Emirates, has regularly paid his accounts promptly by banker's draft. However, payment of his latest account is now 8 weeks overdue. The sum due is £4,235. You wrote to him a month ago, but received no reply. Compose a suitable second letter.

Chapter 9 Complaints and adjustments

Write a letter from the Purchasing Manager, Mr James Jones, of Quick Assembly Kitchens, 92 London Road, Berkhamstead BS4 6TU, to the Sales Manager of Browns Timber Ltd, Maldon Road, Stevenage, complaining about the quality of the last delivery of teak finish wood they have received from the firm. In the past the quality of goods has always been very good but if the quality is not up to the required standard the firm will have to look elsewhere for a supplier.

(PITMAN EBC Elementary)

Use about 100–200 words to reply to the following letter of complaint:

2 Sandford Road
Gillingham
Kent
LA33 O54

25 April 1991

Ace Record Club
Savoy Lane
Doncaster
MA48 L68

Dear Sirs

I am writing to complain that for the past 2 months I have been sent the wrong records.

As you know, members of your club select the cut-price records they wish to buy from the monthly list you send to them. Last month I was sent 2 records by the Beatles instead of the 2 Mozart symphonies I had ordered, and this month you sent me another Beatles' recording instead of the Beethoven sonatas I had asked for.

This is wasting my time and is most annoying. What is the reason for these errors? Have you any problems? Are you understaffed? Is the volume of work too much for you to manage?

Whatever the reason, if this kind of mistake occurs again I shall resign from the club.

Yours faithfully

Charles Bentley
(LCCI EFC2 1991)

3

The East Saxon Omnibus Company, based at The Monument, Westwood, Lancashire PN3 7AJ, is cutting back its services. One of the services it plans to cut is one which brings most employees to work at Brindley's Engineering Ltd at Wordworth Road on the Ferry Estate in Westwood (postcode PN7 3AN).

'Are they mad?' James Brindley asks, when he hears the news. 'Don't they know how important that bus service is to the factory and the community?'

The works foreman at Brindley's says 'If it happens, we'll all have to look for other jobs. Unfortunately most of us are too old to move.'

James Brindley considers other points too in a letter to the bus company:
- No workers, no factory – no factory, no business income for the council – and then who would need bus services?
- Shouldn't they cut back on other services first – like leisure and non-essential, non-peak services?
- Why not simply raise fares a little – or ask for help (and guidance) from local employers?
- Without this bus service, this factory – and others around us – will die.
- Wouldn't be surprised if they don't get all fares the bus crews collect – better not mention that though!

Write the letter Mr Brindley sends to the bus company.
(LCCI EFC3 1991)

Chapter 10 Credit and status enquiries

Your company has received a large order from H. Langford & Co, Derby, a firm with whom you have not previously done business. The firm has supplied two trade references. Write a suitable letter to be sent to both referees, stressing that the order is for £3,000 and requesting relevant advice or information.

2

You are Office Manager at Dunn's Wholesale Confectionery Co. Reply to the following letter welcoming Mr Baird as a new customer, but pointing out that a bank reference is needed before goods can be supplied. If that is satisfactory he can pay monthly, but also add that we stick strictly to payment dates. Mention that Tuesday is our normal delivery day for Glasgow but to save him making special arrangements to receive deliveries, we will ask our local manager to arrange to deliver on Wednesday mornings.

BAIRD'S SWEETS
4 Jutland Road
Glasgow
G62 36R   Telephone 483848

LB/ST

23 April 1990

Dunn's Wholesale Confectionery
200–220 Mars Road
London
EC6 MB5

Dear Sirs

Two days ago I sent to you my first monthly order for confectionery, wholesale value £1,900. I forgot to ask if you deliver on any special day of the week. My shop is closed on Tuesday so if that is your delivery day, I shall have to arrange for somebody to meet your van.

I should like to pay for my goods at the end of each month as I do with my other suppliers. Is this acceptable to you?

I look forward to doing business with you.

Yours faithfully

L Baird

(LCCI EFB1 1990)

Chapter 12 Goodwill letters

Thompson Manufacturing Co have placed a number of important orders over the past year. Their Sales Manager has sent you a Christmas card expressing his thanks and seasonal greetings, together with a gift. Send a suitable letter thanking him for his gift, which you very much appreciate.

2

The Managing Director of Adsons Insulation Ltd, with whom you have had business dealings for over a decade, has just been honoured with an OBE in recognition for his services to local community affairs. Write a letter congratulating him.

3

Your firm J. W. Bright & Sons Ltd, 67 Station Road, Carlsbrook, Essex CM8 9UP, have recently appointed a new office manager – Mr John Green – who will replace Mr Steven Carter. Write a letter to be signed by the Managing Director – Mr J W Bright – to one of your customers, Mr G Cutmore, Quick Autosales, 72 Mersea Road, Colchester, Essex CM8 7YT inviting him and his wife to a reception to mark Mr Carter's retirement and to introduce Mr Green to them. It is to be held on 3 December at 7.30 pm at The Old Anchor Hotel, Kelvedon.

(PITMAN EBC Elementary)

4

Erich Rein, Production Manager of Gunther Engineering, says to you, 'We have just received this letter. Will you please write a reply to it under my name? Jim Billings from the Birmingham branch mentioned this company to me when I was in the United Kingdom recently. He said they'd been very good customers for many years but for the last two they have been late with payments – going well over our 30-day limit – and Jim was wondering if they had cash flow problems. We must be very tactful as we don't want to lose them. Politely decline their request and say that we will ask Jim to contact them to discuss – hopefully – a way out of the problem.'

McArthur Cycle Co Ltd
Grant's Lane
Stoke-on-Trent
UR9 9MB
UK

3 April 1991

Gunther Engineering
Emilien Str 100
2000 Hamburg
Germany

Dear Sirs

For several years your Birmingham works in this country have been supplying us with parts for our cycles and we have been pleased with this service. However, for the last 18 months or 2 years things have deteriorated. We send orders and are told that they cannot be met until we have paid the accounts for previous deliveries. This causes problems for us. We have always paid our bills – even if not always within 30 days – but as we are known customers is this really essential?

Would it be possible to transfer our custom to your branch in the hope of getting more efficient service? If so, I can then give you full details of our requirements.

Yours faithfully

Richard McArthur
Managing Director
(LCCI EFB2 1991)

Chapter 13 Circular letters

On 4 February, Far & Wide Travel, a firm which arranges package holidays, was informed that the Seaside Hotel at Montego Bay, which was to be used during the forthcoming season, had been badly damaged by a hurricane and would not therefore be available to accommodate their clients. As secretary to the Sales Manager, prepare a circular letter to be sent to clients who have reserved holidays at this hotel. Explain that a limited number of vacancies are available at other hotels; holiday price unchanged; same amenities and standards, etc. Some hotels are away from the beach; 5 kms from Montego Bay; have swimming pools etc; free transport provided from hotel to coast during holiday; 20% discount given if booked immediately; money refunded; deposits returned.

(PITMAN EBC Intermediate)

You are the Secretary for a charity organisation (such as Oxfam or Save the Children Fund). Choose some area of the world, suffering from the effects of famine, drought, earthquake or some other disaster. Write a letter to be circularised or printed in a newspaper, appealing for help. Describe the disaster and its effects, the condition of the people and their needs. Ask for urgent help in the form of money, food and clothes.

(PITMAN EBC Intermediate)

You work for Mr Austin Canterbury, Managing Director of Comlon International plc who, following the publication in May of a government-sponsored report on the effects of 'passive' smoking, felt that, perhaps, it was his responsibility to encourage a ban on smoking throughout Comlon. After consulting with union representatives he decided to test the opinion of everybody in the organisation, including his fellow Directors, several of whom are smokers. You were asked to prepare a special newsletter to be sent in his name to all employees.

Use the following notes, made by you during your discussion with Mr Canterbury:

- 20% of Comlon staff – smokers
- 20 years ago most adults in Britain smoked – fashionable
- Today balance has shifted – 2 out of 3 adults non-smokers – but non-smokers still on defensive – no redress if smokers refuse to stop smoking
- Government Report claims non-smokers have between 10% and 30% greater chance of developing lung cancer if working with smokers
- Several complaints received from staff – ill-feeling caused – both sides
- Health hazard to non-smokers
- Smell also unpleasant
- Small fire in waste paper basket in Kensington – discarded cigarette end – no serious damage
- Employees' opinion sought – total ban on smoking will be imposed if a clear majority in favour
- Decision to be made at a special meeting of the Board of Directors on Tuesday 13 June.

Draft a suitable newsletter. You may add any relevant information you feel to be necessary. Use approximately 250 words.

(LCCI PSC 1989)

Chapter 14 Sales letters

1

Your company is shortly to launch a Business Class car rental service intended to appeal particularly to executives. All business customers, whose names and business addresses are kept on file at the Central Reservations Office, are to be informed by letter of the new service, which will become available from Monday 14 August 19.--

As Secretary to John Browning, Sales Manager (UK), you have been asked to compose a letter announcing the new service and incorporating the following points:

Cars need to be booked only one hour in advance. If the preferred car is not available a more expensive model will be supplied at no extra cost. Presentation of a Business Class Rental Agreement will secure reduction of room rates at selected hotels in both this country and abroad. It will secure other benefits and privileges at these hotels, e.g. a free daily paper.

Customers can choose from a wide range of models and all major makes. All cars are given a comprehensive pre-rental check. Rates cover unlimited mileage and personal accident insurance for driver and passengers. There is a round-the-clock emergency service. Telephones are installed in all the prestige cars – a boon to the busy executive. One-way journeys are possible – there is no need to return vehicles to the original hire centres. Cars can be 'dropped off' at any of your locations.

Rates are only slightly above those for the regular and tourist services. Bookings can be made through travel agents, any company location or the

CRO (telephone 071-438-6275). A tariff is enclosed. A list of your locations is also enclosed. Business Class users receive preferential treatment at all Comlon Reservation desks.

(LCCI SSC 1989)

2

The Directors of Comlon International plc have decided to enter the catering equipment market. The company has recently become the sole UK distributor for the Vendeuse range of food-vending machines, which are manufactured in France. The Directors believe that Comlon's reputation for high quality catering will help them to secure a substantial share of the expanding market for vending machines. The Sales and Marketing Director has decided that a letter should be sent to Comlon's industrial and local government customers to announce the company's entry into the vending machine market, and to point out the machine's advantages.

Compose a suitable letter using the following notes:

Sole distributor for UK. Will supply and install the machines on customers' premises. Will stock machines with high quality snacks and hot and cold beverages. Cooked meals (varied menus) can be supplied on a daily basis. The machines will also dispense confectionery. The company will provide an inexpensive and efficient inspection and maintenance service. Research has shown that capital outlay on vending machines can, in the right circumstances, be recovered in a few months. Vending machines provide a round-the-clock catering service – no need for kitchen staff to work unsocial hours. Particularly useful in the evening when main restaurant/canteen/refectory facilities not available. At midday, vending machines can help to ease queuing and congestion in canteens. Comlon will advise on siting of machines. Machines available for hire as well as purchase. Complete enclosed Freepost card for brochure.

(LCCI SSC 1987)

3

You work for Mrs Maria Hayes, Public Relations Manager of Comlon Holidays plc. Information gained from questionnaires completed by Comlon clients suggests that although many clients do rebook with the Company, many other satisfied clients do not. It has been decided therefore to use mail shots to remind previous customers of the services and high standards available from Comlon.

Mrs Hayes has therefore asked you to draft a suitable letter for her to sign. The letter is to be sent to all recent Comlon clients enclosing the latest general brochure and simple form on which customers can request more information about Comlon's holidays – short period tours, package tours and special interest tours. Clients should be asked to specify the departure point from the list offered by Comlon. The high quality of the service and the Company's good name should be stressed. Comlon has also produced a short promotional video (VHS format only) which customers can request on the form. A returnable £5 deposit is required for the video.

Produce the letter and the form.

(LCCI SSC 1990)

Chapter 15 Personnel

Write a letter to your employer regretfully tendering your resignation on health grounds. Say that you are deeply sorry to have to leave after 15 years' connection with the company, but your decision has been made after much careful thought. Include in your letter an appreciation for the help and kindness shown by your seniors, and also how you have enjoyed the pleasant working relationship with your colleagues.

As Managing Director, write a letter suitable to send to two members of staff giving notice of dismissal on the grounds of redundancy. Since the recent computerisation of the Accounts Department, you regretfully have no option but to take these measures in view of fewer staff being needed. Make sure your letter is tactful, sympathetic and helpful.

Write a letter of application enclosing full details of your qualifications and experience, for the following post advertised in your local paper:

Personal Secretary required, male or female, must have good shorthand and typing speeds, some clerical experience and good references. Apply giving full details, salary required, and date of commencement if successful, to The Managing Director, XYZ Company Ltd, High Street, York, YA88 CD2

(PITMAN EBC Intermediate)

Chapter 16 Travel/Hotels

You are considering taking your vacation in Southport and a good friend has recommended the South Shore Private Hotel at which he has stayed on a number of occasions. Write to the proprietor asking if he could provide accommodation for you and a friend for 2 weeks in June. You will require one twin-bedded room with en suite bathroom, and bed and breakfast only.

Comlon is about to launch a range of products which will help reduce the problem of excessive noise from traffic. These products can be fitted to any vehicle and to promote the launch the range will be demonstrated by Comlon's rally team at the Kenyan rally which begins on Tuesday 26 February.

Patrick Hughes will be attending the event and will take with him a group of Comlon's leading clients who will attend the rally at the Company's expense.

On the day before the rally begins there will be a press conference to publicise the new products. Mr Hughes will be giving a presentation at this conference.

You have been put in charge of some of the arrangements and have already telephoned the Grand Hotel, Lenara Road, Nairobi, Kenya, to make the necessary booking.

Mr Hughes now asks you to **write a letter to the hotel to confirm the booking and finalise the arrangements**. You have made the following notes:

- Transport to and from hotel required
- Party to arrive Saturday 23 – 1600
- Party to depart Friday 1 March – 1000
- Bed, breakfast and evening meal required
- Party to comprise:

  Mr Henry Symonds
  Mr James Broome
  Mrs Susan Gale
  Mr Philip Lynch
  Mr Richard Norman and Mrs Norman
  Mr John Schofield and Mrs Schofield
  Mr Peter Reid

  (Philip Lynch vegetarian
  Peter Reid – mobility problems – needs ground floor room or room near lift!)

- Room for press conference Monday 25 at 1000 – need video recorder, audio tape facilities, overhead projector, access to fax.

Mr Hughes will sign the letter.

(LCCI PSC 1990)

Chapter 17 Miscellaneous letters

Your local authority proposes to demolish a building of historical (or architectural) interest in your town, in order to provide space for a supermarket (or an office block). Write a letter of about 100 words to the editor of a local newspaper, either supporting or opposing the proposal. Give sensible reasons to justify your attitude.

(LCCI EFC1 1991)

2

Situation

Mr Roderick MacDonald, Managing Director of Woomera Bio-Technics Pty, 1 Rockingham Way, Melbourne, Victoria, Australia is going to visit your company to discuss the possibility of producing some of Bio–Technics' products in your factory. Unfortunately, you have just received a telephone call from your manager informing you that it is necessary to change Mr MacDonald's programme at short notice.

Task

Using the following notes you made when you received the telephone call, **write a letter** to Mr MacDonald; explain what the changes are, why they have been made and apologise. Send a new programme with your letter. Make up the name and address of your own company and other necessary information.

Write the letter followed by the new programme.

Original programme:

Day 1: Flight arrival 1600. Our driver will meet you and take you to the 'Merlin Hotel'.

Day 2: Leave hotel 0800. Meeting at Head Office all day.

Day 3: Leave hotel 0800. Tour of factory, with the Production Manager, finishing at 1400.

Day 4: Leave hotel 0800. Tour of warehouse facilities, with the Warehouse Manager, finishing at 1200. Further meeting at Head Office, finishing at 1600.

Day 5: Leave hotel 0900. Flight departure 1100.

Telephone notes:

Merlin Hotel no longer available (being refurbished) – room booked at 'Camelot hotel'.

Camelot Hotel nearer so driver will call each day 45 minutes later than originally planned.

The warehouse tour and the factory tour will be on the same day, leaving day four free for a Head Office meeting that will finish after lunch. Give the names of the people Mr M will meet each day.

(LCCI EFB1 1990)

Chapter 18 Agencies

Your company has considerable export business in dress materials with Sri Lanka. Unfortunately, you now find it necessary to raise your prices, which have previously remained static for over 2 years. Write to your agent in Colombo asking his opinion as to whether the market will stand the proposed increases. Enclose a proposed revised price list.

Your company does considerable export business with several companies overseas, with local agents in each country. You have recently become concerned with the sales performance of your agent in Tunisia. Write asking the agent for a full report on the last 6 months, and suggested action he proposes to take to improve sales. Point out tactfully that business between them cannot be continued unless a higher level of sales can be guaranteed in the future.

Chapter 19 International trade

Messrs Dupont et Cie wish to extend their trade in leather handbags in Morocco. They wish to write to Mohamed Benhima, Casablanca, to whom they have been strongly recommended, enclosing catalogues and price lists. Write such a letter, also offering to send goods on consignment, with monthly settlements against acceptance of drafts at 60 days. Suggest a commission of 10% on gross sales.

L Otiendi & Co need to send an indent to their London agents, F Hobson & Sons, for 4,000 metres of cotton cloth in various shades of mauve and green, at a maximum price of £1.60 a metre. The consignment is to be shipped to Mombasa, where it will be handled by F Patel & Co, the buyer's forwarding agents. Write a letter to send along with the indent.

Chapters 20/21 Banking

You are manager of Midminster Bank and have received an enquiry from a company as to the standing of one of your bank's customers. Draft the reply, making up the appropriate details.

2

Write to your bank manager asking for advice on the investment of £2,000. You are looking for a safe investment in an industrial company with prospects of modest return.

3

You have the chance to purchase the bankrupt stock of a competitor on very favourable terms. Unfortunately you lack the necessary capital (£5,000). Write to your bank manager asking for a loan. Mention the security you can offer.

4

Write to your firm's bank enclosing shipping documents and a 60 days after sight draft on your overseas customer. Ask your bank to obtain your customer's acceptance of the draft before handing over the shipping documents, and then to discount the bill and credit your account with the proceeds.

5

Write to your banker with a request to open an irrevocable credit for £1,800 in favour of a British manufacturer to cover a consignment of cutlery. The credit is to be available for one month from the date of your letter. The manufacturer's draft at 60 days will be accepted by the overseas bank's correspondent in Leeds.

Chapter 23 Insurance

1

You have a fire policy covering your warehouse in your town but are now removing to a larger warehouse in the same town. Write to your insurance company asking them to issue a policy increasing the amount of cover from £70,000 to £100,000.

2

As secretary of the insurance company, write in reply to the letter in Assignment 1 explaining that a new policy will be unnecessary and that the present policy should be sent for endorsement of the alterations necessary.

3

Write to your insurers informing them of a fire at your premises that has completely destroyed the top storey. Request early inspection by their representative as you wish to submit your claim without delay since you are anxious to commence rebuilding at once.

Index